EXPANDING WORLD

PHILIP SAUVAIN

STANLEY THORNES (PUBLISHERS) LTD

Designed by Simon Borrough
Maps, graphs and charts by Nick Hawken
Artwork on page 18 by Tim Hayward

First published in 1993 by:
Stanley Thornes (Publishers) Ltd
Old Station Drive
Leckhampton
CHELTENHAM GL53 0DN
England

A catalogue record for this book is available from the British Library

ISBN 0-7487-1233-X

Typeset by Florencetype Ltd, Kewstoke, Avon
Printed and bound in Hong Kong

Acknowledgements

Many of the extracts quoted in this book have been adapted and shortened to improve the clarity and readability of the text while fully retaining the flavour and intent of the originals. Some come from the classic collections of historical documents, such as Everyman's Library. Some are translations from documents in German or French and I am indebted to my daughter Rachel Sauvain for translating a number of sources and picture captions for me.

The extracts from *Chronicle of Youth* by Vera Brittain are included with the permission of Victor Gollancz Ltd, Alan Bishop, the editor, and Paul Berry, Vera Brittain's literary executor.

Grateful acknowledgements are also due to the authors and publishers of the following books which have been invaluable in the research and preparation of this book and in providing contemporary written sources.

Atlas of the British Empire, edited by Christopher Bayly, Hamlyn, 1989.
The Berlin Diaries of Marie 'Missie' Vassiltchikov, edited by George Vassiltchikov, Chatto and Windus, 1985.
Berlin Diary, by William L. Shirer, Hamish Hamilton, 1941
The Boer War Diary of Sol T. Plaatje, edited by J.L. Comaroff, Macmillan, 1973.
Boy in the Blitz, by Colin Perry, Leo Cooper, 1972.
Chips: The Diaries of Sir Henry Channon, edited by Robert Rhodes James, Weidenfeld and Nicolson, 1967.
The Common People, by G.D.H. Cole and Raymond Postgate, Methuen, 1938.
The Concept of Empire, edited by George Bennett, A. and C. Black, 1953.
A Concise History of Warfare, by Field Marshal Montgomery, Collins, 1968.
Contemporary Sources and Opinions in Modern British History, edited by Lloyd Evans and Philip J. Pledger, Frederick Warne, 1966.
The Croker Papers, edited by Bernard Pool, Batsford, 1967.
The Deluge, by Arthur Marwick, The Bodley Head, 1965.
Diaries and Letters, by Harold Nicolson, Collins, 1967.
Diaries of Sir Alexander Cadogan, edited by David Dilks, Cassell, 1971.
Diary of a Country Parson, edited by John Beresford, Oxford, 1935.
The Diary of a Desert Rat, by R.L. Crimp, edited by Alex Bowlby, Leo Cooper.
The Diary of Sir Edward Walter Hamilton, edited by Dudley W.R. Bahlman, Oxford, 1972.
Documents and Descriptions: The World Since 1914, edited by R.W. Breach, Oxford, 1966.
Dresden, 1945: The Devil's Tinderbox, by Alexander McKee, published by Granada, 1982.
D-Day, by Warren Tute, Sidgwick and Jackson, 1974.
Echoes of the Great War: The Diary of the Reverend Andrew Clark, edited by James Munson, Oxford University Press, 1985.
English Historical Documents: 1783–1832, edited by A. Aspinall and E. Anthony Smith, Oxford, 1959.
English Historical Documents: 1874–1914, edited by W. D. Handcock, Oxford, 1977.
English Social History, by G.M. Trevelyan, Longmans, Green, 1944.
European Historical Statistics, by B.R. Mitchell, Macmillan, 1981.
The Faber Book of Reportage, edited by John Carey, Faber and Faber, 1987.
The First Casualty, by Phillip Knightley, André Deutsch, 1975.
Fylingdales Census Returns, Fylingdales Local History Group, 1979.
The Goebbels Diaries 1939–1941, translated by Fred Taylor, Hamish Hamilton, 1982.
The Great War, by Correlli Barnett, Peerage Books, 1979.
The Guardian Omnibus 1821–1971, edited by David Ayerst, Collins, 1973.
Harry S. Truman, by Margaret Truman, Hamish Hamilton, 1973.
Hiroshima Diary, by Michihiko Hachiya, translated by Warner Wells, Gollancz, 1955.
History of the Second World War, by B.H. Liddell Hart, Cassell, 1970.
History of the USSR, translated by Ken Russell, Progress Publishers (Moscow), 1977.
Hitler's Interpreter, by Dr Paul Schmidt, edited by R.H.C. Steed, Heinemann, 1951.
The House that Hitler Built, by Stephen Roberts, Methuen, 1937.
How We Lived Then 1914–1918, by Mrs C.S. Peel, John Lane, 1929.
How We Lived Then, by Norman Longmate, Hutchinson, 1971.
Human Documents of the Age of the Forsytes, edited by E. Royston Pike, Allen and Unwin, 1969.
Human Documents of the Lloyd George Era, edited by E. Royston Pike, St Martin's Press.
I Was There!, edited by Sir John Hammerton, The Waverley Book Company, 1938.
The Imperial Dream, by Edward Grierson, Collins, 1972.
Independent on Sunday, 31 May 1992.
Industrialisation and Culture, edited by Harvie, Martin and Scharf, Macmillan, 1970
Inside the Third Reich, by Albert Speer, translated by Richard and Clara Winston, Weidenfe and Nicolson, 1970.
International Almanac of Electoral History, by Thomas T. Mackie and Richard Rose, Macmillan, 1982.
Into Unknown England, edited by Peter Keating, Fontana, 1976.
Journal of the War Years, by Anthony Weymouth, Littlebury, 1948.
Keep Smiling Through, by Susan Briggs, Weidenfeld and Nicolson, 1975.
The Life of Neville Chamberlain, by K. Feiling, Macmillan, 1946.
The Making of the English Working Class, by E.P. Thompson, Victor Gollancz, 1963.
Mrs Milburn's Diaries, edited by Peter Donnelly, Harrap, 1979.
My Part in Germany's Fight, by Josef Goebbels, Hutchinson, 1935.
My Warrior Sons, edited by Guy Slater, Peter Davies, 1973.
Nazism 1919–45, edited by J. Noakes and G. Pridham, University of Exeter, 1983.
1940: The World In Flames, by Richard Collier, Hamish Hamilton, 1979.
A Norfolk Diary, edited by Herbert Armstrong, Harrap, 1949.
Official Handbook to Dachau Concentration Camp, International Dachau Committee, 1978.
The Opinions of William Cobbett, edited by G.D.H. and M. Cole, 1944.
Otto Dix: His Life and Works, by Eva Karcher, translated by D.L. Jones and J. Gaines, Benedikt Taschen, 1988.
The People's War, by Angus Calder, Jonathan Cape, 1969.
Private, by Lester Atwell, Simon and Schuster, 1958.
The Private Diaries of Sydney Moseley, Max Parrish, 1960.
The Private Papers of Senator Vandenberg, Houghton Miflin, 1952.
R D B's Diary, R.D. Blumenfeld, Heinemann, 1930.
Realities of War, by Philip Gibbs, Heinemann, 1920.
Return Via Dunkirk, by John Charles Austin, Hodder and Stoughton, 1940.
Road to Victory, by Martin Gilbert, Heinemann, 1986.
The Rommel Papers, edited by B.H. Liddell Hart, Arrow.
The Second World War, by Winston Churchill, Cassell, 1954.
Speeches and Documents on International Affairs, edited by Arthur Berriedale Keith, Oxford, 1938.
Strikes: A Documentary History, by Frow and Katanka, Charles Knight, 1971.
Testimony of War 1914–1918, by Peter Liddle, Michael Russell, 1979.
They Saw it Happen: 1689–1897, by T. Charles-Edwards and B. Richardson, Blackwell, 1958.
Torrington Diaries, edited by C. Bruyn Andrews, Eyre and Spottiswode, 1954.
A Touch on the Times, edited by Roy Palmer, Penguin Education, 1974.
U-Boat 202, by Freiherr von Spiegel of Peckelsheim, translated by Barry Domville, Andrew Melrose.
Vain Glory, edited by Guy Chapman, Cassell, 1937.
A Victorian Diarist, edited by the Hon. E.C.F. Collier, John Murray, 1944.
The War 1939–1945, edited by Desmond Flower and James Reeves, Cassell, 1960.
War Letters to a Wife, by Rowland Feilding, The Medici Society, 1929.
War Memoirs, by David Lloyd George, 1933.
The War Poets, by Robert Giddings, Orion Books 1988.
War Report D-Day to VE-Day, edited by Desmond Hawkins, Ariel Books BBC, 1985.
Warriors Without Weapons, by Marcel Junod, Jonathan Cape, 1951.
The Weimar Republic, by Louis L. Snyder, Van Nostrand, 1966.
Women and Children Last, by Hilde Marchant, Gollancz, 1941.
Workers and Employers, edited by J.T. Ward and W. Hamish Fraser, Macmillan, 1980.
The World at Arms: The Reader's Digest Illustrated History of World War II, 1989.
World War I, by David Shermer, Octopus Books, 1973.

The author and publishers would like to thank the following for permisssion to reproduce pictures and photographs in this book (pictures are referred to by page number):.

Australian War Memorial, 151, 174–5; Bildarchiv Preussischer Kulturbesitz, 132 (top), 134 (top left), 136 (bottom left), 146 (bottom), 152 (top), 157, 180 (left), 182; Borough of Darlington Museum, 31; Bridgeman Art Library, 68 (Guildhall Library/Corporation of London), 142 (bottom) (© DACS 1993/Prado, Madrid), 86 (Private Collection), 50 (Royal Holloway anc Bedford New College, Surrey), 16 (Science Museum, London), 38 (top) (Tate Gallery); British Library (India Office), 84 (left); British Waterways, 30; Canadian War Museum/Bruno Bobak, 159; (Governing Body of) Christ Church, Oxford, 85 (middle left); Communist Party Library, 72–3 (middle), 74 (top); Corporation of London/Greater London Record Office (Maps and Prints), 71; Edimedia, 145; Erwitt/Magnum, 172 (top); Mary Evans Picture Library, 17 (left), 34–5 96 (bottom); First Queen's Dragoon Guards Regimental Museum, 59; Fotomas Index, 56–7; Guildhall Library/Private Collection, 66 (top); Hulton Picture Company, 89 (top), 158 (top), 161; Robert Hunt Library, 167 (middle); Imperial War Museum, London, 76, 99 (top left), 101 (right, top and bottom left), 103, 104 (top), 109 (right), 114, 116 (bottom right), 120, 123 (left) 164 (left), 179; Ironbridge Gorge Museum/Elton Collection, 34; David King, 128, 152 (bottom); Labour Party Library, 130–1 (top); Leicestershire County Council, 7 (top); Manchester City Art Galleries, 70, 83; Mansell Collection, 20, 22; Mirror Group Newspapers Ltd, 162 (top), 178 (top); Moro, Rome, 129; Musée de l'Armée, Paris, 105, 148; Museum of London, Cover, 28, 41 (bottom left), 45 (bottom); National Gallery of Scotland, 43 (left); National Maritime Museum, 65 (bottom); National Museums and Galleries on Merseyside, 14–5; National Portrait Gallery, London, 72–3 (bottom), 84 (top); National Railway Museum, York, 8 (top), 32 (top), 33 (bottom left and right); Peter Newark's Military Pictures, 101 (middle left), 122 (top left), 127, 146 (top right), 154 (top), 158 (bottom), 170, 171 (left), 176–7; Barry Page, 124 (left); Popperfoto, 168–9, 178 (bottom), 180–1 (top), 181 (bottom); The Post Office Library, 29; Putnam Publishing Group, 168 (top); Royal Commission on the Historical Monuments of England, 47 (top right); Royal Geographical Society, London, 60 (bottom); Royal Library, Windsor Castle/ © 1992 Her Majesty the Queen, 72 (top); Sheffield City Museums, 46; Staatliche Kunstsammlungen, Dresden, 115; Tate Gallery, London, 4, 54 (top right); TUC Library, 76; Ulster Museum, 43 (right); United Nations, New York, 184; University of Reading, Institute of Agricultural History and Museum of English Rural Life, 6 (top); US Army, 139 (bottom), 153, 175; US Navy, 155, 174 (bottom); Victoria and Albert Museum, 64, 85 (bottom right).

All other illustrations and photographs were supplied by the author.

Every effort has been made to contact copyright holders. The author and publishers apologise to anyone whose rights have been overlooked, and will be happy to rectify any errors or ommissions.

Contents

Expansion, trade and industry in Britain 1750~1900

1 The Agricultural Revolution

FOCUS

▶ *WHAT were the main changes brought about by the Agricultural Revolution?*
ATIA ■ ATIC ■

▶ *HOW and WHY did they affect Britain?*
ATIB ■ ATIC ■

Reaping corn in the middle of the eighteenth century

Enclosing the open fields

Between 1750 and 1850, great changes took place in the countryside. New methods of farming were introduced. This is why this period is sometimes called the Agricultural or Agrarian Revolution. It was part of the Industrial Revolution – the period when Britain changed from a rural to an industrial country where most people lived in towns.

In 1750, large areas of the country were still farmed as huge, unfenced open fields divided into narrow strips of land (see photograph on pages 10–11). These open fields were not evenly spread across England. In many areas, the land had already been enclosed. This means dividing it up into separate fields and farms.

Source 1.A Arthur Young in 1771

The profit [per sheep] *in enclosed fields is 11s* [55p]. *In the open fields it is only 2s 3d* [11p]. *This is a very great difference. In the Vale of Evesham the average fleece is 9lb* [4kg] *in the enclosures, but only 3lb* [1.6kg] *in the open fields. Can there be a stronger argument for enclosing?*

Experts like Arthur Young (Source 1.A) urged farmers to enclose the land. This could only be done with the agreement of the people holding most of the land. If they did agree to it, then Parliament passed a special Enclosure Act after officials had surveyed the land and drawn maps to say how it should be divided up. After enclosure farmers were given land according to the number of strips they had held in the open fields. This cost a lot of money and there were also legal fees to pay. All these costs had to be met by the villagers. In addition, they had to pay for new roads, farm buildings, hedges, walls and fences.

Disadvantages of the open field system
Farmers had to grow the same crops as their neighbours. They grew wheat and then barley in the first two years and then left the land fallow (without crops) for a year to let it recover its fertility.
All the village animals grazed in the meadows (cattle), on the commons (sheep and cattle) and in the woods (pigs). Each farmer had the right to graze a certain number of animals in these areas. It was difficult to breed good quality animals since the livestock were not kept apart from each other.
Because the strips and commons were scattered, people built their homes in the village itself instead of among the fields. They wasted time going from strip to strip.
Since their holdings were small and scattered, there was little point in farmers buying expensive machinery, draining the land, or spreading fertilisers.
There were no hedges, so weeds from a lazy farmer's land quickly spread to neighbouring strips.

1.1 How did Arthur Young try to persuade farmers to accept enclosure? AT2/L5
1.2 What would you have wanted to know before accepting his statistics as proof that enclosure worked? AT2/L5
1.3 Look at the maps of Waltham. How did the village change after the land was enclosed in 1771? AT1A ■
1.4 Who gained most? AT1B/L6
1.5 What effect did enclosure have on Meriden? AT1A/L6
1.6 Give reasons for thinking that Byng may not be a reliable source of information about the effects of enclosure. AT2/L5
1.7 What do you think were the three most powerful arguments (a) for, (b) against, the enclosure of the open fields? AT1B/L6

The Lincolnshire village of Waltham before (top) and after (bottom) enclosure ▶

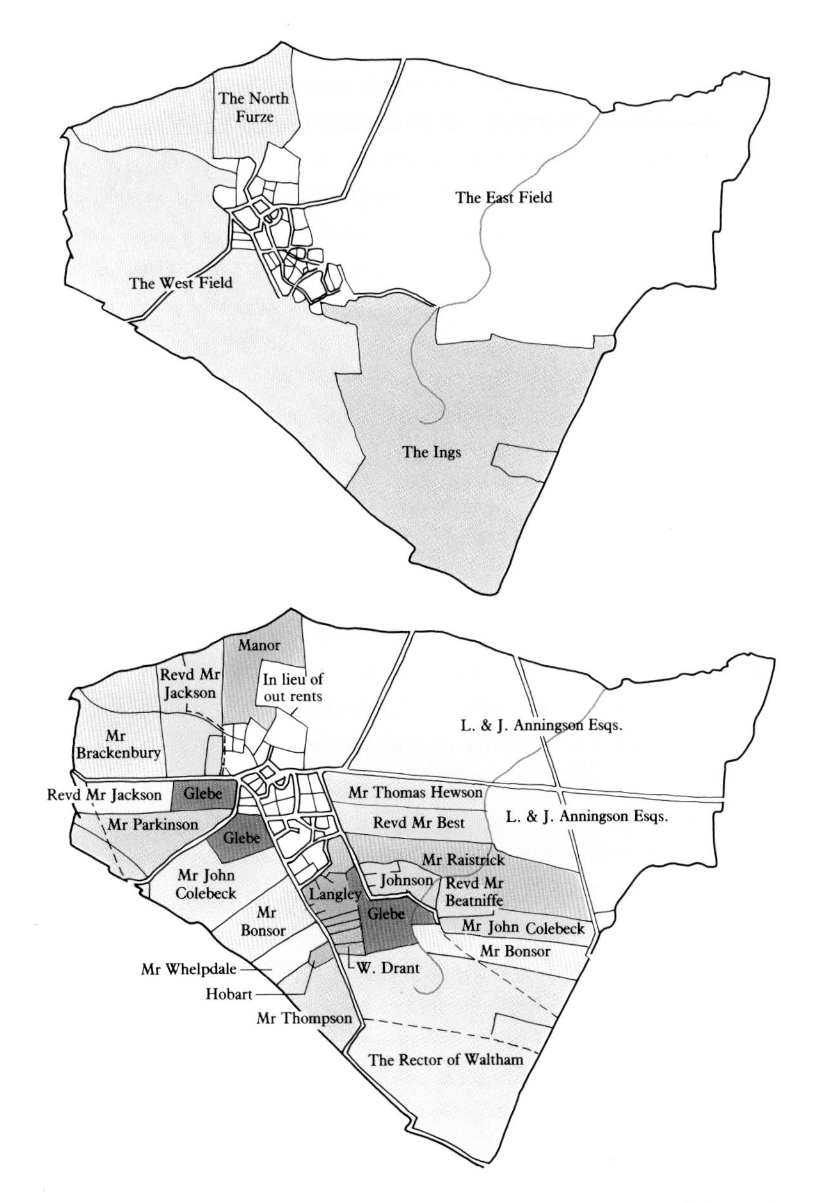

Source 1.B The effects of enclosure in 1789

Ah, lackaday, Sir, that was a sad job and ruined all us poor folk. Those who then gave into it, now repent it. We once had our garden, our bees, our share of a flock of sheep, the feeding of our geese; and could cut turf for our fuel. Now all that is gone!

Source 1.C John Byng's views on enclosure in 1789

As a sportsman I hate enclosures, and as a citizen, I look on them as the greedy tyrannies of the wealthy few.

Enclosure meant that farmers could rotate their crops, and therefore increase the amount of land cultivated each year. There was no longer any need to leave each field fallow every third year. Farmers who used the Norfolk rotation, for instance, grew wheat in the first year, a root crop, such as turnips, in the second, barley in the third, and clover in the fourth.

The order in which these different crops were grown helped to put fertility back into the soil. When the farmers hoed between growing plants, they cleaned the land of weeds. When sheep grazed on the harvest stubble, their tiny feet trod manure well into the soil. Crops with longer roots took nutrients from the soil at a deeper level than did the others.

Effects of enclosure

However, there was a price to pay. Enclosure brought poverty to thousands of farm workers. Poor people could not afford to pay their share of the costs of enclosure. They had to sell their land to their richer neighbours. Many became farm labourers instead of farming their own land. In 1789 the travel writer John Byng visited Meriden, near Birmingham, and talked to a woman there about the enclosure of the village fields (Sources 1.B and 1.C).

◀ *A Victorian advertisement*

New machines and implements

Enclosure made it easier for farmers to use new methods. They could use new implements and machinery. The Rotherham plough, invented in about 1760, made ploughing easier when the ground was hard. Improvements in the iron and steel industry (page 16) enabled Robert Ransome (see the advertisement) to make an iron plough in 1808. Patrick Bell invented a reaping machine in 1827. Andrew Meikle made a threshing machine to separate the ears of corn from the stalks when the corn was fed into a revolving drum. This engine, 'gin' for short, was turned by a gang (team) of horses walking round in a circle. Round or octagonal buildings, called 'gin-gang houses', were built on farms to make use of them. They were later adapted to use steam power instead of horses.

'Gin-gang house' at the Beamish Museum in County Durham

1.8 How can you tell from the photograph that this 'gin-gang house' used steam power rather than horse power?
1.9 Look at Source 1.D. A landowner called Sir Tatton Sykes noticed that grass grew better near his dog's kennels. What did he deduce from this?
AT3/L3

Fertilisers

Source 1.D From a magazine published in 1845

Every scrap of farm manure, and every drop of animal liquid, is collected and preserved. The droppings of sea-birds, called guano, are imported from South America at many pounds per ton. Crushed bones are regarded as one of the finest manures for light turnip soils. How our forefathers would have laughed at the use of bones, soot, night-soil and urine.

By 1850, as you can see from Source 1.D and Source 1.N on page 11, most farmers were spreading different types of fertilisers on their land to help them grow bigger and better crops. Some built underground tanks and pits to store manure to stop it being ruined by exposure to sun and rain. Farmers near the towns used human manure. It was called *night-soil* (page 47) because it was carted away at night. They also used soot and a special type of clay called *marl* which contained lime.

Some farmers also improved their lands by draining their fields. They dug deep trenches under the top soil and filled them with stones. Rain water collected in these underground channels and drained away into a river or pond.

Robert Bakewell on horseback

1.10 Look at Sources 1.E, 1.F and 1.G. How can you show that the historian G.M. Trevelyan made a mistake in Source 1.E? AT2/L5

1.11 Write the report you think a farm manager might have written to his rich employer after attending the demonstration at Louth in 1857. AT1C/L5

1.12 Look at the pictures on these pages and at Source 1.H. If you had been a farm worker at this time, would you have been happy about this? Give your reasons. AT1A/L6

Source 1.H Newspaper description of a demonstration at Louth in Lincolnshire in 1857

The steam traction-engine with three double ploughs, ploughed about 8 acres in one day of ten hours. The cost for labour and coal was £1.12s [£1.60]. *Six single ploughs pulled by eighteen horses in the same time would have ploughed only 4½ acres. This would have cost about £2.11s* [£2.55]. *The cost of the engine with the ploughs would be about the same as the eighteen horses; while the wear and tear would be the greater on the latter.*

New ways of breeding livestock

Farmers also used new methods to improve the quality of their animals. One of the leading breeders was Robert Bakewell from Dishley in Leicestershire. Like Thomas Coke of Holkham in Norfolk, he picked the finest animals from a flock or herd and only bred from these. Mating the largest rams with the fattest ewes produced lambs which fattened quickly and grew bigger than normal. However, the meat was fatty and of poor quality. Nonetheless, visitors were impressed. These methods were soon copied and improved by other farmers. By 1800, pedigree bulls, cows, rams and ewes were fetching very high prices at auction.

New methods

Many farmers learned about these new methods from books, such as those written by Arthur Young. They visited show farms on special open days, such as the annual sheep-shearings at Woburn Abbey in Bedfordshire. Later, historians gave 'Turnip' Townshend and Thomas Coke much of the credit for these new methods. Viscount Townshend was a famous politician who took up farming in Norfolk in 1730. Thomas Coke, who later became Earl of Leicester, started farming at Holkham Hall in Norfolk in 1776 when he was 22.

Source 1.E G.M.Trevelyan (writing in 1944)

Both Townshend and Coke introduced into Norfolk new crops and new methods – above all, root crops and the marling of light land. Their example put their backward county at the head of English agriculture.

Source 1.F Daniel Defoe (writing in 1722)

Suffolk is also remarkable for being the first where the feeding of sheep and cattle with turnips was first practised in England.

Source 1.G Arthur Young (writing in 1771)

This county (Norfolk), before the great works done by enclosing and marling was all a wild sheepwalk [rough grazing for sheep]. *Through the skill of many great farmers, it has grown in value to an amazing degree.*

Steam power

The first efficient steam-engine was invented by James Watt in the 1770s (page 14). By 1850, steam traction-engines were being used to plough the land (Source 1.H) and thresh the corn after the harvest (see the picture below).

A steam traction-engine threshing corn in the 1850s

Livestock carried by the Liverpool and Manchester Railway in the 1830s

Effects of the Agricultural Revolution

The Agricultural Revolution greatly increased the amount of food grown in Britain. In 1698 Gregory King estimated that England produced 67 million bushels of corn a year. Only 150 years later, the yield of corn in 1846 was put at 250 million bushels. During this time the sheep population rose from 12 million to 30 million and the number of cattle grew from 3 million in 1774 to 10 million a century later.

Better roads and the coming of the railways made it easier to bring this food to the towns. Trains brought fresh milk, cattle and sheep into London each day. Farmers now had a great incentive to produce as much food as possible from their land. They built model farms and used all the latest methods and labour-saving machinery to improve production.

1.13 Sources 1.J and 1.K are both taken from the same popular magazine published on 5 September 1846. How can you tell the writer wanted readers to sympathise with the Dorset farmworkers? AT2/L5
1.14 How can these extracts be used as evidence about the living conditions of farmworkers at that time? AT3/L6

◀ *A model farm in Oxfordshire in 1858*

1.15 How and why was the Agricultural Revolution responsible for the Captain Swing riots? AT1B ■
1.16 What was the point of the *Punch* drawing? What was the attitude of the cartoonist to the farmworkers at this time? AT1C/L6
1.17 The picture *The Last Load* was drawn in 1872 for The *Illustrated London News*. How was this artist's attitude different from that of the *Punch* cartoonist? AT1C/L6
1.18 Which artist do you think was probably nearest in summing up what life was like for the farmworker at this time? AT2/L7 AT3/L7

Britain changed from a land of peasant farmers growing their own food to one of employers (farmers) and employees (farmworkers). Labour-saving machinery meant that fewer workers were needed on the land. Many farmers no longer took a leading part in village life. The richer farmers became gentlemen and mixed with fashionable society. Their new houses and farm buildings were built next to their fields. William Cobbett saw this in Northumberland in 1832 (Source 1.I).

Source 1.I

I saw in one place more than a hundred corn-stacks in one yard, each having from six to seven Surrey wagon-loads of sheaves in a stack; and not another house to be seen within a mile or two of the farm house.

Empty, broken-down buildings were to be seen along many village streets (Source 1.J). Some of the old village occupations disappeared, such as those of the cowherd, swineherd and hayward. Ploughs and other field implements were now made in town factories and not by village smiths and carpenters.

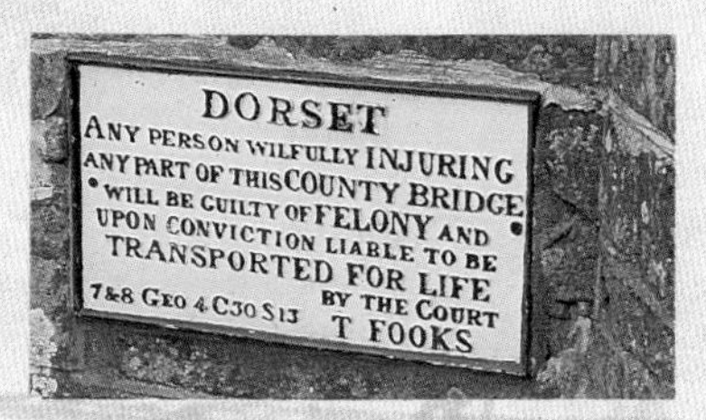

A sign dating from 1828 on a bridge in Dorset

Source 1.J Newspaper account of a Dorset village in 1846

The first feature which attracts the attention of a stranger on entering the village is the total want of cleanliness which pervades it. A stream of filth meanders down each street and collects in pools which lie rotting in the sun.

Poverty and distress

However, the new farmers did not always prosper. Prices for wheat and barley fell sharply at the end of the Napoleonic Wars in 1815. Parliament passed the Corn Laws to keep out foreign corn (see page 67) but farmers still found it hard to make a good living. Many economised by buying new machines and sacking their farmworkers, or cutting their wages to save costs.

Source 1.K Farmworker's cottage in Dorset in 1846

Dishes, plates and other articles of crockery seem almost unknown. Bread is the chief kind of food. In no single instance did I see meat of any kind. A labourer and his family – in all eight persons – are the occupiers of a hut, in which there is but one bedroom. There is a small opening about a foot square which serves as a window. The furniture – a rickety table and two or three broken chairs. Want, famine and misery are the features of the village.

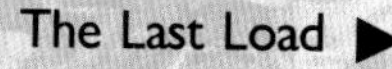
The Last Load ▶

Captain Swing

The poverty in the countryside (Source 1.K) led to violence in the 1830s and 1840s. Hayricks and corn stacks were set on fire and threshing machines destroyed. Many of these outrages were said to be the work of the mythical Captain Swing (Sources 1.L and 1.M). Some of the rickburners were executed, such as James Passfield, aged 23. He was convicted at Essex Assizes of setting fire to a farmer's stackyard.

Source 1.L Letter received by a farmer in 1830

Your name is down amongst the Black Hearts in the Black Book and this is to advise you and the likes of you, to make your wills. Ye have been the Blackguard Enemies of the people on all occasions, ye have not done as ye ought.

[SIGNED] *Swing*

Source 1.M

At the Huntingdon Assizes, Gifford White, aged 18, was sentenced to transportation for life for sending a letter to a farmer, threatening to burn his farm and the farms of others.

'The home of the rick-burner' printed in Punch *in the early 1840s*

Agriculture: The impact of the Industrial Revolution on a local area

The changing countryside

The Industrial Revolution affected all parts of the British Isles, even those far from the coalfields and cotton mills. As you have seen, steam-engines were used on farms as well as in factories. Railways and canals criss-crossed the country. No matter where you live, you can be sure the Industrial Revolution made a great impact on your area.

One of the biggest changes was to the landscape. Many beautiful parts of the countryside, such as the valleys of the West Riding close to Halifax and Huddersfield, were transformed into black, smoking, industrial areas without regard for the effect this had on the environment.

This horse-drawn plough was still in use in West Norfolk in 1956 when the photograph was taken

Sources of information

Even if your local area is part of an urban area today, such as Greater London, it would have been very much closer to the countryside in 1750. If you are going to measure the impact of the Industrial Revolution on your area, therefore, you will need to know something of what it was like at the start of this period.

You can find out some information using old maps, paintings and engravings, street names (such as those referring to a common, green, field, wood or meadow) and from local histories in the library and old documents in a local archive collection. You can also find out from investigations in the area:

1 If the fields still have traces of the old medieval 'ridge and furrow' pattern (like those in the photograph), you can plot the direction of the ridges on a sketch map. If the ridges in a number of adjacent fields all follow the same line of direction, you may even be able to suggest that this area was one of the old open fields before it was enclosed to form separate fields.

2 If hedges separate the fields in your area, see if you can identify the shrubs in the hedge. If there are two or three different species, this may be a sign that the hedge is over a hundred years old.

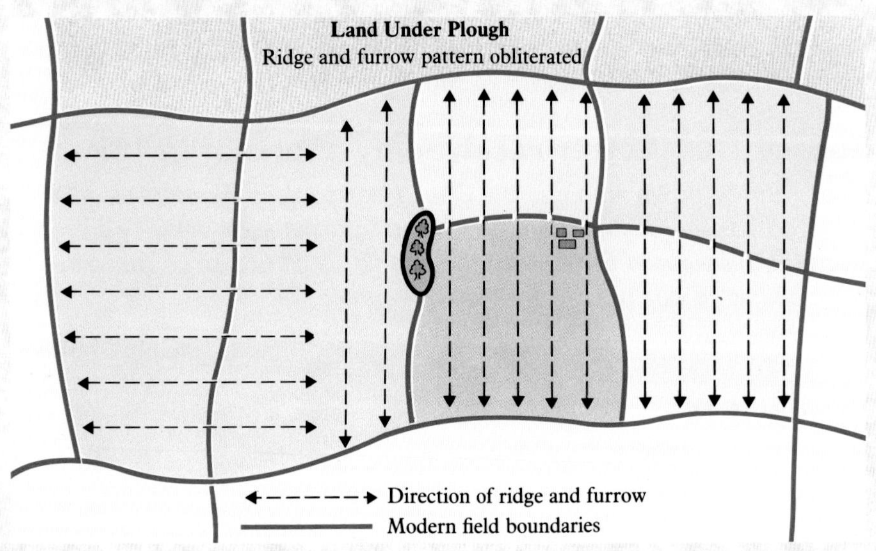

This map shows how the medieval 'ridge and furrow' pattern cuts across modern field boundaries on the farm shown in the photograph

3 If you are lucky, you may be able to find a local history book in the library with a copy of an old enclosure map. You can then compare the fields and buildings shown on the map with the field boundaries and farms of today.

4 If you visit an old farm, look at the farm buildings. When were they built? Many date back to the time when the fields were enclosed. Do the outbuildings on the farm resemble those of the model farm shown in the picture on page 8? Can you see a 'gin-gang house' like the one on page 6?

5 Exhibits on display in your local museum may tell you about the countryside and about farming in your district at the time of the Industrial Revolution. You may be able to see advertisements for farm machinery in copies of old local newspapers. There may be paintings or sketches of local farms in your nearest art gallery.

6 Illustrations in books in the local history section of the public library will show you how farming methods changed with the introduction of new machines and the coming of the railway. There are many modern collections of old photographs taken in the Victorian period.

7 If you talk to older friends and relatives who have lived in your area all their lives, they may be able to tell you about the machines and implements used in the fields when they were young. Some may even remember seeing a steam traction-engine threshing corn in a farmyard or the horse-drawn plough teams which could still be seen less than forty years ago. They may also be able to remember stories and anecdotes told to them by a grandparent or great-grandparent born in the middle of the nineteenth century!

8 If you visit your local archives office, you may be able to find documents like the one below. In this agreement, Martin Taylor (the tenant farmer) accepted in 1858 that it was his duty to spread lime and all the 'Dung and Manure' from the farm on these fields every year. In other words the document shows the importance farmers put on adding fertilisers to the land (page 6).

The direction followed by these ridges and furrows are the same on either side of the modern field boundaries. This suggests the fields were once part of a much bigger field – perhaps a medieval open field ▼

Source 1.N

This legal document was drawn up when a Yorkshire farmer agreed to take on the tenancy of a farm near Whitby in 1858. ▶

***Memorandum** of an Agreement made this* Fifth *day of* October *in the Year of our Lord, One Thousand Eight Hundred and* Fifty Eight *BETWEEN Jacob Coulthirst, of Fylingdales, in the County of York, Farmer, of the one part, and* – – Martin Taylor – – – *of the Township of* Fylingdales – – – *in the said County, Farmer, of the other part.*

THE said JACOB COULTHIRST hath let to Farm, and the said Martin Taylor hath taken ALL that Messuage or Farm House, with the Farm, Lands, and Grounds thereunto belonging, or therewith held, used, or enjoyed; containing by estimation Thirty Two – – – Acres, or thereabouts, situate and being in the Township of – – Fylingdales – in the said County of York, now in the occupation of – – – Thomas Newton – TOGETHER with the Barns, Byers, Stables, Buildings, and Appurtenances, to the same belonging, TO HOLD the said Premises with the Appurtenances, from the Sixth day of April next, for the term of One Year, and so on from Year to Year, until Six Month's Notice shall be given by either party to quit the same Premises, at and under the Yearly Rent of Thirty Four Pounds – of lawful English Money, payable Half-Yearly, by equal portions, on the Eleventh day of October, and the Sixth day of April, in every year: the first payment thereof to be made on the Eleventh day of October, next. AND ALSO to observe, perform, and keep the several stipulations and Agreements following, that is to say: That he, the said – – Martin Taylor shall and will discharge all Taxes and Assessments, Lay Charges,

2 The Industrial Revolution

◀ A small weaving workshop in the middle of the eighteenth century

FOCUS

▶ WHAT is meant by the Industrial Revolution?

ATIB ■ ATIC ■

▶ HOW and WHY did industry change between 1750 and 1900?

ATIA ■ ATIB ■ ATIC ■

The domestic system

Source 2.A Birmingham in 1785, by Thomas Newte

Many nailers work in their own cottages and employ every hand in the family, whether male or female.

The changes in farming took place at a time when Britain was already on its way to becoming the world's first great industrial nation. At first these industries, even those producing metal goods (Source 2.A), were on a small scale. They were carried on in people's homes or in workshops employing a handful of workers. This is why it was called the 'domestic system'. Workers used hand tools or simple machines which took their power from a waterwheel.

The woollen industry

In 1750 the most important domestic industry was still the manufacture of woollen cloth. Daniel Defoe described the cloth industry of Halifax at about this time (Source 2.B).

Source 2.B

The houses were full of cheerful men. Some were at the dye-vat. Some were working at the loom. Others were dressing [cleaning and trimming] *the cloths. The women and children were carding* [brushing wool with prongs to separate the fibres] *or spinning the wool. All were employed from the youngest to the oldest.*

The invention in 1733 of the flying shuttle caused a crisis in the woollen industry. It doubled the output of a handloom weaver. Twenty spinning-wheels were needed to supply yarn to one loom. Inventors therefore tried to find a way of increasing the amount of yarn a spinner could produce. In 1764 James Hargreaves invented the spinning jenny for use in his own home. At first he kept his invention secret since it enabled one spinner to do the work of eight. But when, in 1767, he sold a few of the new spinning jennies to make extra money, a mob of spinners broke into his house and destroyed his machines.

Source 2.C

A map of the woollen industry in the middle of the eighteenth century

In 1771 Richard Arkwright opened a cotton-spinning mill at Cromford in Derbyshire using another new spinning machine. This was the water frame. It was powered by a water-wheel. Each frame could spin four spindles at a time and the mill was a great success. Arkwright built other cotton mills as well and later adapted them to use steam power.

2.1 Look at the map of the woollen industry. Which was your nearest centre of wool production at the start of the eighteenth century?
2.2 Look at the picture on the left and at Source 2.B. How did the domestic industry differ from a factory industry today? AT1A ■
2.3 Look at the photograph showing weavers' cottages in the West Riding of Yorkshire. What is unusual about the windows? Can you think of a reason for this? AT1C/L5
2.4 Look at the sources. How and why did the use of steam power and new machinery change the textile industries of Lancashire and Yorkshire? AT1A ■
2.5 Why did Oldham prosper? AT1B/L4
2.6 Was it true to say that 'Machines is th'ruin of poor folk'? Did the destruction of Hargreaves's spinning jenny in 1767 achieve anything? Can you think of any similar changes taking place in Britain today? AT1A ■

Weavers' cottages at Thurlstone in Yorkshire

Arkwright's second cotton mill at Cromford in Derbyshire

Arkwright ran his mills effectively (see Source 3.A on page 20). He put his workers on 13-hour shifts so that his machines worked night and day. By 1782 he was employing over 5000 cotton workers. Other manufacturers soon followed his example. Even better machines were invented, such as Samuel Crompton's spinning mule in 1779 and the 'self-acting' (automatic) mule in 1830. The power loom invented by Edmund Cartwright in 1789 further speeded up the weaving of cloth.

By the 1820s, steam power, using coal as the fuel, had taken the place of water power. This gave the valley towns on the coalfields of Lancashire (Source 2.G), the West Riding of Yorkshire and central Scotland a great advantage. They grew rapidly. At the same time, many of the centres of the textile industry shown on the map declined.

The new methods brought disaster to many skilled craft workers such as the woolcombers, carders, hand spinners and handloom weavers. They were replaced by unskilled workers. Many of these were children (see page 20). Their job was simply to check that the machines were working properly.

Source 2.D At work in Bradford

Power looms		Handcombers	
1836	2768	**1845**	10 000
1850	29 539	**1857**	almost nil

Source 2.E Statement from a Manchester spinner recorded by Henry Mayhew in about 1850

Twenty years ago I could earn £2.10s [£2.50] *every week. In 1837 the 'self actors' came into common use. One girl can mind three pairs. That used to be three men's work. She got 15 shillings* [75p] *for work which had given three men £7.10s* [£7.50]. *Out of one factory, 400 hands were flung* [sacked] *in one week. Nothing could be done. We were told to go and mind the three pairs, as the girls did, for 15 shillings a week.*

Source 2.F Extract from Mrs Gaskell's novel *Mary Barton* set in Manchester in 1838

'Bless thee lad, do ask 'em to make th'masters break th'machines. There's never been good times sin' spinning jennies came up.'
'Machines is th'ruin of poor folk,' chimed in several voices.

Source 2.G Oldham in Lancashire in 1825

Sixty years ago there was not a cotton mill. At present there are no fewer than sixty five, of which all, except two, have been built during the present century. These mills, which are wholly employed in spinning cotton, are all worked by steam, and there are, within the same limits, one hundred and forty steam-engines used in the various processes of manufacturing and mining.

The closeness of Oldham to Manchester [the great market for cotton goods], *the advantages of water, but above all the abundant supply of coal from the mines in the surrounding townships, have made this one of the most extensive and rapidly growing centres of manufacture in the county.*

The Age of Steam

By 1750, the first steps towards the use of steam power had already been taken. Thomas Newcomen had invented a steam-engine in 1712 to pump out water from coal mines (see photograph on page 24). But his engine had several drawbacks. It could only work in an up-and-down motion. It was also very large and heavy and used a lot of coal.

The use of steam power grew rapidly, however, when James Watt, in partnership with Matthew Boulton, built a more effective steam-engine in 1776. Watt's steam-engine produced three times as much power from a tonne of coal. Nonetheless, it still went up and down instead of round and round like a water-wheel or windmill. Five years later, however, Watt and his foreman William Murdock invented a way of turning this up-and-down motion into rotary motion.

James Watt

Unlike a water-wheel (see photographs on pages 24–5), the new steam-engine could be used anywhere in Britain. It could power machines in factories, traction-engines on farms, ships at sea, and locomotives running on railway lines. It changed the world. James Watt's steam-engine was undoubtedly the most important single invention of the Industrial Revolution.

Coal mining

By 1800 there were at least 500 Boulton and Watt steam-engines in Britain. New factories were built to make use of this cheap and efficient source of power. At the same time, the iron and steel industry was also growing rapidly. It used coke (see page16) to smelt iron ore (natural deposits of iron from the ground). Large quantities of coal were needed, therefore, to make iron and to heat the boilers sending steam to the steam-engines. As you can see from Source 2.H, coal production rose sharply.

Source 2.H

Coal production in tonnes			
1750	1800	1850	1900
6 million	10 million	50 million	230 million

Most of the coal close to the surface had been mined. The demand for more coal could only be met if seams deep below the surface were mined as well. But there were problems (Source 2.I). The solutions to these problems made the coal mines of 1844 (Source 2.J) and 1877 (see picture opposite) very different from those in operation at the start of the century (see the picture in the centre).

Source 2.I Problem
The pits soon filled with wate… Efficient pumps were needed.
A gas called 'fire-damp' (a mixture of air and methane gas) sometimes escaped when coal was excavated in a mine. Flames and sparks could ignite causing an explosion.
A gas called 'choke-damp' (carbon dioxide) sometimes escaped as well. It suffocated miners if there was no fresh a… underground to clear it.
As mine shafts became deeper the ropes which lowered the miners began to snap.

Painting of a coal-mine in about 1800 ▼

2.7 Compare the two mining pictures. How did coal-mines change between 1800 and 1877? AT1A ■

2.8 How was a coal-mine in 1844 (Source 2.J) different from a coal mine today? AT1A ■

2.9 Look at Source 2.J and at Source 3.Q on page 27. What risks did miners run in a coal-mine in the 1830s and 1840s? AT1C/L5

ution	Problem	Solution
omas Newcomen designed his am-engine to pump water of the coal mines.	*Women and children were used to pull heavy wagons laden with coal along underground railways.*	*Pit ponies who spent their whole lives in the mines were used to pull the waggons instead.*
Humphry Davy invented the ty lamp in 1815. A sheet of tal gauze stopped the flame n an oil lamp igniting the gas, let enough light through to	*Finding a cheap way to transport coal on the surface was another big problem.*	*Canals were used from 1761 onwards (page 30). Wagons running on wooden rails were used in the North-East by 1750 (page 32). The Stockton and Darlington steam railway opened in 1825 (page 31).*
n Buddle invented an exhaust np in 1790. It sucked out the air from one mine shaft, wing in fresh air down ther shaft.	*Tunnel roofs often collapsed when the coal was removed.*	*Wooden pit props were used to support the roofs of the tunnels.*
e cables were introduced to e and lower the metal cages d by the miners.	*Long working hours made the miners sleepy and careless.*	*Shorter working hours were introduced.*

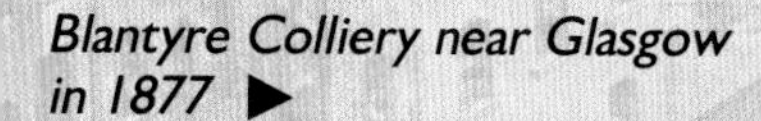

Blantyre Colliery near Glasgow in 1877 ▶

2.10 Draw a graph to show the rise in coal production between 1750 and 1900. When was the fastest period of growth? Write a brief paragraph explaining your graph. AT1C/L5

2.11 What problems had to be solved in order to meet the increased demand for coal in the nineteenth century? AT1B/L5

Source 2.J A Durham coal mine in 1844

I had to wait a few minutes, till a huge deep iron tub, containing about two tubs of coal, emptied its load. We were then swung off and let down, sinking the eighteen hundred feet [550 metres] *in what seemed to me little more than two minutes. The tub was brought to a level with a kind of gallery, along which was a tramway for wagons. A few candles and lamps gave light to the scene.*

Every hundred yards or so [about 90 metres] *a horse and laden wagons go tearing and clanking past. At intervals along the passage, I found it closed up with coarse wooden doors, each attended by a boy. He opened it for the passing of the wagons and then shut it again. These form a part of the arrangements for ventilating the mine. Every two yards* [1.8 metres] *a wooden beam prevented falls of the sandstone ceiling.*

At length we came to two human figures, almost naked, the one using a pick against the solid wall of coal, the other shovelling the resulting loose materials into a wagon.

The iron and steel industry

As you have seen, the rapid growth of the iron and steel industry was one of the main reasons why coal mining became Britain's most important industry in the nineteenth century.

The rise of the iron industry began in 1709 when a Shropshire manufacturer called Abraham Darby used coke for the first time to smelt iron ore. He made the coke by heating coal to drive off the gases it contained.

Darby owned an ironworks at Coalbrookdale. He had discovered that a strong blast of air could raise the temperature in a coke-fired furnace high enough to melt the iron in iron ore. It produced molten iron which could be poured into a mould. The charcoal-burning furnaces which had been used before then had not been able to do this. The iron they produced had had to be hammered in a forge before it could be used.

Darby kept his invention to himself. This is why most of the new coke-burning blast furnaces were still in Shropshire in 1750. In the next forty years, however, the industry changed rapidly. Other manufacturers were soon using coke as well (Sources 2.K and 2.L). By 1788 nearly five tonnes of pig iron were being smelted with coke to every tonne smelted in a charcoal-burning furnace.

◀ *This painting shows Abraham Darby's ironworks at Coalbrookdale in about 1780. The Darby family built the world's first iron bridge across the River Severn between 1779 and 1781 (see page 25)*

Henry Cort was another important inventor of the eighteenth century. At his ironworks in Hampshire he developed the 'puddling' (stirring) process in 1784. This helped to turn brittle iron into a tougher metal called wrought iron. Cort could make 15 tonnes of bar iron in the time it took other ironmasters to make a tonne of wrought iron in a forge. These new methods caused a sharp rise in iron production, as you can see from Source 2.M.

Source 2.M

Iron production in tonnes						
1786	1806	1826	1846	1866	1886	1906
70 000	250 000	650 000	1 800 000	4 600 000	7 100 000	10 300 000

Source 2.K The Carron ironworks in Scotland in 1760

We visited a flourishing ironworks, where, instead of burning wood, they use coal, which they have the art of cleaning in such a way as to free it from sulphur, that would otherwise make the metal too brittle for working.

Source 2.L Rotherham in 1769

Rotherham is famous for its ironworks. Near the town are two collieries, out of which the iron ore is dug, as well as the coals to work it with. These collieries and works employ nearly 500 hands. The ore is here worked into metal and then into bar iron, and the bars sent into Sheffield to be worked.

2.12 What great advantage did Rotherham have as an iron-producing centre in 1769?

2.13 What effect did the writer of Source 2.N think the new process would have on the price of steel? AT3/L3

2.14 Draw a graph to show how the production of iron rose between 1786 and 1906 using the figures given in Source 2.M. Explain your graph. When did the industry grow at its fastest rate? AT1A/L5

Iron was still unsuitable for many manufacturing processes. What was needed was a tougher form of iron, called steel. This was made by burning off impurities in the raw iron. In 1740, Benjamin Huntsman of Sheffield discovered an expensive but effective way to do this, making high-quality steel in a coke-burning furnace. But the method he used only produced small quantities. This is why there were still only five steel manufacturers in Sheffield by 1770. By 1856 there were 135. This was because Henry Bessemer had invented a new steel-making process (Source 2.N). It drastically changed the way in which steel was made.

An iron and steel works in about 1890

Source 2.N Description of the Bessemer process printed in a magazine in November 1856

This new process of Mr.Bessemer's consists merely in forcing air through the molten pig iron. The molten iron is received red-hot into a sort of basin with holes at its bottom, communicating with a very powerful pair of blast-bellows, worked by steam. The air blast is turned on before the red-hot liquid metal is received into the basin.

The fierce air-blast forces the carbon combined with the iron into a furious combustion. A bright flame and an eruption of sparks burst from the mass. The sulphur and phosphorus are burned off with the carbon.

There is to be one roasting and one melting, in the place of half-a-dozen tedious and costly fusings; air is to be blown through the molten liquid, and presto! In a few short minutes, huge masses of the finest iron are to be ready for the hammer and the anvil. If this promise be fulfilled, the best steel, which is now worth from £20 to £30 the ton, will be furnished in any required quantity at the cost of £6 the ton.

The main advantage of the Bessemer process was that it could turn twenty times as much iron into steel as Huntsman's method but in less than a quarter of the time. Good quality steel was now cheap and plentiful. This had a major effect on the engineering and metal-working industries, such as those making weapons, railway rolling stock, machine tools and cutlery. By the end of the century scenes like the one in the picture above could be seen in all the great iron and steel centres of Britain, such as central Scotland, South Wales, Sheffield, the Black Country around Birmingham and Middlesbrough on Teesside.

A Bessemer converter at work in about 1880

2.15 What did the Bessemer Converter convert? Which stage in the process is illustrated in the picture?
2.16 Compare the pictures of the two ironworks. How did the iron industry change between 1780 and 1890?

AT1A ■

'The Workshop of the World'

Engineering, too, was thriving. Visitors to Britain were impressed with what they saw (Source 2.O).

Source 2.O An American visitor in Birmingham in 1811

In one place five hundred persons were employed in making plated ware of all sorts, toys and trinkets. In another place, three hundred men produced ten thousand gun-barrels in a month.

In 1855 a forge in Leeds was supplying steam-hammers to India, Australia and Italy, steam-engines to Egypt and machine tools to Russia. It had developed out of small workshops where skilled smiths and other craftsmen had shaped tools, weapons and implements in the past. By 1851, when Queen Victoria opened the Great Exhibition in Hyde Park, Britain had become 'The Workshop of the World'. If foreign buyers wanted a railway, steamship, or a pin, they bought it in Britain.

Agricultural machinery at the Great Exhibition in 1851 ▶

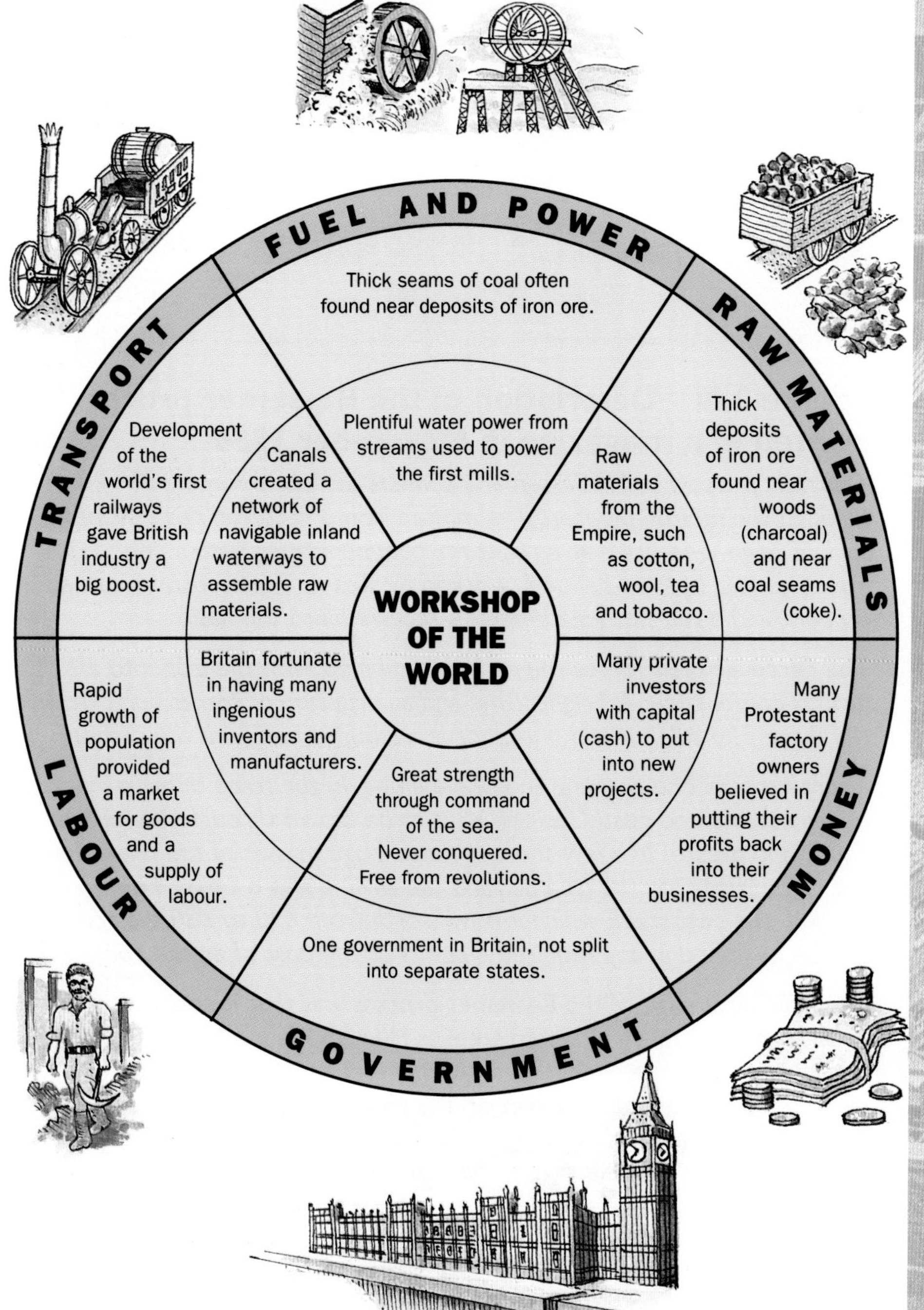

◀ *Why Britain became 'The Workshop of the World'*

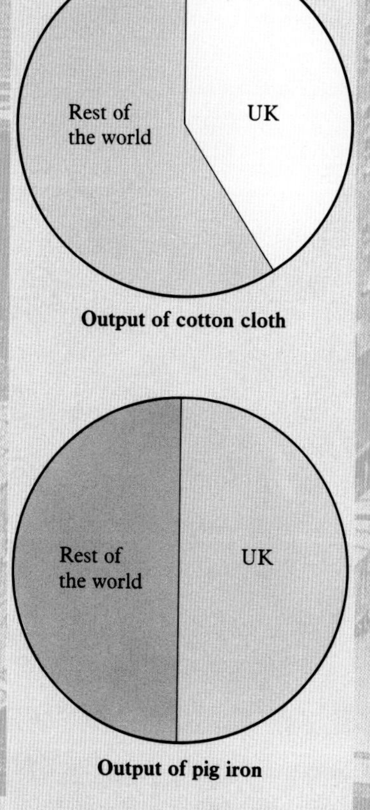

Pie charts showing output of cotton cloth and pig iron in Britain in about 1870

2.17 How do the pie charts support the idea that Britain was 'The Workshop of the World'?
2.18 Draw a bar chart to compare the growth in output of the British industries shown in the table in Source 2.P.
2.19 Which of the industries recorded in the bar chart made most progress in the space of 80 years? By how many times did each of these industries grow in the space of eighty years? AT1A/L7
2.20 Why did Britain become 'The Workshop of the World'? AT1B ■

Time Line

- **1767** Hargreaves's spinning jenny
- **1771** Arkwright's mill at Cromford
- **1776** Boulton–Watt steam-engine
- **1784** Cort's puddling furnace
- **1789** Cartwright's steam power loom
- **1815** Davy's safety lamp
- **1851** The Great Exhibition
- **1856** Bessemer converter

Oil and cake mills in Liverpool in 1899

Source 2.P

	1800	1880
Coal production	10 000 000 tonnes	147 000 000 tonnes
Iron production	200 000 tonnes	7 700 000 tonnes
Cotton imported	22 000 tonnes	650 000 tonnes
Shipping launched	50 000 tonnes	660 000 tonnes

New factories, mills and works making foodstuffs, chemicals, soap, animal foods and many other new products were becoming a familiar sight in Britain by the end of the nineteenth century.

3 Changes in working conditions

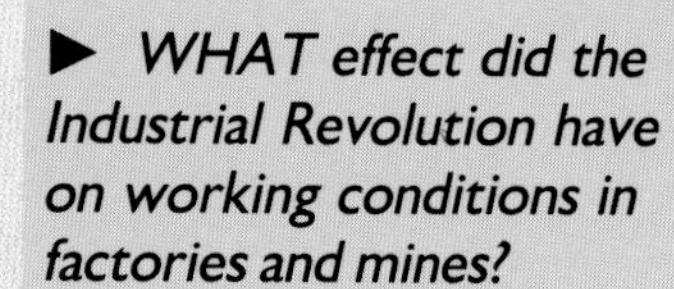

► *WHAT effect did the Industrial Revolution have on working conditions in factories and mines?* AT1A ■ AT1C ■

► *HOW and WHY did working conditions improve?* AT1B ■ AT1C ■

◄ *Children going to work in a woollen mill in Yorkshire in about 1813*

Working conditions in textile mills

Working conditions in many factories at the start of the nineteenth century were appalling. Visitors described the constant shriek of the machines and the clatter of the looms. The air was dusty, smelly, stiflingly hot in summer and bitterly cold in winter. Long working hours made the workers tired and careless. Accidents were common, especially since the machines were usually unguarded. It was easy for someone to get their hair or hands caught up in a machine.

What made matters worse was the fact that thousands of young children worked in these factories. They were paid very low wages and forced to do the dirtiest of jobs. They were also small. This was very useful. They were made to crawl under power looms, crouch down in the narrow tunnels of a coal-mine, or climb up narrow chimneys with a brush.

Some employers did their best for the children they employed. Joseph Farington, a famous artist, saw this for himself when he visited Richard Arkwright's mills at Cromford in 1801 (Source 3.A). He saw the factory children in church on Sunday and noted that they were sent to school there each week.

Source 3.A Children at work in a cotton mill in 1801

August 22 1801 *In the evening I walked to Cromford and saw the children coming from their work out of one of Mr Arkwright's factories. I was glad to see them look in general very healthy and many with fine, rosy complexions. These children had been at work from 6 or 7 o'clock this morning and it was now about 7 in the evening. One of them, a boy of 10 or 11 years of age, told me his wages were 3s 6d* [17.5p] *a week. A little girl said her wages were 2s 3d* [11p] *a week.*

Working conditions for adults also varied. After visiting two cotton mills near Bolton in 1844, a lady writer spoke highly of the working conditions she had seen (Source 3.B).

3.1 Look at Source 3.A. Was Richard Arkwright an ideal employer? How long did the children work on each shift? What form of discrimination was practised in his mills?

3.2 Look at the picture showing the inside of a cotton mill in about 1840. Which evils of the factory system does it illustrate?

3.3 Look at Source 3.B. What were the writer's conclusions? Did she base them on facts or on opinions? Was she in a good position to say there could be no workers 'better off, more comfortable, or more happy than the factory operatives of the north of England'? AT2 ■

3.4 Imagine you are a textile worker in the nineteenth century. Write about the working conditions in the place where you work, saying why you think they are good or bad. AT1C ■

Source 3.B At work in a cotton mill near Bolton in 1844

The working rooms are spacious, well-ventilated and lofty. They are kept at a pleasant temperature. Like all parts of the factory, they are exceedingly clean. There are a number of windows in each room. I saw that great care had been taken to box-up dangerous machinery. I was told that accidents were very rare. When they did occur, they were the result of the greatest stupidity or negligence.

My opinion is, that as long as the masses have to earn their bread by the sweat of their brows, we cannot expect to see them better off, more comfortable, or more happy than the factory operatives of the north of England.

Inside a cotton textile mill in about 1840

Cruelty and neglect

Although many mills and factories were well-run, there were many bad employers. Working conditions began to improve slowly when Parliament passed a series of laws called the Factory Acts. These controlled the circumstances in which women and children could be employed and the hours they were to work.

Much of the pressure to change the laws came from a small number of well-meaning people who took up the cause of the workers. Even then, the laws were only passed by Parliament after Government officials reported heart-rending examples of the disgraceful working conditions in which women and children were employed. You can see extracts from some of these reports in Sources 3.C and 3.D.

Source 3.C Cruelty to children near Wolverhampton

In Willenhall the children are shamefully and most cruelly beaten with a horsewhip, strap, stick, hammer, handle, file, or whatever tool is nearest at hand, or are struck with the clenched fist or kicked.

Source 3.D Child labour near Nottingham

If the statement of the mother be correct, one of her children, four years of age, works twelve hours a day with only an interval of a quarter of an hour for each meal at breakfast, dinner and tea. The child never goes out to play. Two more of her children, one six and the other eight years of age, work in summer from 6 a.m. till dusk. In winter they work fifteen hours from 7 in the morning till 10 at night.

The Factory Acts

Slowly Parliament passed a number of laws to protect women and children at work. The pressure to do so was led by Lord Shaftesbury and a number of factory reformers who included Richard Oastler and the manufacturer Robert Owen. Oastler described the appalling conditions in which children worked in Bradford. He called it 'Yorkshire slavery'.

In 1833, Parliament bowed to this pressure and passed an important Factory Act. It banned the employment of children under 9 years of age, but only in textile mills. It put restrictions on the employment of other children as well. Government inspectors were appointed to make sure the Act was carried out. It was followed by further Factory Acts in 1844, 1847 and 1850 regulating textile mills. The last of these limited the working day for all workers to 10½ hours. The 1847 Act cut the amount of time that women and boys under 18 could work. The 1844 Act did the same and made the manufacturers box in and protect dangerous machines. By 1850 all workers had the right to a 5½ day working week. Saturday afternoons and Sundays were holidays.

Nonetheless, it was not until 1874 that children under 9 years of age were banned from working in factories not covered by the earlier laws. This minimum working age was raised to 12 years by 1901. Despite these improvements, living and working conditions in many mills and factories were still appalling. R.H. Sherard investigated some of these for a popular magazine in 1896 (Sources 3.E and 3.F).

Source 3.E Combing wool in Bradford in 1896

The noise is deafening – a grinding, screeching noise. The whole place vibrates. The heat is very great, and the air is full of a yellow, noisome [nasty] *dust. And the smell – the horror of it when it comes to you from the heated rooms in which the wool is scoured of the grease.*

Source 3.F Processing chemicals in Widnes in 1896

The foul gases which belched forth night and day from the many factories, rot the clothes, the teeth, and, in the end, the bodies of the workers. They have killed every tree and every blade of grass for miles around. One sees numerous and fine children, but never any old people. The certainty of a shortened life, the possibility of a sudden and terrible death, and constant risks of painful accidents are well known to all the chemical workers in these alkali factories.

Conditions in the coal mines

Conditions were no better in the coal-mines. In many ways they were much worse. A report published in 1842 shocked people with its vivid and horrifying descriptions of the conditions in which children and women were working underground (Sources 3.G to 3.K).

Source 3.G A trapper (aged 8)

All his work is to open the door and then allow the door to shut of itself. He sits alone and has no one to talk to. He has no light. His hours are passed in total darkness. He knows nothing of the sun.

Source 3.H Mining near Halifax

In many collieries in this district the children work all day long in water and mud. In some the men actually hew the coals in water.

A coal miner in 1813

3.5 What reasons are there for treating Sources 3.E and 3.F with caution? AT2 ■

3.6 What are the strengths and weaknesses of Sherard's account compared with Source 3.B on page 21? AT2/L7

3.7 Look at the *Punch* cartoon showing people at work in a coal-mine. How does it support what you know about conditions in the coal-mines from Sources 3.G to 3.K. AT3/L5

3.8 What was the point of the *Punch* cartoon? What was the artist's attitude to the mine owners? AT1C/L7

3.9 Write a long caption for the *Punch* cartoon, explaining what it shows for the benefit of a foreigner who knows nothing about the Industrial Revolution in Britain. AT1C ■

3.10 Which of the Sources 3.A to 3.K do you think could have been exaggerated or even untrue? AT2/L5

3.11 Write a short account of changes in working conditions, (a) using Sources 3.A and 3.B only, (b) using Sources 3.C to 3.K only. What difference does it make if you use some sources but leave out others? AT2/L6

3.12 Why do you think the workers put up with these appalling working conditions for so long? AT1B ■

3.13 Look at the photograph of the Victorian coal-mine at the Beamish Open Air Museum on page 27. What impression of the Industrial Revolution do you think tourists get when they visit an industrial relic like this? AT2 ■

3.14 How and why have working conditions in factories and mines changed since the period of the Industrial Revolution? AT1A ■

Source 3.I The Yorkshire coalfield

In one case a child was regularly taken into the pit of his father at three years of age. It was made to follow him to the workings, there to hold the candle, and when exhausted with fatigue, was cradled upon the coals until his return at night.

Source 3.J Evidence from a drawer in a coal pit

Betty Harris (aged 37) from Bolton: *I have a belt round my waist, and a chain passing between my legs, and I go on my hands and feet. The road is very steep, and we have to hold by a rope. It is very hard work for a woman. My cousin looks after my children in the day time. I am very tired when I get home at night. I have drawn till I have had the skin off me.*

Source 3.K Speech by Lord Ashley in Parliament in 1842

In Oldham the tunnels are so low only little boys can work in them, which they do naked, and often in mud and water, dragging sledge-tubs by the girdle and chain.

As a result of this pressure and the evidence in the report, the Government brought in the Coal Mines Act of 1842. The new law banned the employment underground of (a) boys under 10 years, (b) women and girls, whatever their age. An Inspector of Mines was appointed to see that the Act was carried out. In addition there were new rules to try to make life safer underground. No child under the age of 15, for instance, was any longer to be put in charge of machinery.

This cartoon in Punch *was printed in 1843. The magazine explained the drawing with these words: 'It is gratifying to know that though there is much misery in the coal mines, there is a great deal of luxury results from it'*

Industry: The impact of the Industrial Revolution on a local area

This water-wheel was used to crush lead ore at the Kilhope lead mine in the Pennines near Alston in Cumbria

Newcomen pumping engine at Elsecar Colliery, near Barnsley

In some areas, such as the West Country and the Pennines, the ruins of disused kilns like this one near Coniston in the Lake District can still be seen. When a forge, kiln or mine was abandoned in the past, the workers did not clear the site afterwards. They left it in ruins after stripping away any machinery they wanted to keep

The beginnings of the Industrial Revolution

If you study the impact of the Industrial Revolution on your local area, you will need to know what it was like in 1750. Pictures and paintings in your local museum and art gallery and in books on local history in the library will help you to find out about this. Look out for scenes like the colliery in 1800 (on page 14) and the millworkers of Wigan (on page 83).

You will also find that some evidence of the old domestic industries of the early eighteenth century can still be seen today, such as weavers' cottages (see page 13), disused kilns, windmills and water-wheels. Newcomen steam-engines, like the one in the photograph above, were sufficiently rare for their arrival in the district to be commented on in local records. Luckily, local historians in the Victorian period were fond of compiling lists of local events like this. Some of their books have been reprinted in modern editions, such as *Swindon* by William Morris (1885), *The Local Records of Stockton and Neighbourhood* by Thomas Richmond (1868) and *Annals of Bristol* by John Latimer (1887).

There may be a book like this for your area. You will find it in the local history section in your local library. For instance, *Historical Records of Northumberland and Durham* by John Sykes (1866) was reprinted in 1973. It contains a reference to the arrival of a Newcomen steam-engine on Tyneside in 1763 (Source 3.L).

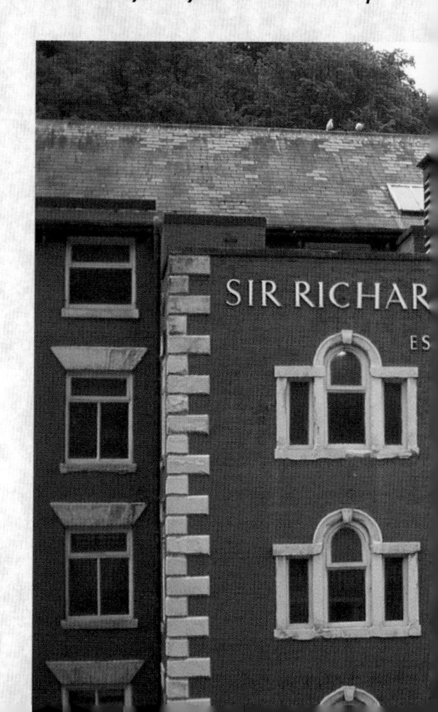

The remains of a water-wheel at Wortley Forge near Sheffield. It provided the power for a heavy hammer which was used to produce wrought iron in the early years of the Industrial Revolution

Woolpack inn sign

Look at the factories in your town today. Are there any signs like this one at Cromford in Derbyshire, telling you when the company was founded or when the factory buildings were erected?
▼

Source 3.L

23 February 1763 *A fire engine cylinder was landed at Wincomblee coal staith* [a landing place], *on the river Tyne, for the use of Walker Colliery. It surpassed everything of the kind which had been seen in the north. It did honour to Colebrook Dale Foundry in Shropshire, where it was manufactured.*

This was the first bridge in the world to be made of iron. It spans the River Severn at Ironbridge near Telford in Shropshire. It forms the centrepiece of the outstanding group of museums which commemorate the origins of the modern iron and steel industry in and around Coalbrookdale

Industrial archaeology

Direct reminders of the mines, mills and factories of the Industrial Revolution can be seen today in many areas. The study of these relics is called Industrial Archaeology. It is worthwhile plotting the position of these remains on a large scale map of your district. It will help to show where the industries of your area were concentrated and how they relate to the growth of the urban areas.

You may be able to find out more from visits to industrial buildings open to visitors, such as Wortley Forge near Sheffield and Kilhope Lead Mine near Alston in Cumbria. Some of the outstanding achievements of the early pioneers of the Industrial Revolution have been carefully preserved in special museums. The 'gin-gang house' shown in the photograph on page 6 is at the Beamish Open Air Museum in County Durham.

Other clues can help you to judge the impact of the Industrial Revolution on your area. Inn signs often tell you about the industries of an area in the past, such as the Woolpack. Surnames (Weaver, Webb, Webster, Webber), street names (Forge Terrace, Mill Road, Ironpit Lane) and place names (Pitsmoor, Forge Rocher, Coalpit Dike, Smithy Wood) can be found in many of the towns which flourished during the Industrial Revolution.

Sources of information

Early nineteenth-century colliery at the Beamish Open Air Museum near Durham

Old directories (see below) and local histories can also tell you something about the effect of the Industrial Revolution on your area. Norfolk, for instance, is usually thought of as a rural county. You might think it the last place to find out about the Industrial Revolution. But Norwich, like Devonshire and the Cotswolds, had a woollen and worsted industry in 1750 which was the equal of the West Riding at that time. If you live in Norfolk, or in any other area with an important craft industry at that time (such as iron-making in Kent or Sussex), you could try to find out what happened when steam-powered machinery was first introduced.

Although Norwich was a long way from a coalfield, boats and barges could reach the city along the rivers Yare and Wensum. As a result, the city's textile industries did not collapse straight away when steam power was introduced. Instead, the local worsted and woollen manufacturers brought in coal by sea from Newcastle upon Tyne. They used it to fuel the new steam-engines in their factories – as you can see in these extracts from a handbook called *White's Gazetteer and Directory of Norfolk, 1845* which was reprinted recently (Sources 3.M, 3.N and 3.O). As you can see, by then the industry was already on the decline. Norwich could not compete because coal was much more expensive there than it was in Bradford or Huddersfield.

Source 3.M The woollen industry in Norwich in 1845

Here are now nearly 700 power looms; and since 1841 more cloth has been woven in workshops and factories than in the houses of the weavers, large numbers of whom are often unemployed.

Source 3.N Rising unemployment

In 1840 there were 1021 unemployed looms, making the total numbers 5075.

Source 3.O The Norwich workhouse in 1845

The workhouse in Bridge Street has accommodations for about 600 paupers. Those who are able to work are employed in the manufacture of worsted and cotton goods.

Source 3.P

It was dark before we reached Sheffield; so that we saw the iron furnaces in all the horrible splendour of their everlasting blaze. This Sheffield, and the land all about it, is one bed of iron and coal.

Monument at Silkstone Church

The inscription records the names and ages of fifteen of the 'twenty-six persons' who were killed. What was the age of the youngest 'collier'? What was the age of the oldest? What was the average age? What do you know about the other eleven victims? ▶

Travel journals

Similar descriptions of towns and their industries can be found in the journals of travellers and writers. Some of these are quoted elsewhere in this book, such as Daniel Defoe in the early eighteenth century (page 12) and the clergyman H.B.J. Armstrong in 1855 (page 47). John Wesley visited most parts of Britain in the eighteenth century and wrote about them in his diary (which you will probably find in your local library). William Cobbett wrote a famous book called *Rural Rides* which describes the places he visited in about 1830, such as South Yorkshire (Source 3.P).

Working conditions

You may also be able to find out about working conditions in the mills, factories and mines of your area. If you visit an industrial site like Wortley Forge (on page 25) or the coal-mine at Beamish (opposite), you can try to picture for yourself what working conditions were like over a hundred years ago.

At Silkstone Church, near Barnsley, a monument in the churchyard records the names of the victims of a terrible mining disaster in 1838. You can see what happened in Source 3.Q. This extract is taken from a book called *The Annals of Yorkshire* which was published in 1862.

Source 3.Q

4 July 1838 *A terrific storm of thunder and hail did immense damage to property and caused a great loss of life. In the neighbourhood of Stainborough, Dodworth, and Silkstone, near Barnsley, the storm was very violent. In the valley of the south-west side of Dodworth, the water rose to such a height that it reached the entrance of a coal-pit in the hillside, belonging to R. Clarke, Esq., called the Moor-Side Pit. The water rushed in, so that in a short time it was filled. A number of colliers were at work in the pit, and twenty-six persons perished in the water, eleven of them females.*

4 The Transport Revolution

◀ The turnpike at Hyde Park Corner in the eighteenth century

▶ *WHAT effect did the Industrial Revolution have on methods of transport?*
ATIB ■ ATIC ■

▶ *HOW and WHY did these changes affect people in Britain?*
ATIA ■ ATIB ■ ATIC ■

Turnpike roads

Roads in the middle of the eighteenth century were in an appalling state. You can see what the traveller Arthur Young thought about some of them in Source 4.A.

Source 4.A Road near Wigan in Lancashire in 1769

I measured ruts four feet [1.2 metres] *deep, floating with mud from a wet summer. What must it be like after a winter? The only mending it receives is the tumbling in of some stones.*

The reason why the roads were often bad was because their upkeep was left to local people and they regarded it as a nuisance. In wet or dusty conditions it was often hard to tell where the road began and the fields ended. As a result, travel in a coach or carriage was very slow and very uncomfortable.

By 1750, however, travellers in some areas were able to use much better roads. These were the turnpikes. They were built by groups of local business people called Turnpike Trusts. Travellers paid a small toll to the keeper at the turnpike gate. This barred them from going through and using the road without paying. The money was used to keep the road in good condition. The writer Arthur Young thought many of them were very good (Source 4.B).

Source 4.B

Kendal to Windermere
Turnpike; now making. What is finished, is as good, firm level a road as any in the world.

Brentford to London
Turnpike. Excellent. But much too narrow for such vast traffic.

The road builders

Road surfaces improved after 1750 (see Source 4.P on page 37). This was largely due to the work of three outstanding civil engineers who built many of the new turnpike roads between 1770 and 1830. John Metcalf and Thomas Telford believed in building roads with strong foundations and good drains. John McAdam used a cheaper method. Instead of putting down solid stone foundations, he laid a shallow layer of small granite chips on top of a platform of medium sized stones. The weight of carts and coaches pressed the stone chips together to make a smooth, hard-wearing 'macadam' surface.

The Golden Age of Coaching

By 1830 there were over 35 000 kilometres of turnpike roads in Britain and about 3000 stage and mail-coach services a day. They were

4.1 What improvements in journey times were achieved between (a) London and Exeter (b) London and Edinburgh? Show them on a graph. AT1A ■

4.2 Why is the travel journal of a foreign visitor especially useful as a source of information about everyday life in Britain? AT3/L5

4.3 What would be the danger of relying on Source 4.D as evidence of what it was like to travel in 1782? AT2 ■

4.4 The Golden Age of Coaching was a colourful period in British history. Use these sources, the pictures here, and the photographs on pages 36–7, to describe its main features. AT1C/L4

4.5 How would your answer to question 4.4 differ if you made no mention of Sources 4.D and 4.E? AT2/L6

4.6 What differences would you expect to see if C.P. Moritz and Charles Dickens both wrote captions for the picture of *Quicksilver* below? AT2/L7

Source 4.D By the French traveller C.P. Moritz in 1782

This ride from Northampton to Leicester I shall remember as long as I live. The coach drove from the yard through a part of the house. The inside passengers got on in the yard. We outside passengers had to clamber up on the main street because there was no room for our heads to pass under the gateway.

The machine now rolled along with prodigious rapidity over the stones through the town. Every moment we seemed to fly into the air. From Harborough to Leicester I had a most dreadful journey. It rained all the time. As before we had been covered with dust, so now we were soaked with rain.

Source 4.E From John Cabbell's diary for 1833 (see page 37)

Nothing more bleak, chilling and miserable than starting at daybreak of a cold frosty morning, the roads hard and slippery and the cold penetrating through every pore.

called 'stagecoaches' because they ran in stages – from one coaching inn to the next. At each new inn, fresh horses were harnessed while the passengers took refreshments. Many coaches travelled at night using carriage lamps to light up the road ahead. In addition to passengers, they also carried newspapers, letters and parcels. Travelling on a smooth 'macadam' surface made coach journeys much more comfortable.

Fifty coaches left London each day for Liverpool. Forty went to Birmingham and another thirty to Edinburgh. They had special names, such as *Tally Ho!*, *The Telegraph*, *The Royal Liverpool* and *Quicksilver*. You can read what travellers thought about these coaches and the roads in Sources 4.D, 4.E, 4.F and the handwritten diary entry on page 37. As you can see from the table (Source 4.C), journey times were now much shorter than they had been a hundred years earlier.

The mail coach Quicksilver *passing the* Star and Garter *at Kew Bridge in 1835. Notice the turnpike in the distance*

Source 4.C Coach services to and from London

Year	Destination	Distance	Length of journey
1658	Exeter	274 km	96 hours
1754	Edinburgh	652 km	264 hours
1784	Edinburgh	652 km	60 hours
1797	Exeter	274 km	25 hours
1825	Edinburgh	652 km	43 hours
1836	Exeter	274 km	17 hours

Source 4.F By the novelist Charles Dickens in 1837

The pavement ceases, the houses disappear; and they are once again dashing along the open road, with the fresh air blowing in their faces, and gladdening their very hearts within them.

Poor people travelled by stage-wagon (see the photograph on page 37). These huge goods vehicles with their large wheels, were pulled by teams of four, six, eight or ten horses. They trundled slowly through the countryside at speeds of only 5 k.p.h. They also carried parcels, packages and heavy items which could not be taken on the stagecoach. This is why the people who ran them were called carriers (page 37).

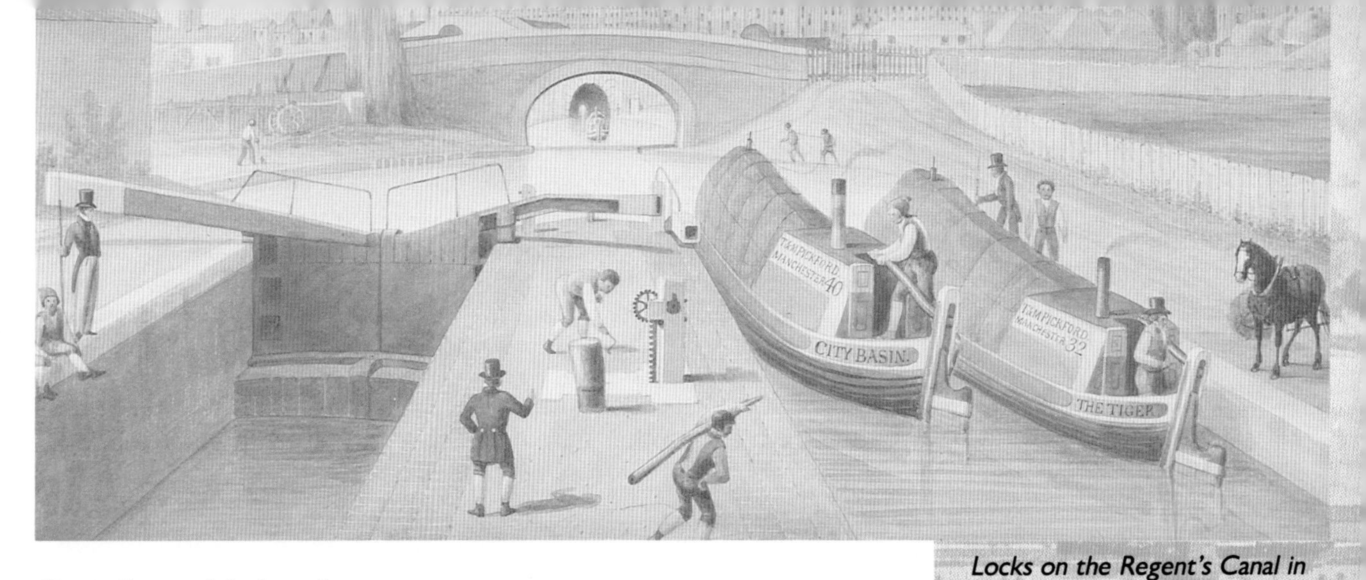

Locks on the Regent's Canal in North London in the 1820s

Canals and inland waterways

In 1750 heavy goods such as corn were usually carried over longer distances by sea or along a navigable river. For instance, coal from Newcastle was taken in wagons to the river Tyne and loaded on to a boat. It reached London by sea after sailing down the Tyne and up the Thames. Although some ports, like King's Lynn on the Great Ouse, owed much to river transport, many other rivers could not be used. They were either too shallow or flowed too fast. The areas with the best navigable rivers, such as East Anglia, were not always the ones which most needed a cheap inland waterway.

When the demand for heavy and bulky raw materials like coal began to grow, manufacturers were keen to find a way of lowering the cost of moving heavy goods. The Duke of Bridgewater's solution was to get James Brindley and an army of construction workers to dig a canal from his coal mines at Worsley in Lancashire to Manchester where the coal was sold (Source 4.G).

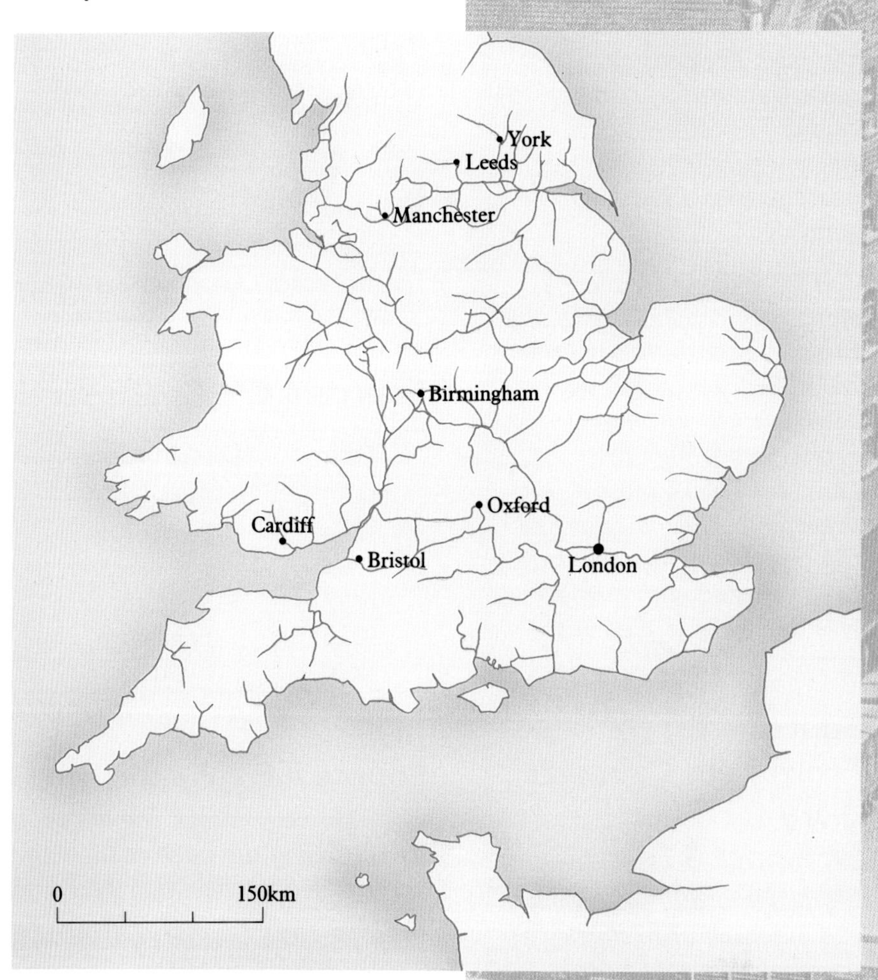

By 1840 there were 6400 kilometres of navigable inland waterway in Britain

Source 4.G From a letter written in 1763

It [the aqueduct carrying the canal over the river Irwell] *is as high as the tops of trees. Whilst I was surveying it with a mixture of wonder and delight, four barges passed me in the space of about three minutes, two of them being chained together and dragged by two horses. I hardly dared to walk. I almost trembled to look down on the river Irwell beneath me.*

This navigation begins at the foot of some hills, in which the Duke's coals are dug, from whence a canal is cut through rocks which daylight never enters. In some places, where Mr.Brindley has been forced to

4.7 What is a 'navvy'? How do you think this name started with the canal builders?
4.8 What problems did Brindley have to solve in constructing the canal? How did he alter the landscape?
AT1C/L5

4.9 Which parts of England and Wales were a long way from an inland waterway in 1840? Why?
4.10 Look at Source 4.Q on page 37. Was your nearest town served by an inland waterway in the nineteenth century? What effect did this have on the town? AT1B/L5

carry his navigation across a public road, he has sunk the road gradually, so as to pass under his canal, which forms a bridge over the road.

Brindley's canal greatly reduced the cost of sending coal from Worsley Colliery to Manchester. It had cost £2 a tonne by pack-horse and 60p a tonne by river before the canal was built. After 1761 the cost fell to only 30p a tonne and the journey took far less time.

Other factory owners saw the benefits a canal could bring to their industries. Josiah Wedgwood, the pottery manufacturer, helped to plan the Grand Trunk or Trent and Mersey Canal which was begun in July 1766. When it was opened he could bring china clay all the way from Cornwall by water to his pottery works in Stoke-on-Trent.

Many other new canals were built in the next forty years, such as the Grand Union Canal linking London and the Midlands. The prospect of huge profits (see Source 4.O on page 36) attracted people who rushed to invest money in new projects. But many canals were built which never paid their way.

The opening of the Stockton and Darlington Railway in 1825

The coming of the railways

On 27 September 1825, a long train pulled by a steam locomotive carried the world's first rail passengers on the new Stockton and Darlington Railway. Some spectators were frightened as the train speeded along at 20 k.p.h! You can see what happened in Source 4.H. Afterwards the railway was used mainly to carry coal. But it was followed in 1830 by the world's first regular passenger service between Liverpool and Manchester. The age of the railway had arrived.

4.11 Why were the canals vital to the new industries growing up in the years before the coming of the railways?
AT1B ■

4.12 In what ways does the picture support the evidence in Source 4.H? AT3/L6
4.13 Use the painting and Source 4.H to write a letter to the editor of the *Scots Magazine* in 1825 commenting on the new railway.

Source 4.H From the *Scots Magazine* in 1825

All along the line people on foot crowded the fields on each side, and here and there a lady or gentleman on horseback. A few miles from Stockton the railway runs parallel and close to the turnpike road. This gave them a fine opportunity of viewing the procession. Horses, carriages, carts and other vehicles travelled along with the engine and her immense train of carriages. At one time, the passengers on the train had the pleasure of cheering their brother passengers on the stage coach which passed alongside. They saw the striking contrast between the engine with her six hundred passengers and load, and the coach with four horses and only sixteen passengers.

The Liverpool and Manchester Railway in the 1830s

The first railways

Two things led to the invention of the modern railway system. These were (a) the use of railway lines to make it easier for horses to pull heavy coal wagons and (b) the invention of the steam-engine. In 1769 the traveller Arthur Young wrote about the coal wagons pulled by horses, which ran on wooden railways near Durham (Source 4.1). Twenty years later, they had been replaced by iron rails and the wagons were fitted with flanged wheels to stop them slipping off the rails.

The 'steam horse'

In 1803, Richard Trevithick, an engineer from Cornwall, built the first 'steam horse' – a steam-engine which could move under its own steam. In 1808 he raced his *Catch Me Who Can* locomotive on a round track at Euston in London. These early locomotives were slow, unreliable and expensive to run. It was cheaper to use a horse.

In 1814 a colliery engineer called George Stephenson demonstrated a steam locomotive at Killingworth Colliery, near Newcastle upon Tyne. It could pull 30 tonnes of coal at a speed of 6.5 k.p.h. Eleven years later his steam-engine *Locomotion* opened the Stockton and Darlington Railway in 1825 (see page 31).

The Liverpool and Manchester Railway

It was obvious by now that a steam railway system could be built to carry passengers and freight. When the Liverpool and Manchester Railway opened in 1830 it became the first passenger railway in the world to use steam locomotives. Well over half a million pounds was raised to pay for the new railway. This was a huge sum of money at that time. Rich people bought shares in the railway at £100 each.

Building the railway meant big changes to the countryside and also to Manchester and Liverpool. Over 60 bridges and viaducts were erected and a tunnel was dug under part of Liverpool. Embankments and cuttings carved through solid rock kept the railway track as level as possible. A large area of soft bogland – Chat Moss – was drained and special foundations were laid to stop the railway line sinking.

The new railway was opened on 15 September 1830 by the Prime Minister, the Duke of Wellington. He and a number of other distinguished guests set off in the first train. Within a month the railway was carrying over 1200 passengers a day. By the end of the year it was moving heavy goods as well. In 1831, in its first full year, nearly half a million passengers travelled on the railway. By 1835 the investors in the railway were being paid £10 a year for each £100 share they owned. This was very much more than they got on savings in a bank. This is why everyone wanted to invest in the new railway companies formed to build similar railways in other parts of Britain.

In 1837 the Grand Junction Railway linked the Manchester and Liverpool Railway to Birmingham and the Midlands. In 1838 the London to Birmingham railway was opened. It was followed in 1841 by the Great Western Railway from London to Bristol.

Source 4.1 By Arthur Young in 1769

The tracks of the wheels are marked with pieces of timber let into the road for the wheels of the wagons to run on. By these means one horse can pull with ease 50 or 60 bushels [2 tonnes] *of coal.*

Replica of Locomotion *at the Beamish Museum in County Durham*

4.14 Look at the pictures on the right. How did a First Class railway compartment differ from the Third Class?
4.15 How did the stagecoach (see page 28) affect the way in which the first railway carriages were designed? Why were they called 'railway carriages' or 'coaches'? Why was the official on board called a 'guard'?

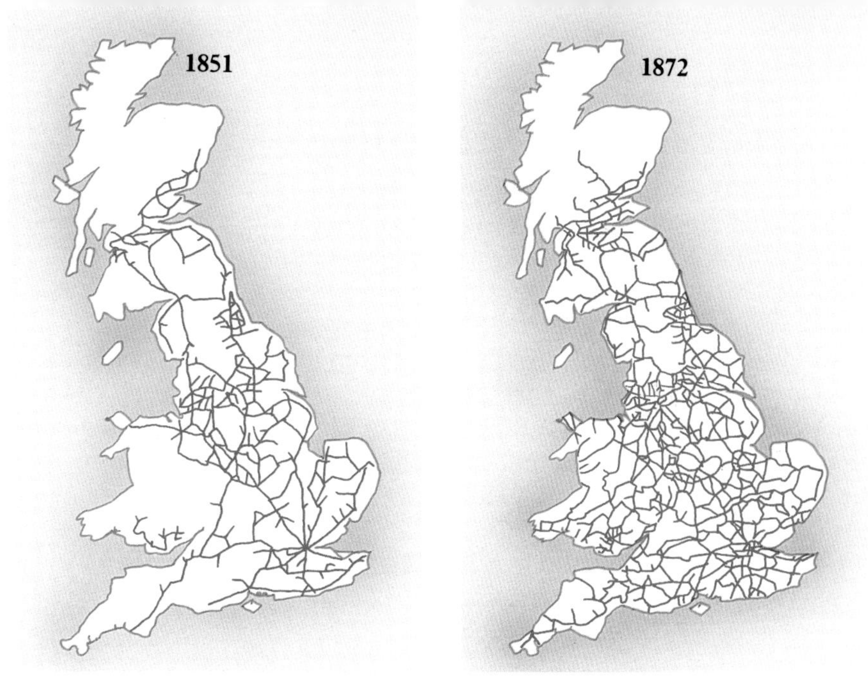

The railway system in Britain in (a) 1845, (b) 1851, (c) 1872

4.16 Use Source 4.J to draw graphs showing how the railways grew in importance between 1842 and 1902. AT1A ■

4.17 Work out the number of passengers carried on the railways in each year for every kilometre of railway line. How did the numbers change between the dates shown below? AT1A ■

1842–52	1862–72	1882–92
1852–62	1872–82	1892–1902

4.18 What do these maps and statistics tell you about the coming of the railways in Britain?
AT1A/L5 AT1B/L5 AT1C/L5

Source 4.J The growth of the railways

Date	Length of line	Passengers
1842	3000 km	18 million
1852	11 800 km	89 million
1862	18 600 km	180 million
1872	25 500 km	423 million
1882	30 000 km	682 million
1892	32 700 km	864 million
1902	35 700 km	1188 million

Railway mania

The expansion of the railway system was so fast, however, that many people in the 1840s lost money buying shares in new railways which failed to make a profit. This period of 'railway mania' was chaotic. There were many accidents. The railway companies were accused of putting profit before safety. They were also accused of neglecting poor people who could not afford the high fares. This is why Parliament made a law in 1844 forcing the companies to run at least one train a day to every station on the line at a cost of no more than a penny a mile (about 1/4p a kilometre).

Departure – Third Class *was the first of two pictures painted in 1855 by the artist Abraham Solomon. He called the second picture* Return – First Class

How the railways affected Britain

At first many people were against the railways. They included the people who stood to lose money, such as shareholders in canals, owners of stagecoaches and coaching inns. Turnpike-keepers, stable lads and canal workers all stood to lose their jobs. Hunters complained because they could not chase a fox through tunnels, across embankments, cuttings or viaducts. Farmers said sparks from locomotives set fire to their straw and frightened their livestock. People in villages and town suburbs complained because they were cut off from their neighbours by the railway line. But it was not long before the railway could be seen to bring benefits to everybody – as you can see in Sources 4.K to 4.N.

Source 4.K Clearing the site for a new railway – from *Dombey and Son* by Charles Dickens

Houses were knocked down and streets broken through and stopped. Deep pits and trenches were dug in the ground and huge heaps of earth and clay thrown up. Everywhere were bridges that led nowhere, temporary wooden houses, piles of scaffolding.

Source 4.L After the new railway was opened – from *Dombey and Son* by Charles Dickens

The new streets formed towns within themselves. Bridges that had led to nothing, led to villas, gardens, churches, healthy public walks. There were railway journals in the newsagents. There were railway hotels, boarding houses; railway maps, views and timetables; railway cabs; railway omnibuses, railway streets and buildings.

4.19 What was the point of the two pictures entitled *The Driver of 1832* and *The Driver of 1852*? What similarities did the artist point out? AT1C/L3

Source 4.M From a magazine written in 1856

Coal is carried at an average of a half-penny [0.13p] *per ton per mile. The old charge by the canals was three halfpence. These iron roads save people two-thirds of their time in travel and two-thirds in fares and tolls. They have given us the penny post, which could not have existed without them. They have criss-crossed the country with telegraph-wires. They have reduced the cost of many goods. Railways bring to London its meat, fish and milk.*

Source 4.N A cheap day excursion to Brighton in 1856

The railway has done it all. The turnpike road has become deserted and grass-grown. Great credit is due to the managers of the South Coast Railway for giving the workers the chance to breathe the invigorating sea-breeze and to give them a change from whizzing wheels, blazing furnaces and other implements of labour.

The Driver of 1832

The Driver of 1852

4.20 What evidence is there that the coming of the railway harmed the turnpike roads? AT1B/L4

4.21 What were the main benefits brought by the railways? How did they benefit the factory owner? How did they benefit the worker? Draw a diagram like the one on page 18 to show how Britain benefitted from the invention of the railway. AT1B ■

Time Line

1761 Worsley and Manchester Canal
1784 First mail-coach service
1803 Trevithick's steam locomotive
1825 Stockton and Darlington Railway
1830 Liverpool and Manchester Railway
1845 Railway mania begins
1858 Launch of the *Great Eastern*

How the coming of the railway affected Britain
The railways directly helped the growth of industry. They created a huge new demand for coal, machine tools, iron rails, steel plate, steam-engines, timber planking, bricks, stones and mortar.
In future, when new factories were built, they were almost always erected next to a railway line. Factories wishing to use steam-powered machinery could now be built away from the coalfields, since coal could be taken there cheaply and quickly by rail.
Passenger and cargo ports, such as Southampton and Liverpool, thrived with the coming of the railways. Ferry ports like Dover, fishing ports such as Grimsby and Fleetwood, and seaside resorts like Brighton, Blackpool and Bournemouth, also prospered.
Hundreds of thousands of new jobs were created, such as engine-drivers, railway guards, stationmasters, cleaners, porters and engineers. Some jobs were lost, such as those of the hostler, coachman and turnpike-keeper. On the whole, however, the railways created many more jobs than they destroyed.
Towns and cities grew even bigger, because people from outlying districts could now afford to shop there. This helped the growth of chain and department stores in the towns. Commuters could live at a distance from their work. Suburbs grew up around the railway stations outside London and the big cities.
There were many other unforeseen effects as well. The Great Exhibition of 1851 was visited by over six million people. Many travelled to London on cheap day trips to see it.
Many new public schools were built in the 1840s and 1850s since pupils could travel easily by rail from any part of the country.
The Government realised that policemen and soldiers could be rushed by train to break up disturbances in distant parts of Britain.

Shipping

The Industrial Revolution had a similar effect on the development of shipping. The wooden sailing ship of 1750 was replaced by the iron or steel ship, first using a steam-driven paddle wheel, and later a steam-powered screw propeller.

The invention of the iron steamship opened up new markets for British goods. It also played a big part in ensuring the supremacy of the Royal Navy in the nineteenth century and in helping Britain to annex a large empire (see Chapters 7 and 8). Ships took troops, guns, farmers, miners and settlers to the colonies. The numbers of people travelling overseas increased dramatically since ships were bigger and much more comfortable. They were also quicker and safer.

◀ *Brunel's* Great Eastern. *This was the biggest ship of its time and could carry 4000 passengers. It was so large it had to have an electric telegraph system to link the engine room with the Captain on the bridge. Seven masts carrying 5500 square metres of canvas, two huge paddle wheels on either side of the ship and a giant screw propeller 8 metres across gave it the power it needed*

Transport: The impact of the Industrial Revolution on a local area

This toll-house is at Great Whelnetham near Bury St Edmunds. Notice the distinctive shape of the building with its six sides – so the turnpike-keeper could always keep an eye on the traffic

Sources of information

Old gazetteers and directories in your public library (see page 26) can help you to find out about the changes in transport in your area during the Industrial Revolution. Some list the coaching inns and stage and mail-coach services provided in your town.

Old local newspapers can often tell about the effect of these changes on your area. You may be able to find copies on display in the local museum, in the library, in a local archive collection, or in a newspaper office. The items shown here are taken from a local newspaper published in the Midlands – The *Birmingham and Lichfield Chronicle* for Thursday, 24 October 1822. This one edition alone tells us about the golden age of coaching, the profits which could be made from the canals, and about the first steam ra

TALLY-HO!
A NEW DAY COACH TO LONDON,
FROM THE NELSON HOTEL, (late DOG INN),
BIRMINGHAM.

THE Public is respectfully informed, that a NEW DAY COACH, called the TALY-HO! has commenced running to and from the NELSON HOTEL (late the Dog Inn) Birmingham, and the GOLDEN CROSS, Charing Cross, London; leaving both houses at six o'clock in the morning, and arriving precisely at half past seven the same evening, through Coventry, Dunchurch, Daventry, Towcester, Stony Stratford, and intermediate places.

*** Passengers and Parcels booked in London at the Golden Cross, Charing Cross; Cross Keys, Wood-street; and Three Cups, Aldersgate-street; and in Birmingham at the Nelson Hotel.

30s. INSIDE—15s. OUTSIDE.
Parcels 1d. per lb.

Performed by
W. RADENHURST and Co. Birmingham,
W. HORNE and Co. London,

who will not be accountable for any kind of luggage or parcels, above £5 value, unless entered and paid for accordingly; but pledge themselves that every attention and dispatch shall be used for the safe delivery of parcels, &c. committed to their care.

N. B. Passengers and Parcels booked at the above offices to all parts of the kingdom.

An advertisement from the Birmingham and Lichfield Chronicle, *24 October 1822*

irmingham and  Lichfield Chronicle.

421.—VOL. LIX.]—[*Price 7d.*

Remember, O my friends, the laws, the rights,
The generous plan of power delivered down,
From age to age, by your renowned forefathers.
Oh! let it never perish in your hands!
But piously transmit it to your children.

THURSDAY, OCTOBER 24, 1822.

Source 4.O
Extract from a letter in the *Birmingham and Lichfield Chronicle*, 24 October 1822

SIR, In the present state of the country, when the profits of all trades and agriculture are so greatly reduced, the Birmingham Canal Company continue to exact their full tonnage [the top rate for using the canal] *and derive an income amounting to near £80 000 a year, which is principally drawn from the trade and industry of Birmingham and its neighbourhood.*

The original shares in this concern it is well known cost only £100 each, but their shares are now currently selling in the market at £2500 or £2600 each. The canal, instead of being an advantage to the town of Birmingham, becomes rather an oppressive tax.

I have been led into these reflections by a conversation which I have lately had with a friend, who has been visiting the collieries of the North of England, and inspecting the *steam rail-roads* which are used there. He informs me that steam engines work there upon rail roads so as to carry coal eight or ten miles, at the tonnage of only 5d. per ton, which is about the distance that the coals are brought to Birmingham upon the canal. The engines or machines are said to cost but 150*l.* or 200*l.*; and travelling upon small carriages by means of small cog wheels, draw 15 or 20 coal carriages after them, carrying about three tons each, say from 40 to 60 tons in the whole. If such steam roads were established between Birmingham and Wednesbury, it would compel the Canal Company to make a reasonable reduction in their tonnages, and would prove an incalculable advantage to the town of Birmingham. The undertakers of such a concern would certainly derive sufficient advantage to themselves, as they might of course charge 5d. per ton, as is done in the North, and the town and trade of Birmingham would still save full 1s. per ton upon all coals, cokes, &c. used in e various manufactories.

I am, Mr. Editor, yours,
VERITAS.

◀ *The concluding half of the letter begun in Source 4.O*

This turnpike gate is at Hunters Bar in Sheffield. You are unlikely to find a gate like this in your town but you might find a street or place name, such as Kenton Bar (Newcastle upon Tyne) or Bootham Bar (York)

Source 4.P
White's Directory of Norfolk, 1845

The turnpikes in Norfolk are better than those of most other counties in England, being generally raised higher than the adjacent lands, well drained by trenches on each side, and having a firm bottom composed of gravel, flint and chalk.

Source 4.Q
White's Directory of Suffolk, 1844

Stowmarket was in a declining condition during the last century, till the River Gipping was made navigable to it from Ipswich in 1793. Since then it has doubled its buildings and population [1761 inhabitants in 1801; 3043 in 1841], *and has enjoyed a considerable traffic in corn, malt, coal, etc., being nearly in the centre of the county* [Suffolk], *and there being no other navigation within the distance of many miles.*

How did the railway affect your town? Is there a Station Hotel or a Victorian station, like this one at Audley End in Essex? Were rows of terraced houses built nearby?

Look at the hotels and inns in your area. Do any of them have a porte-cochere? This was an archway in the middle of the inn which led through to the courtyard and stables at the back. It was because there was an arch like this that C.P. Moritz had to climb on to the coach in the main street instead of in the inn yard (Source 4.D)

You may be able to see other documents in your local museum, such as posters advertising stage-coaches or railway excursions. The extract below is from the diary of John Cabbell, a well-to-do young Scotsman who travelled around Europe in 1833. In it he describes his journey by stagecoach from Edinburgh back home to Glasgow. You can use it to work out the average speed of a stagecoach between Edinburgh and Glasgow in 1833 (distance 72 km = 45 miles).

Old handbooks, such as *White's Gazetteer and Directory* (see page 26), can sometimes tell you about the roads in your district (Source 4.P).

The extract quoted in Source 4.Q (from a *Directory* for Suffolk) shows the effect a new inland waterway had on a small market town. You may be able to find similar information about your area.

started at 11, in a perfect purgatory of a Coach, six inside, oh! it was a sad squeeze, and along the most miserable country possible, the road most excessively dull – The inventor of sixinside Coaches ought to be well squeezed; well, arrived in Old Glasgow at 4 Oclock

Fieldwork

Almost every area has buildings or clues, like those you can see on this page. They show some of the striking changes in transport which took place during the Industrial Revolution.

You can plot the position of the coaching inns, railway stations, turnpike roads, canals and railways you find out about on a large-scale map.

Long lines of packhorses carrying packs of wool crossed streams by narrow, humpbacked bridges like this one at Stokesley in North Yorkshire

This memorial is to John Catchpole, a carrier, who died at Palgrave in Suffolk in 1787

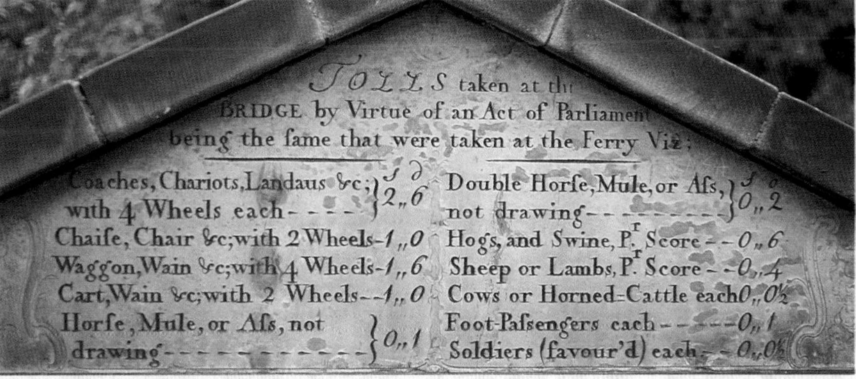

The tolls charged to travellers can sometimes be seen on a tollboard like this one on Cavendish Bridge in Leicestershire

5 Population changes

► *HOW and WHY did the population of Britain change between 1750 and 1900?*

ATIA ■ ATIB ■ ATIC ■

Differences between rich and poor were much greater in Victorian times than they are today. Derby Day was one of the few occasions when you could have seen all classes of Victorian society together in the same place at the same time. When William Frith painted this famous picture in the 1850s, the population of England and Wales had doubled in only fifty years

Growth of population

Source 5.A Growth of population 1751–1901

Year	England and Wales	Scotland	Ireland
1751	6 500 000	1 300 000	3 200 000
1801	8 900 000	1 600 000	5 200 000
1811	10 200 000	1 800 000	6 000 000
1821	12 000 000	2 100 000	6 800 000
1831	13 900 000	2 400 000	7 800 000
1841	15 900 000	2 600 000	8 200 000
1851	17 900 000	2 900 000	6 600 000
1861	20 100 000	3 100 000	5 800 000
1871	22 700 000	3 400 000	5 400 000
1881	26 000 000	3 700 000	5 400 000
1891	29 000 000	4 000 000	5 400 000
1901	32 500 000	4 500 000	5 400 000

We know precise details about the population of Britain since 1801, because the Government has sent officials every ten years since then to count the people of the United Kingdom. You can see the sort of details they asked for in Source 6.Q on page 52. Estimates are used to calculate the population before 1801.

As you can see from the table in Source 5.A, the population of the British Isles grew rapidly between 1751 and 1901. There were five times as many people living in England and Wales in 1901 as there had been in 1751. This meant that at least five times as much food had to be grown or imported. Five times as many houses had to be built. Five times as many jobs had to be found.

Agricultural improvements helped to provide much of the food. The Industrial Revolution provided the jobs and houses. At the same time, the rapidly expanding population gave farmers and manufacturers an ever-growing market for their products.

Most Victorian families were large. Families of ten were commonplace and even Queen Victoria had nine children. In most of these families, only one or two years separated children from their older or younger brothers and sisters – like this prosperous family returning home from church on Christmas morning in 1855

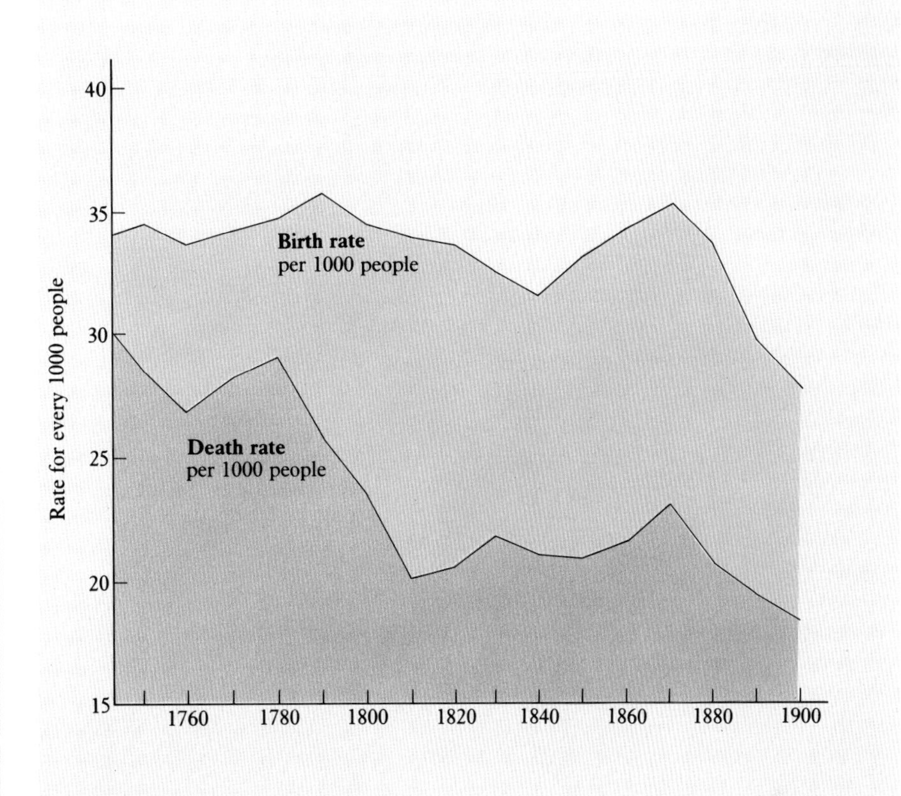

The graph shows the rise and fall of the birth and death rates in England and Wales between 1750 and 1900. As you can see, the death rate usually rose or fell in line with the birth rate. At all times it was much higher than it is today. This was because many children died when they were very young. We call this a high rate of infant mortality

5.1 Draw graphs to show the growth of population in England and Wales, Scotland and Ireland using the statistics in Source 5.A. AT1A/L5

5.2 What happened to the population of Ireland between 1751 and 1901? How was it different from the population of England and Wales? AT1C/L5

5.3 Work out the percentage increase in population in England and Wales between (a) 1751 and 1801, (b) 1801 and 1851, (c) 1851 and 1901. Which fifty-year period saw the steepest rise in population? AT1A/L7

5.4 Look at the graph. Why did the population grow? Was it because the birth rate rose or because the death rate fell? AT1B/L4

5.5 When were the birth and death rates at their highest? When were they at their lowest?

5.6 Write a paragraph to say what happened to the death rate. What was its general direction between (a) 1750 and 1810, (b) 1810 and 1870, (c) 1870 and 1900? What happened to the birth rate at these times? AT1A/L7

5.7 When would you have expected the population of England and Wales to grow at a (a) faster, (b) slower, rate than average? Give reasons. AT1A/L7

Births and deaths

The rate of population growth depends on whether there is an increase or decrease in (a) the birth rate, (b) the death rate, (c) the rate of immigration (people coming to live in the country), (d) the rate of emigration (people leaving the country for good). If there are more deaths than births, the population falls. If there are more immigrants than emigrants, the population rises (provided the number of deaths stays the same as the number of births).

The population of Ireland actually fell between 1841 and 1871. In many of the rural counties of Great Britain, too, the population rose only slowly throughout this period. In 1801, for instance, Suffolk and Warwickshire both had about 210 000 inhabitants. By 1901 Suffolk's population had grown slowly to 375 000. The population of Warwickshire, on the other hand, had grown to nearly 1 100 000. Suffolk was a farming county. Warwickshire had a coalfield and important metal industries.

In other words, the growth of population in the nineteenth century was not the same across Britain. It was directly affected by the changes begun by the Industrial Revolution. People from rural areas went to the towns in search of jobs and a better life. This is why the industrial areas of Clydeside, South Wales, Tyneside, Lancashire, the West Riding of Yorkshire, Warwickshire and London all experienced a much steeper rise in population than the rest of Britain. By contrast, the population of the rural counties of Sutherland (Scotland), Herefordshire (England) and Cardiganshire (Wales) all fell between 1851 and 1901.

Diseases and poor living conditions

As you have seen, the birth rate was always high throughout this period. Few people practised any form of birth control at this time. As a result, half the people in the factory towns were under 20 years old. Young couples started their families in their teens. Having ten or more children was usual, although many infants died before the age of five. Standards of medical care were much lower then and the children of the poor were badly fed and often brought up in insanitary conditions.

As you can see from the graph on page 39, the annual death rate fell from nearly 30 per 1000 people per year in the 1750s to 20 per 1000 in 1810. However, living conditions in the new factory towns could not keep pace with the rapid growth in population this fall in the death rate helped to cause. As a result, the death rate began to rise again. In Liverpool, for instance, it rose sharply from 21 per 1000 in 1831 to 35 per 1000 in 1841. Drains and sewers could not cope with the extra numbers. Water supplies were no longer adequate and were often contaminated with sewage. Rubbish and filth piled up in the streets. Vermin, such as lice, rats and mice, thrived. Overcrowded, dirty, damp, badly-ventilated homes were the breeding grounds for disease, as you can see from the table in Source 5.B.

5.8 What use as a source of information is the *Punch* cartoon A Court for King Cholera when studying living conditions at this time? AT3/L5

5.9 Why were woollen garments 'seldom or never washed'?

5.10 Why was it possible for poor people to wear cotton clothes in 1835?

5.11 Draw up a table to show how some effects of the Industrial Revolution helped (a) diseases to spread, (b) helped get rid of them. AT1B/L5

5.12 Look at the picture on the right. How did the artist show the appalling effects of the famine in Ireland in the 1840s? AT1C/L6

5.13 Look back at the population figures on page 38. When was the greatest fall in the population of Ireland?

The killer diseases

Source 5.B

Disease	How it was spread	How it was eliminated
Smallpox	Spread by contact with infected people. Caused 10 per cent of deaths in London in 1750.	Introduction of vaccination by Edward Jenner in 1796. By 1850 only 1 per cent of deaths were due to smallpox.
Typhus *Infantile diarrhoea*	Carried by insects and other vermin which thrive in filth and rubbish.	Cheaper soap and better water supplies made it easier to keep clothes and homes clean.
Scarlet fever *Whooping cough* *Diphtheria* *Measles*	Spread by droplet infection – by infected people coughing.	Less of a problem as families became much smaller and the worst slums were cleared.
Tuberculosis *(Consumption)*	Damp dark rooms helped the bacteria which caused some forms of tuberculosis to thrive.	The abolition of window tax in 1851 helped to ensure that new houses would not be deprived of the sunlight which helps to kill the bacteria.
Typhoid fever *Dysentery* *Cholera*	Spread rapidly when drinking water and food were contaminated with excreta from people carrying these diseases. Cholera epidemics in 1831–2, 1849 and 1865 killed 150 000 people.	Treated water supplies and effective drains, sewers and refuse disposal, as well as water closets (flush lavatories) and more hygienic cooking facilities did much to solve the problem.

Source 5.C Francis Place, in 1835, looks back to the 1780s

Cotton cloth took the place of woollen garments, which were seldom or never changed, and seldom or never washed. Cotton brought in a degree of cleanliness which has been increasing ever since.

Source 5.D Why people are living longer (in 1884)

The expectation of life is now about three years longer than in 1837–54. This is probably due to abolishing the duty on soap and the window-tax, as well as to better water supply and drainage.

A working-class street in London in the 1830s

Some improvements were due to advances in medical care. However most came about because of effective sanitation, cleaner homes and an adequate diet. The Industrial Revolution played its part in this, since it made possible the widespread use of cotton (Source 5.C), soap (Source 5.D), and coal. Together with improvements in water supplies, this meant that the poorer classes were better able to boil water, have baths (in a tin bath in front of the fire), wash clothes and scrub their homes. Cheaper coal also meant their houses were warmer and drier.

This Punch *cartoon,* A Court for King Cholera, *was printed in 1852*

Diet and starvation

The improvements in agriculture meant that by the end of the nineteenth century many more people were enjoying a better, healthier diet. They were eating more bread, potatoes, meat, dairy products, fresh vegetables and fruit. They got the protein, calories and vitamins they needed to help them resist diseases. But the poorest people still lived close to starvation level. People suffering from malnutrition were much more likely to catch epidemic diseases.

Starvation had been a problem in earlier centuries. This was because communications were so poor that relief could not be sent to the aid of the needy without great difficulty. Yet despite the coming of the railway and the great improvements in agriculture, there was a terrible famine in Ireland in the 1840s when the potato crop failed (see Source 5.H on page 42). As many as a million people may have died and vast numbers were forced to emigrate.

These starving people in Ireland were trying to get into, not out of, the workhouse

Emigration and immigration

Emigration overseas played an important part in population change in the nineteenth century. It accounted for much of the decline of the population in Ireland. Nearly 13 million people from Britain as a whole emigrated between 1851 and 1900.

Source 5.E Emigration from Victorian Britain

Period	England and Wales	Scotland	Ireland	Grand total
1815–34	100 000	30 000	400 000	530 000
1835–60	1 000 000	250 000	2 600 000	3 850 000
1861–80	1 600 000	300 000	1 400 000	3 300 000
1881–1900	3 000 000	500 000	1 300 000	4 800 000

Two main reasons – push and pull – caused this massive emigration. Poverty at home pushed people out while the attractions of a new life overseas pulled them away from Britain. You can see this, and how it affected the emigrants, in Sources 5.F to 5.L.

Source 5.F 1844: Recollections of an emigrant

We had been longing for the hour of sailing. Now, when it arrived, we would have delayed it if possible. When the afternoon came, how we strained our eyes to catch a distant glimpse of the Welsh coast, perhaps for the last time in our lives.

Source 5.G 1846: An advertisement in a local newspaper – *The Northampton Herald*

FREE EMIGRATION to SOUTH AUSTRALIA, via Southampton. First class ships of large tonnage with the best arrangements and equipment. The undersigned are authorised to grant a free passage [journey] *by these ships to this healthy and eminently prosperous colony, to agricultural labourers, shepherds, male and female domestic and farm servants, miners, and mechanics of various trades, of good character. The demand for labour in the colony is urgent, with remuneration* [pay] *ensuring the comfort of every well-conducted man and his family.*

◀ *1848:* Punch *suggests a remedy for the unrest (see page 75) in Britain*

5.14 Look at Source 5.A (page 38) and Source 5.E. What percentage of the 1831 populations of (a) England and Wales, (b) Scotland, (c) Ireland, emigrated between 1835 and 1860? What percentage of the 1881 populations did so in 1881–1900? Which country suffered the greatest loss of population as a result of emigration? AT1A ■

5.15 What do you think would have been the effect on Britain had emigration not been possible at this time? AT1B ■

5.16 Why did the Government offer free travel to South Australia in 1846? What sort of settlers were they trying to attract? Were they always successful? AT3/L4

5.17 What were the reasons for encouraging emigration according to these sources? What were some of the arguments against it? AT1B/L5

Source 5.H 1847: W.E. Forster, a Liberal politician, visits an Irish village

Out of a population of 240, I found thirteen already dead from want. The survivors were like walking skeletons, the men gaunt and haggard, stamped with the livid mark of hunger, the children crying with pain, the women in some of the cabins too weak to stand.

1871: An Irish emigrant lands at Liverpool. Many people from Ireland settled in mainland Britain in the nineteenth century but immigration from outside the United Kingdom was not an important reason for population growth in the period before 1901

5.18 What cure did *Punch* suggest for unemployment and unrest in Britain in 1848? What was the attitude of the artist to emigration? AT1C/L7

5.19 Imagine you are a Scottish or Irish emigrant at this time. Write a letter to a friend describing what happened and your feelings before, during and after the journey. AT1C/L6

5.20 Use the sources and pictures on these pages to write an account of emigration from Britain in the nineteenth century. AT3/L6

5.21 What difference would it make to your answer to question 5.20, if you only used some of these sources (such as Source 5.K) and ignored the rest? What does this tell you about using evidence from the past? AT2/L6 AT3/L6

1851: A special ship filled with emigrants leaves Belfast

Source 5.I 1853: A report on emigration from Scotland in *The Illustrated London News*

Since the end of May 1852, the Highland and Island Emigration Society has sent to Australia about 3000 persons. This has been done to relieve distress caused by excess of population in Scotland and at the same time solve the problem in Australia caused by a lack of workers.

Source 5.J 1853: A report on The Female Emigration Fund in *The Illustrated London News*

A grand total of 1071 young women rescued from the brink of starvation in London are now – at least the vast majority of them – comfortably settled in marriage, or service, amid the plenty of Australia. The gold fever has attracted a vast male emigration, and the balance of sexes in Australia is more uneven than ever.

Source 5.K 1869: Charles Dilke, a Radical politician, visits Australia

Many of the convicts' women went out from England as Government free emigrants, taking with them money obtained by the robberies for which their men had been convicted. The Female Emigration Society and the Government competed with each other in sending out to Sydney the worst women in all London, to reinforce the ranks of the convict girls in Australia.

Source 5.L 1899: An opponent of emigration speaks out in a magazine for farmers

Many have been led away by the highly coloured statements of emigration agents. They contrast poverty and decay [in Britain] *with the homes of freedom and plenty beyond the seas* [in the United States]. *By such tricks, thousands have been persuaded to leave comfortable homes and good friends for dreary wastes* [the Prairies] *or crowded cities* [New York and Chicago]. *We know many people who have emigrated full of hope and who have returned after great expense and loss of time.*

6 Changes in living conditions in the towns

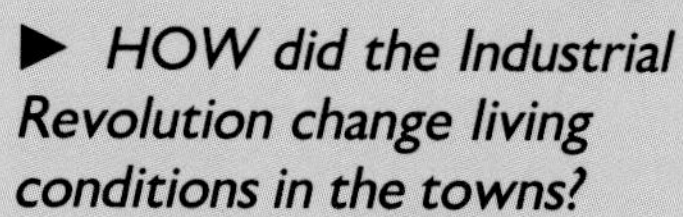

► *HOW did the Industrial Revolution change living conditions in the towns?*
ATIA ■ ATIB ■

► *HOW and WHY was religion affected by the Industrial Revolution?*
ATIB ■ ATIC ■

► *WHAT was the Poor Law and how did it work?*
ATIC ■

The rapid growth of the towns

Source 6.A City populations 1751–1901

	1751	1801	1851	1901
London	750 000	1 100 000	2 685 000	6 586 000
Dublin	129 000	165 000	272 000	373 000
Manchester	45 000	75 000	303 000	605 000
Liverpool	35 000	82 000	376 000	704 000
Norwich	35 000	36 000	61 000	80 000
Birmingham	25 000	74 000	233 000	523 000
Glasgow	24 000	77 000	357 000	776 000
Sheffield	13 000	31 000	135 000	409 000
Leeds	12 000	53 000	172 000	429 000
Bradford	6 000	13 000	104 000	280 000

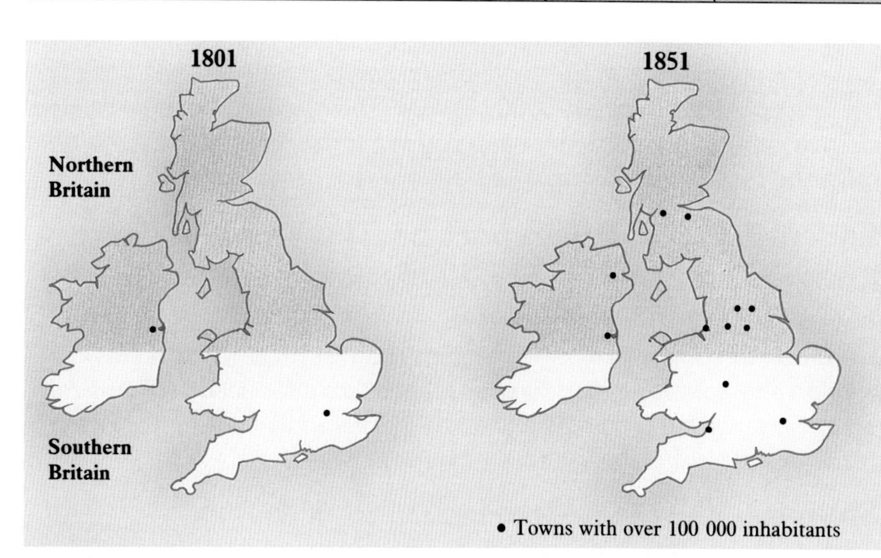

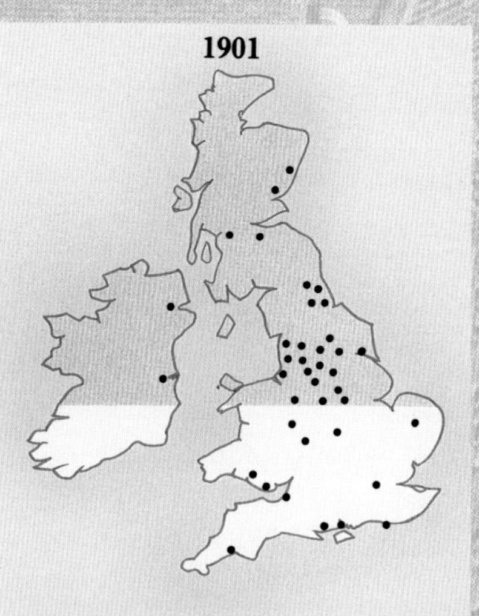

The major towns and cities in Britain in 1801, 1851 and 1901

In 1750 London was the only large city in Great Britain. With the spread of industry, however, many old market towns such as Leeds, Birmingham and Manchester became industrial centres. Thousands of factories were built. The use of steam power meant that smoking chimneys dominated the city skylines. Rows of terraced houses for the workers were built close to their place of work. Visitors who came back to a town after twenty years could hardly recognise it.

The growth of the suburbs

The towns grew so rapidly that ordinary workers often found it hard to find somewhere to live (Source 6.C). There was no cheap public transport in the early years of the nineteenth century, so they had to live close to their jobs. Large families crammed into single rooms. Many took in lodgers as well. Middle-class workers, however, could afford to travel to work each day by train or horse bus. They moved out to new homes in the suburbs (Source 6.B).

6.1 Look at the maps. How many more big towns were there in 1851 and 1901 than in 1801? How many of these towns were (a) in the North, (b) in the South? What does this tell you about the effect of the Industrial Revolution on Britain's towns? AT1B/L6

6.2 Look at Source 6.A. Roughly how many times bigger was London in 1901 compared with 1751? Which of these cities grew most rapidly between 1751 and 1901? Why? Which two cities grew at the slowest rate? Why? Draw a graph to show your findings. AT1A/L7

Leeds Town Hall in 1858

Pentonville Road, London, in 1884

6.3 How does Source 6.B help us to understand what was wrong with city life in the 1840s? What were the advantages of the suburbs? AT3/L5

6.4 What can Source 6.C tell us about the way in which London expanded in the nineteenth century? AT3/L5

6.5 What do you think the town councillors of Leeds wanted people to think when they looked at the new Town Hall? AT2/L5

6.6 Do any of the buildings in your town look like this? When and why were they built? AT1C/L5

Source 6.B A writer praises London's suburbs in 1844

Here are no stinking gasometers, nor tall chimneys belching smoke, nor any smelly dunghill and stagnant pools to offend the nostrils of the passer-by. The houses in the suburbs each possess a small garden. Their occupants are principally superior clerks, heads of firms, or gentlemen who have to visit the City daily. They live in the suburbs both on account of its cheapness to themselves, and its healthfulness for their families.

By 1871 the population of London was growing each year by about 100 000 people. The better-off workers were now able to live in the suburbs as well. The railway companies ran workmen's trains and there were cheap fares on the horse-drawn trams (see picture on the left). Huge new suburbs sprang up around the edge of the old London. You can see some of the effects in Source 6.C. Similar suburbs were built round every town in Britain (see maps on pages 52, 53 and 55).

Source 6.C By Thomas Wright, a working man, in 1868

I received three weeks' notice that the house in which I lived was, with some forty others, to be taken down at one fell swoop for the extension of the City and Suburban Company's railway line. The district was one of the most densely populated in the metropolis and I had been hearing, with constantly increasing frequency during the last two years, that houses were getting dreadfully scarce.

Local government

The rapid growth of the towns created many problems. Public services, such as the supply of fresh water, could not keep pace. Half of Manchester and most of Liverpool were without mains drains in 1830. Towns like these had to be given the power to make improvements. This is why Parliament passed a law in 1835 called the Municipal Corporations Act. The people of each borough could now elect a town council to control street lighting, the supply of gas and water, the police and to deal with housing and public health.

In 1842 Edwin Chadwick shocked people in an official report on the 'labouring classes'. He claimed that on average people in the countryside lived longer than people in the industrial towns. He blamed four main causes for this – dirt, dampness, overcrowding and contaminated water. He recommended that the town authorities should be made to clean the streets regularly and take measures to provide homes with better drainage, ventilation and water supply. Parliament took note and passed the Public Health Act in 1848. It gave town councils the new powers they needed to insist on better standards of water supply, street cleansing and refuse collection.

Although some councils were reluctant to raise rates to pay for improvements, others regarded it as their duty to do so. They were very proud of the achievements of their towns. They built solid and impressive town halls and lit the streets with gas lamps. Many provided amenities for the use of poor people, such as public baths (for washing, not swimming) and public parks where working people could enjoy fresh air and exercise in an area of green space close to the town centre.

Painting of Sheffield in 1854

Housing

Since few slum children went to school, the small cramped homes and dark narrow alleyways and courts of many Victorian towns always teemed with people. Despite their large families, the homes of many workers were often only 'one-up, one-down' (one room upstairs, one downstairs). It was impossible to keep a tiny house like this clean when it was always packed with people. There was no bathroom or kitchen. The lavatory was an earth toilet in a wooden hut in the back yard. This was shared by the people in the neighbouring houses as well. Water came from a pump outside which was also shared. Lack of a piped water supply meant that clothes were often washed in dirty water to save people going out to fetch fresh water from the tap. These overcrowded and unclean homes helped to spread disease (see page 40). You can read what people thought of some of the worst of these houses in Sources 6.D, 6.E and 6.F.

Source 6.D By Thomas Wright, a working man, in 1868

There were twenty houses in the Court – ten on each side – and each house consisted of four small apartments, two upstairs and two down, of an average size of eleven feet by ten [3.4 by 3 metres]. *In eighteen of these houses there were two, and in some instances three, families living. Each house had an average of at least ten inhabitants.*

Source 6.E *The Bitter Cry of Outcast London* in 1883

To get into them you have to go through courts reeking with poisonous and stinking gases arising from sewage and refuse. Courts which the sun never reaches, which are never visited by a breath of fresh air.

Source 6.F *The Bitter Cry of Outcast London* in 1883

Eight feet square – that is about the average size of very many of these rooms. Walls and ceiling are black with filth. What goes by the name of a window is half of it stuffed with rags or covered by boards to keep out wind and rain. As to furniture – you may see a broken chair or an old bedstead. More commonly you will find rough boards resting upon bricks, an old box turned upside down, or, more frequently still, nothing but rubbish and rags. Every room in these rotten and reeking tenements houses a family, often two.

6.7 Which source – 6.D, 6.E or 6.F – would you have chosen in order to shock a politician into doing something to improve working-class housing? Give reasons. AT2/L6

6.8 Use these sources and the picture of Kensington to write a report on slum housing in Victorian London. AT3/L4

6.9 What does The Silent Highwayman tell us about London in 1858?

6.10 Look at the map. After a cholera epidemic killed 500 people in Soho in September 1854, Dr John Snow plotted each death on a street map showing the position of the water pumps. When he removed the handle to Pump E, the epidemic cleared up. Why? What had he proved? AT3/L5

6.11 What can Source 6.H tell us about town problems in the nineteenth century? AT3/L5

6.12 In what ways were these problems caused by the Industrial Revolution? AT1B ■

6.13 How have town problems changed since 1900? In what ways are they still the same? AT1A ■

This Punch *cartoon was printed on 10 July 1858 at a time when there were many complaints about the stench from the Thames*

Slum homes in Kensington in about 1850 ▶

Source 6.G
A Norfolk clergyman visits London in 1855

Took the children by boat from Vauxhall Bridge to show them the great buildings. The ride on the water was refreshing except for the stench.

Source 6.H
Sheffield in about 1860

Perhaps the most hideous town in creation. All ups and downs and back slums. Massive volumes of black smoke veil the sun and the blue sky even on the brightest day. More than one crystal stream runs sparkling down the valleys, and enters the town. But they soon get polluted and creep through it heavily charged with dyes, clogged with decaying rubbish and bubbling with poisonous gases.

6.14 Compare the painting and Source 6.H in helping us to know what Sheffield was really like at this time. AT2 ■
6.15 Which do you think is likely to be the more reliable source of information? AT3 ■

Pollution

As you can see from Source 6.G and the *Punch* cartoon on the left, London had a major problem in the middle of the nineteenth century. The Thames stank so much in July 1858, even the work of Parliament and the Law Courts was affected. The reason was not hard to find. Many of London's lavatories eventually emptied into the Thames, even though this was the main source of the city's drinking water. Many others emptied into cesspits which were cleaned up after dark by night-soil workers. When leakages from cess pits seeped into water supplies, cholera and typhoid fever spread rapidly (see page 40).

A big improvement to London's problems came in 1859 when work started on a new mains drainage scheme. When it was completed, huge sewers dumped London's sewage into the Thames estuary well away from the city so the tide could wash it out to sea.

As you can see from the painting opposite, industrial cities like Sheffield were also heavily polluted by smoke and fumes from factory chimneys. Charles Reade described Sheffield in a novel (Source 6.H).

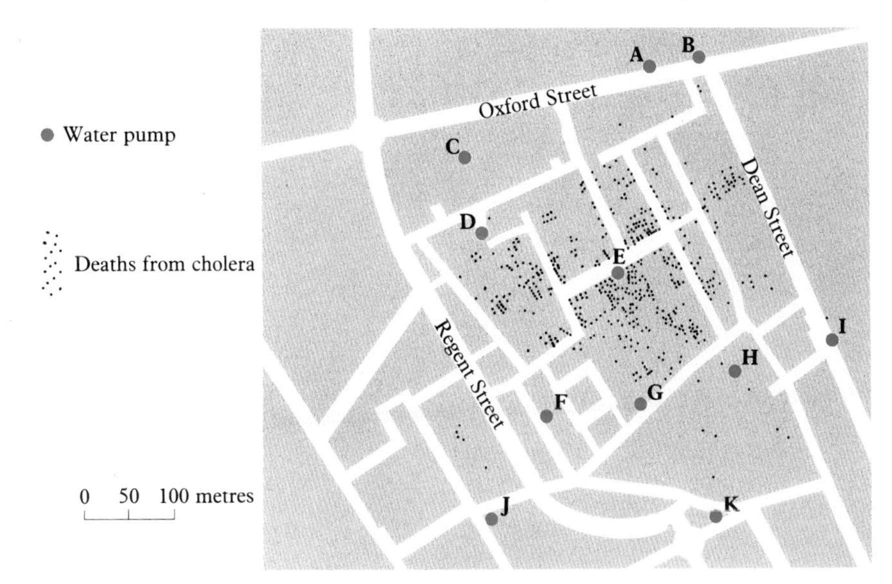

Dr John Snow's map of the cholera epidemic in Soho in 1854

Religion and social reform

The Industrial Revolution even affected religion. The Nonconformist churches, such as the Methodists, appealed to the growing numbers of industrial workers (Source 6.I).

As the towns grew in size, thousands of Anglican, Roman Catholic, Methodist, Baptist and Congregational chapels and churches were built. The Church played a big part in many people's lives, so new churches were built to cater for their needs.

Many people in the Church of England had gained renewed faith in their form of Christianity through the Evangelical Movement. They included William Wilberforce (see page 65) and Lord Shaftesbury (see page 22). The Evangelical Movement played a leading part in social reform – pressing for changes in living standards and the way in which people lived their daily lives. They held Evangelical revivalist meetings which attracted thousands of people (Source 6.J).

These meetings and the rapid growth of the Nonconformist churches gave rise to the idea that all Victorians were strict churchgoers. In fact, a survey in 1851 showed that only half the people of Britain regularly went to church. Even fewer slum-dwellers went to church (Source 6.K). Scenes like the picture below were more typical of the slums.

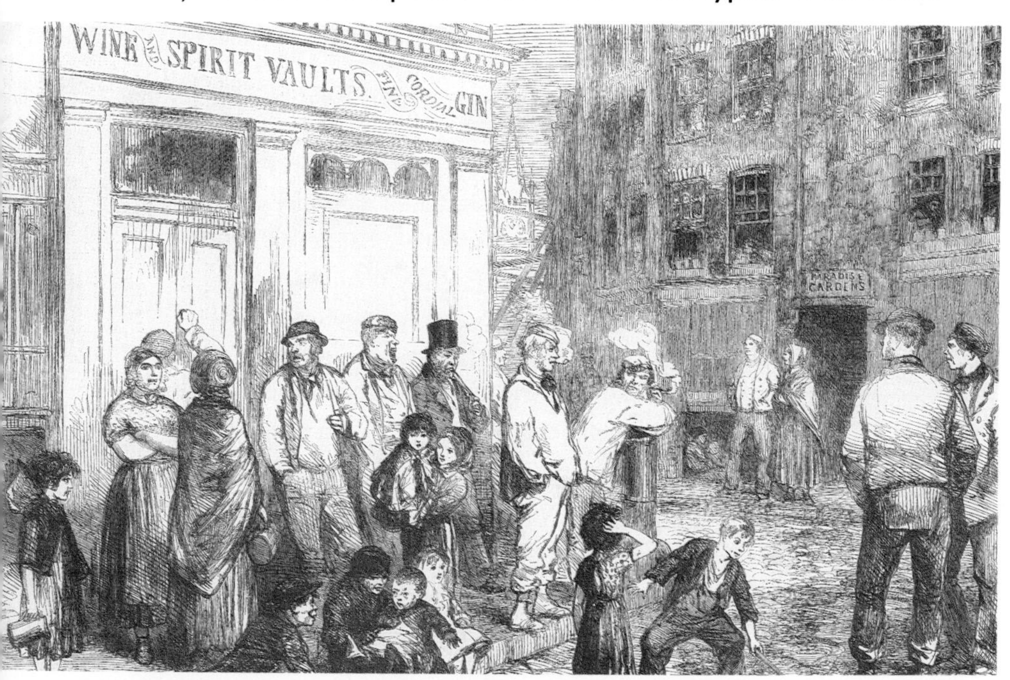

'Sunday Morning' in London's slums in 1856

In the second half of the nineteenth century many well-to-do Victorians were shocked to discover what it meant to be poor. They saw pictures like '*Sunday Morning*' in their magazines and paintings of distressing scenes in art galleries (page 85). They bought pamphlets, such as *The Bitter Cry of Outcast London* which was published in 1883 (Source 6.K). They blamed poverty for an increase in drunkenness and crime. Many volunteered to do social work, such as helping to distribute food or serving hot meals in a soup kitchen.

Members of the Evangelical Movement and Nonconformists worked as missionaries in London's East End. The University Settlement Movement, for instance, started a working-class club in the East End in 1884. You can get some idea of the work it did from Source 6.L.

Source 6.I
The views of a working man in 1868

The worshippers of some sects – notably the Primitive Methodists – are almost all from the working classes. The Dissenting [Nonconformist] *sects have the greatest attractions. Their services and ministers are considered simpler and more practical than those of the Church.*

Source 6.J
From a Norfolk vicar's diary

8 January 1859 *A wonderful revival of religion going on everywhere so far as preaching is concerned. Special evening services are now being held at St Paul's, Westminster Abbey, Exeter Hall and St James's Hall in London.*

Source 6.K
Survey quoted in *The Bitter Cry of Outcast London* in 1883

Out of 2290 persons living at Bow Common, only 88 adults and 47 children ever attend a place of worship. One street off Leicester Square contains 246 families, and only 12 of these are ever at the house of God.

6.16 Look at the picture of the Salvation Army poster and at Source 6.M. How and why was the Salvation Army organised on military lines? AT1C/L5

6.17 Why was *Sunday Morning* drawn? What was the artist hoping to achieve with this picture? AT1C/L6

6.18 What is the value of *Sunday Morning* as a source of information about the Victorian Sunday? AT3/L5

6.19 Which reasons do you think may explain why drunkenness was seen as a great problem in the Victorian slums? AT1B/L6

6.20 What do these sources tell you about the attitudes of the working classes to church-going in the Victorian period? AT3/L6

6.21 What was the approximate proportion of the working classes who went to church in 1883 according to Source 6.K? Why do you need to treat these figures with great caution? AT3/L7

6.22 Look at the Salvation Army Chart. Explain what it shows. What part were the Salvation Army able to play in rescuing society? AT1C ■

This is part of a Salvation Army chart published in 1890. It was called In Darkest England and the Way Out ▼

Source 6.L From a magazine published in 1890

It comprises, besides the club proper, a dispensary [issuing medicines], *a young men's institute, a mothers' club, a children's club, co-operative stores paying a good dividend and supplying goods to a thousand customers on a Saturday night, a library, a boot and shoe productive society, a cabinetmaker's productive society, a book shop, athletic, dramatic, debating, dancing societies, and a band.*

The churches performed many other acts of charity at a time when the Government did little to help the poor. The Salvation Army was probably the leading Nonconformist group involved in social reform. It was founded by General William Booth in 1878 and organised like an army. The Army did much to help the very poorest people. Booth called them the 'submerged tenth' – the poorest 10 per cent of the population. He called the slums 'Darkest England' and thought the solution to poverty was temperance (giving up alcohol). He got children to sign the pledge and encouraged them to join the Band of Hope.

Source 6.M Salvation Army successes in 1890

Mrs W. – of Haggerston slum *Heavy drinker; wrecked home, husband a drunkard, place dirty and filthy, terribly poor. Saved now over two years. Home A1. Plenty of employment. Husband now saved also.*

Mr A.M. – in the Seven Dials slum *Was a great drunkard. Heard the Captain speak on 'Seek first the Kingdom of God!'. Called out and said, 'Do you mean that if I ask God for work, He will give it me?' He was converted that night, found work, and is now employed in the Gas Works, Old Kent Road.*

When Sir Luke Fildes (Source 6.N) painted this picture in 1874, he got 21 vagrants to pose for him in his studio

Caring for the Poor

Many people lived in conditions of appalling poverty in the eighteenth and nineteenth centuries. There was no National Health Service then. Nor were there any Government pensions or sickness and unemployment benefits. Nonetheless there was a system, called the Poor Law, by which paupers – very poor people unable to support themselves – could obtain some relief from distress.

The money came out of a 'poor rate' which was paid by local people according to the value of the property they owned. Some of it was used to look after sick, elderly and disabled paupers who lived in the poor house or workhouse (see the photograph on page 55). The unemployed – the 'able-bodied poor' – were given money but had to work for it, repairing roads and doing other manual jobs.

In 1834, however, the Government changed the system. They brought in a new law called the Poor Law Amendment Act. In future, only the paupers who lived in the workhouse would be given any aid. Those entering the workhouse would be divided into four groups and live in separate buildings or wards.

The helpless paupers, those who were old, sick or disabled, occupied one part of the building. They were often better cared for there than outside the workhouse, since doctors were employed to look after them free of charge. Many poor people outside the workhouse could not afford to pay a doctor's fees.

The children were housed in another block where they were educated and trained to be servants or apprentices. This was at a time when only a few of the children outside went to school.

The able-bodied paupers (the unemployed) were not so lucky. They were to be given every possible encouragement to find a job and support themselves. To the Victorians this meant making life as hard for them as possible in the workhouse. Husbands and wives were separated from each other and their children taken away from them. The food they were given was of poor quality, tasteless, and barely adequate. They were treated as if they were in prison. They could be punished for swearing, uncleanliness, pretending to be ill, playing cards, and misbehaving during prayers.

Source 6.N How Sir Luke Fildes painted the workhouse

I saw an awful crowd of poor wretches applying for permits to lodge in the Casual Ward. I made a note of the scene and after that often went again, making friends with the policeman and talking with the people themselves.

6.23 How did Sir Luke Fildes paint his picture of the homeless queuing up outside a workhouse so that it would arouse the sympathy and anger of the people who saw it? Could a picture like this be painted in Britain today? AT1A ■ AT2/L7

6.24 What value can be attached to this painting as evidence about London's homeless in 1874? AT3/L5

6.25 Is there any reason to question whether this painting is a reliable and accurate record? AT3/L7

6.26 Look at Sources 6.O and 6.P. Why do you think two members of the middle class took such trouble to endure discomfort in this way? What were their motives? Were they the same? AT1C/L6

6.27 What difference would it make if you used Source 6.O instead of Source 6.P to write a description of life in a workhouse? AT2/L6

6.28 Which of the two accounts do you think is more likely to give a realistic and unbiased picture of life in a workhouse? Write a paragraph to explain your choice. AT3 ■

Dinner in the Marylebone workhouse in London in about 1900

Unfortunately, the harsh discipline aimed at deterring the idle scrounger also penalised people who were out of work through no fault of their own. This is why the system was later modified to allow some payments to be made to people not resident in the workhouse. These included the hundreds of thousands thrown out of work when new machines were introduced (see page 13).

We know what the workhouses were like from paintings and drawings and from newspaper reports (Sources 6.O and 6.P).

Source 6.O A workhouse in 1837

Having become weary of the abuse and praise applied to the system, a friend got permission to inspect and see a workhouse ten miles [16 km] *from London. For two or three days he lived there during the day. Although he slept elsewhere, he ate nothing but the diet of the house.*

'I could myself live permanently in the house with comfort were I inclined or permitted to do so' [he wrote.] *'The situation is splendid, and commands a variety of the finest views imaginable. The women and female children have what may well be called landscape gardens of their own. The whole apartments are airy and roomy. Everything is kept as clean as a new shilling and wears an air of comfort.'*

Source 6.P A workhouse in 1866

An adventurous gentleman tested the accommodation provided for the houseless poor by passing a night with the casuals in Lambeth Workhouse. He got himself up in a beggarly dress, his buttonless coat being tied with twine. He was readily admitted and supplied with a thick slice of bread, called in 'casual' language 'toke'. The cold was severe. There were neither bags of straw nor rugs for the entire number, so that shivering men and boys were huddled together, sometimes four on one bag.

Imagine a space about 30 feet by 30 feet [9 metres square], *a dingy whitewashed wall, the fourth side of the shed boarded in and the remaining space hung with flimsy canvas, with a gap at the top. This shed was paved with stone, the flags thickly encrusted with filth.*

Population and towns: The impact of the Industrial Revolution on a local area

Using the census

How your nearest town grew in size as a result of the Industrial Revolution can be measured in different ways. Books about the town will tell you its population at different census dates. You can draw graphs from these figures. You may find separate population figures for the different parishes or wards in your town. From these you will be able to see which parts of the town grew rapidly and which grew slowly or even declined in population.

For instance, the Norfolk *Directory* referred to on page 26 stated that the population of the parish of St John Maddermarket in the centre of Norwich was 1698 people in 1801 but only 738 in 1841. By contrast, the suburb of Heigham grew from 544 persons in 1801 to 6050 in 1841. Figures like these can be plotted on a town street map to show which parts of a town grew faster than the others.

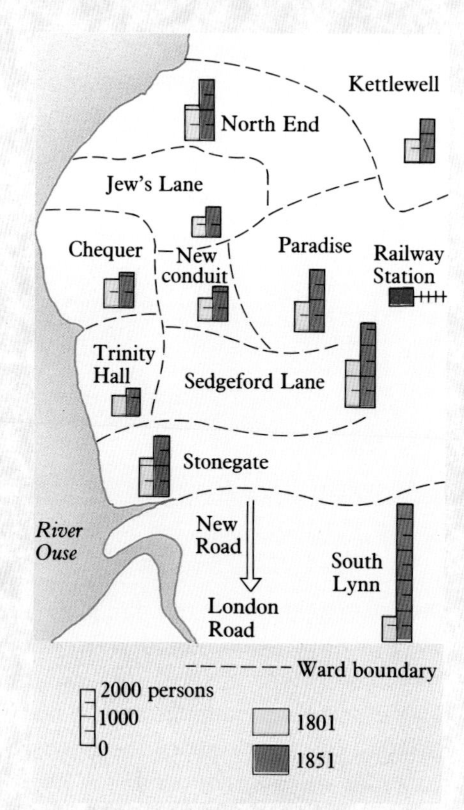

This map shows how the different wards in the Norfolk town of King's Lynn grew between 1801 and 1851. Can you suggest reasons why the town expanded in this way?

You may even be able to see copies of the original census forms which were filled in by hand when the people of your area were counted over a hundred years ago. These census forms tell us about the people living in every street (Source 6.Q).

Statistics like these can be shown on a map or as a series of graphs, showing the numbers of servants employed, the proportion of women to men who were heads of the household (but denied the vote – see page 81), occupations, size of family, places of birth, etc.

Source 6.Q From the 1851 Census Return for Robin Hood's Bay in Yorkshire

Name and surname of each person	Relation to head of family	Marital condition	Age	Rank, profession or occupation	Where born
Elizabeth Gordon	Head of family	Widow	70	Shipowner's widow	Robin Hood's Bay
Elizabeth Steel	Daughter	Married	38	Schoolmaster's wife	ditto
James Steel	Son-in-law	Married	37	Schoolmaster	ditto
William Steel	Grandson		3	At home	ditto
Margaret Anderson	Servant	Unmarried	19	House servant	Kettelness

Making a map to show how your town grew

You can draw a map to show how your town grew during the Industrial Revolution if you use clues to help you date the buildings, or look at old street maps of your town (like those on page 55).

Studies in a cemetery

You may also be able to find useful information about the effect of the Industrial Revolution on the people of your area if you visit a local cemetery. From the dates given on the tombstones, you can work out whether the average age of the people who died before 1800 was higher or lower than that of the people who died between 1800 and 1850, or between 1850 and 1900. To do this, simply add up the ages of all the people recorded in the cemetery in each group and find the average age by dividing by the number of people on your list. Family tombstones can sometimes tell you about the average size of families during this period and about the rate of infant mortality (the proportion of children that died).

Bricked-up windows in King's Lynn

Victorian terraced houses near Sowerby Bridge in Yorkshire

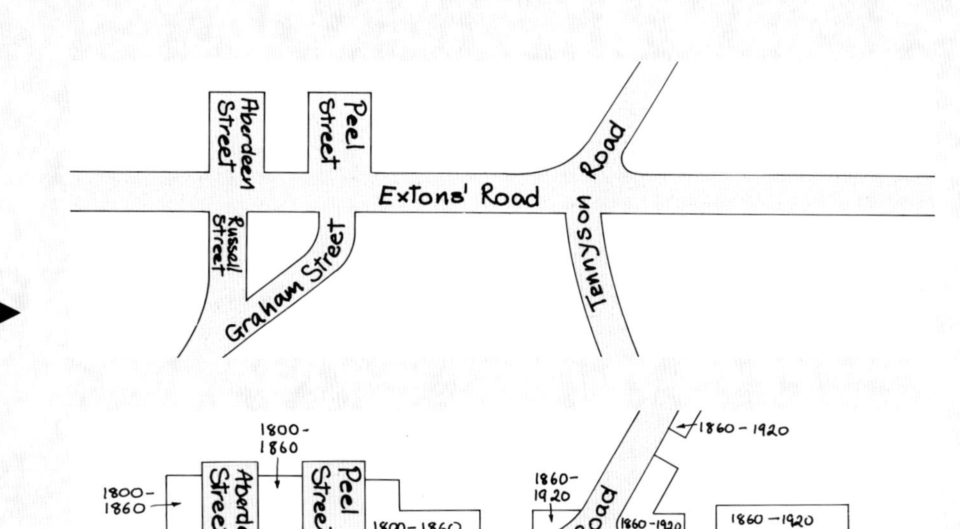

1. Draw an outline map of a group of streets. ▶

2. Draw in roughly the position of each row of houses. Use the clues in the table (below) to help you note down the approximate age of each building. ▶

3. Colour in the map to show the main building periods. It will show you how part of your town grew in the Victorian period. ▶

Street names	Victorian streets were often named after famous people or notable events, such as Balaclava Street, which was named after the battle in 1854, Albert Square (Prince Albert died in 1861) and Coronation Street (Queen Victoria was crowned in 1838). Peel Street, Aberdeen Street, Russell Street and Graham Street shown on the map were named after four politicians who were famous in the 1840s and 1850s. Tennyson Road was named after the poet who died in 1892.
Date stones	The actual date when a building was begun or completed can sometimes be seen on one of the walls. There are four main places to look: (a) on a headstone near the roof, (b) on a foundation stone near the ground, (c) on the top of a drainpipe, (d) on a stone or board above the front door.
Bricked-up windows	The special tax on windows, which encouraged people to brick them up to avoid paying tax, was not abolished until 1851.
Names of buildings	You can also find buildings named after famous events and people, such as Lucknow (after the relief of Lucknow in 1857) and Khartoum Villas (General Gordon was killed at Khartoum in 1885).
Style of building	Houses built before the 1860s often front straight on to the street. Terraced houses built later than this sometimes have a tiny garden or courtyard at the front. Houses with bay windows were often built in the 1880s and 1890s.

This view of the marketplace in Norwich was painted in 1806 by John Sell Cotman. Norwich was then the sixth largest city in England and still a centre of the woollen industry (page 26). Its growth in the nineteenth century was much slower than that of the industrial towns on the coalfields (page 44). As a result, fewer of its old buildings were pulled down to make way for the new. This is why this view is still recognisable today – as you can see if you compare it with the photograph

Comparisons

In your local library you should be able to find copies of old engravings and paintings, like Norwich in 1808 (above) or Sheffield in 1854 (page 46). You will also see old photographs of your town, like the street scene in Edinburgh (below). You can compare pictures from different dates to find out about the effect of the Industrial Revolution on your area. If you can't identify the viewpoint, look out for a church tower or spire (like the church in the pictures of Norwich), or some other landmark you know was already standing when the picture was made.

You may also be able to compare old maps of your town at different dates, like those of part of London on the opposite page. They will also tell you how your town has grown.

Street furniture

Despite the widespread use of steam power as a result of the Industrial Revolution, transport in towns was still dependent on the horse in the nineteenth century. This is why towns had to have stables. Many of these have been pulled down but some have been preserved and converted into Mews cottages. They can sometimes be found along a cobbled street behind a row of very grand houses. Streets and roads had to have troughs to water the horses. Stone-mounting blocks with steps helped riders to mount their horses. Iron tethering rings were used to 'park' your horse when you went into a shop! Not surprisingly, the streets were covered in horse manure. Most houses had footscrapers outside so visitors could scrape their boots before entering.

Footscraper in Saffron Walden in Essex

Princes Street, Edinburgh, in about 1900

An early Victorian pillar box in Framlingham in Suffolk. Victorian letter boxes can be identified from the monogram VR ('Victoria Regina')

Gas-lamp in London

Water-pump in Elm Hill, Norwich

Horse trough in Hoylandswaine in South Yorkshire

Mounting-block and tethering ring in Alston in Cumbria

Many of these features of a Victorian street can still be seen today. They are called 'street furniture'. They can be a powerful reminder of what it was like to live in a town at the height of the Industrial Revolution. You may also be able to see remnants of the old gas-lamps which once lit the streets and the pillar-boxes which people used to post letters after the introduction of the Penny Post in 1840.

Town buildings

Many other buildings in your town can help you to know more about the effect that rapid growth had on towns during the Industrial Revolution. Leeds Town Hall, for instance, still looks much the same as it did in 1858 (page 45). Was the town hall in your town built at this time? Is there a Victorian hospital, school or workhouse? Are there any Victorian shops, pubs, corn exchanges (page 85), churches or chapels?

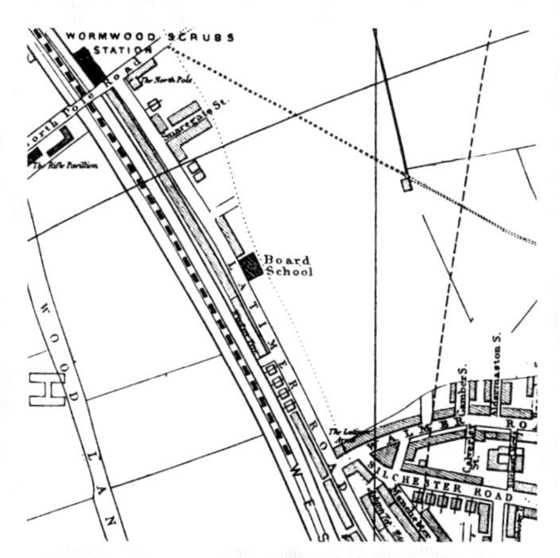

Map of part of London in 1880

This workhouse in Stowmarket in Suffolk was built in 1781 and was used until recently as a hospital for the elderly

Map of part of London in 1923

Victorian School in Dent, Yorkshire

Victorian shop in Bury St Edmunds

Victorian pub in Oldham

7 The growth of the British Empire

► *HOW and WHY did the British Empire expand between 1750 and 1900?*
ATIA ■ ATIB ■ ATIC ■
► *HOW did this expansion affect the people of Britain and the Empire?*
ATIA ■ ATIB ■ ATIC ■

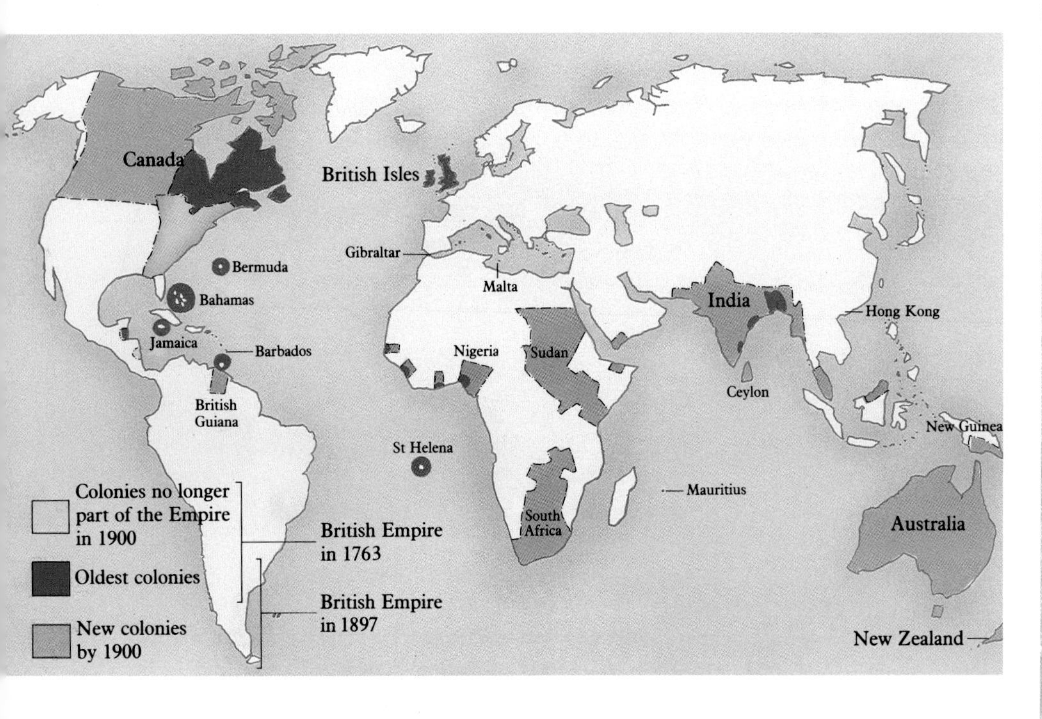

◄ *The British Empire in 1763 and 1897*

7.1 How did the British Empire change between 1763 and 1897? AT1A/L4
7.2 Why do you think red was always used to show the British Empire on a map?
7.3 How can the painting be used to explain the British victory at Quebec? How can you tell the British soldiers from the French? AT3/L5
7.4 What are the drawbacks to using a painting like this as a source of evidence about an historical event? AT2/L4

The growth of the Empire

In 1763 (see the map), Britain was already an important colonial power. In the next fifty years or so she lost the United States but gained other territories. Some were acquired by discovery, such as Australia. Others, such as Canada and much of India, were seized during a succession of wars fought mainly in Europe. During the Napoleonic Wars, for instance, Britain annexed colonies owned by Holland, Spain and France. They included the Cape Colony in South Africa, Ceylon (Sri Lanka), Mauritius, the Seychelles, St Lucia, Guyana, Tobago and Trinidad.

Throughout the nineteenth century, further colonies were added. Many were islands in the oceans, which were acquired for their ports and used to supply British ships with fresh water, food and coal. They were especially important along the vital sea routes patrolled by the Royal Navy, such as the Suez Canal route to India through the Mediterranean (Gibraltar, Malta, Cyprus), the Suez Canal (Egypt), the Red Sea (Sudan, Aden), and the Indian Ocean (Socotra, Maldive Islands).

In 1914 the British controlled a worldwide empire with a land area 250 times greater than Britain itself and a population 10 times the size. It had become the largest empire in history and most people in Britain were very proud of the fact. There were two different types of empire. On the one hand, were the lands with many White settlers. These had climates similar to those of Europe. Most were self-governing, such as Canada, Australia, New Zealand and South Africa.

On the other hand, were the Black colonies of the Tropics, such as the Gold Coast (Ghana), Nigeria, Jamaica and Trinidad. These lands were not attractive to permanent White settlers because of the hot climate. They were exploited, nonetheless, for their minerals, plantation crops and other raw materials. Unlike the territories with many European settlers, none gained their independence until after the Second World War – not even India, a land with a much longer history of civilisation than Britain.

North America

Many battles were fought by British soldiers to amass this huge empire. One of the most decisive in North America was fought near Quebec City in 1759. It forced France to abandon French Canada. In 1776, however, the American colonists, most of them descended from British settlers, declared their independence from the British Crown (Source 7.A). After a short war they became the United States of America.

Source 7.A American Declaration of Independence, 1776

We hold these truths to be self-evident, that all men are created equal, that they are endowed by their Creator with certain unalienable Rights [rights which cannot be surrendered], *that among these are Life, Liberty and the pursuit of Happiness.*

Whenever any Form of Government becomes destructive of these ends, it is the Right of the People to alter or to abolish it, and to institute new Government.

Canada continued to be governed as a British colony until serious riots in 1837 forced the British Government to take action. Lord Durham went to Canada to see what could be done to prevent a recurrence of the events of 1776. In his report, he said the provinces of Canada should be united and given their independence within the British Empire. This was carried out in 1867 when the Canadian provinces at that time (Ontario, Quebec, New Brunswick and Nova Scotia) became a self-governing dominion of the British Empire.

7.5 What reasons did the Americans use in Source 7.A to justify their claim to independence? AT1B/L5

7.6 The first US President, George Washington, owned 300 Black slaves on his plantation in Virginia. What does this tell you about the extract from the Declaration of Independence in Source 7.A? AT1C/L7

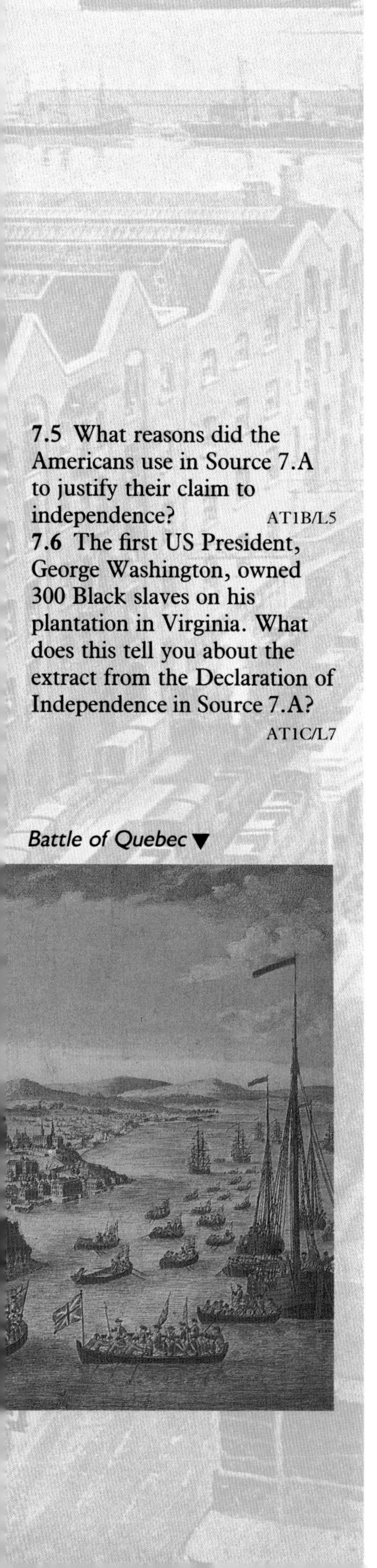

Battle of Quebec ▼

Australia and New Zealand

Before 1776, British convicts sentenced to transportation were shipped out to North America to work as slaves on the cotton and tobacco plantations there. After the American War of Independence, they were sent to Australia instead. This had been acquired by discovery after Captain Cook sailed round New Zealand in 1769–70 and landed at Botany Bay, on the site of modern Sydney.

When merino sheep (noted for their fine wool) were introduced into Australia in the early years of the nineteenth century, settlers who were not convicts went to live there as well. Huge sheep stations grew wool for the West Riding woollen mills (page 13). Further expansion came as emigrant farmers (page 42) settled along the fertile coastal plains. Cities, such as Melbourne, Sydney and Adelaide grew and prospered. Thousands of Europeans joined the Gold Rush in 1851. By this time the Australian settlers were very proud of their country and the separate states, such as New South Wales, had become self-governing. They united in 1901 to form a new dominion within the British Empire.

In the meantime, New Zealand had been settled by traders and whalers and later by farmers. In 1840 the British Government acquired North Island after signing the Treaty of Waitangi with Maori leaders. The country became a dominion in 1907.

Christmas in India *from the Christmas issue of* The Graphic *in 1881*

India

In 1600 Queen Elizabeth I granted a charter to the merchants of the East India Company. It gave them the exclusive right to trade with the Mughal Empire in India and also with the countries of the Far East. The Company grew as its trading posts at Surat, Bombay, Agra and Ahmadabad prospered. In the eighteenth century, however, as the Mughal Empire began to break up, the East India Company took a more aggressive role in order to protect its interests. Robert Clive led the Company's private army to victory over the French and their Indian allies at the battles of Arcot (1751) and Plassey (1757).

The British presence in India grew rapidly. By the start of the nineteenth century the East India Company itself had succeeded the Mughal Emperors as ruler of much of India, although not without criticism back in Britain (Source 7.B).

In general, the Company left the Indian princes free to rule their own kingdoms under the protection of the Company and with the advice of its officials. Indian soldiers, called sepoys, were recruited into the Indian army and fought under British and Indian officers.

Unlike Canada and Australia, India was not attractive to permanent White settlers – as you can see in Source 7.C.

Source 7.C Charles Dilke, a Radical politician, in India in 1867

Settlement in the hot plains is limited by the fact that English children cannot be reared there. You can have no English comfort in a climate which forces your people to live out of doors, or else in rocking-chairs or hammocks. Nightwork and reading are all but impossible in a climate where multitudes of insects haunt the air. The civilians and rulers of India are extremely jealous of the European settlers.

Indian opposition to the British in India built up over the years. Many Indians resented seeing people of a different race, religion and culture exploiting their country and growing rich on the proceeds. Only a few of the British who lived there made any effort to adapt themselves to the customs and beliefs of the Indian peoples. Instead, they tried to make India as British as possible, despite the climate. Palatial homes looked after by armies of Indian servants and social events, such as picnics, fox-hunting (without foxes) and tea parties, brought reminders of 'home'.

Source 7.B By William Cobbett in 1808

What right, in God's name, have we to do this? Conquests in India are not at all necessary either to our safety or our comfort. There is no glory attending such conquests and their accompanying butcheries. We must be actuated by a sheer love of gain; a sheer love of plunder.

7.7 What reasons did William Cobbett give in 1808 to explain the conquest of India?
7.8 What lesson could have been learned from Charles Dilke's message to Britain after his visit to India in 1867? AT1C/L5
7.9 What do you think was the most important cause of the Indian Mutiny? AT1B/L6
7.10 How did the Indian Mutiny demonstrate the ignorance of the British in their dealings with the Indian peoples? Why did the sepoys object to the use of the new cartridges? AT1C/L6

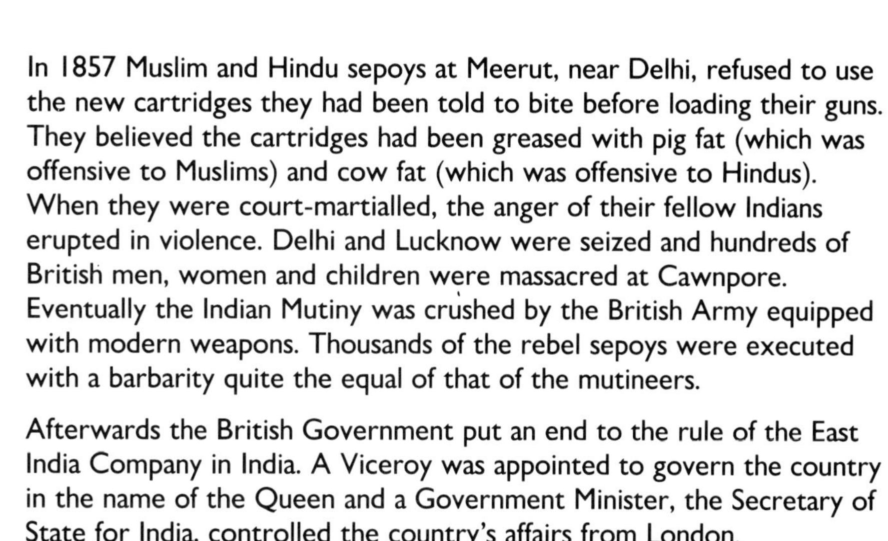

In 1857 Muslim and Hindu sepoys at Meerut, near Delhi, refused to use the new cartridges they had been told to bite before loading their guns. They believed the cartridges had been greased with pig fat (which was offensive to Muslims) and cow fat (which was offensive to Hindus). When they were court-martialled, the anger of their fellow Indians erupted in violence. Delhi and Lucknow were seized and hundreds of British men, women and children were massacred at Cawnpore. Eventually the Indian Mutiny was crushed by the British Army equipped with modern weapons. Thousands of the rebel sepoys were executed with a barbarity quite the equal of that of the mutineers.

Afterwards the British Government put an end to the rule of the East India Company in India. A Viceroy was appointed to govern the country in the name of the Queen and a Government Minister, the Secretary of State for India, controlled the country's affairs from London.

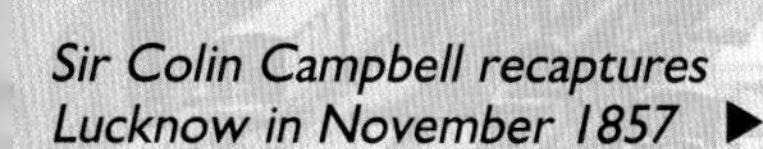

Sir Colin Campbell recaptures Lucknow in November 1857 ▶

In the years which followed, the British authorities made some attempt to bring the benefits of modern technology to India. They built railway lines, hospitals, clinics, schools and universities. Indian students, like Gandhi and Nehru, later to become important figures in Indian politics, studied in Britain. But the British authorities did little to encourage Indians to think they would eventually govern themselves like Canada or Australia. This was criticised by a number of people in Britain at that time, as you can see in Source 7.D.

Source 7.D Speech by Richard Cobden, 16 October 1857

I do not believe in the possibility of the Crown governing India under the control of Parliament. India must be ruled by those who live on that side of the globe. Its people will prefer to be ruled badly by their own kith and kin, than submit to the humiliation of being better governed by a succession of temporary ministers from Britain.

Instead, the British Prime Minister, Benjamin Disraeli, persuaded Queen Victoria to take the title of Empress of India in 1877. Like many other politicians at that time, he regarded India (with a population at least five times that of Britain) to be the brightest 'jewel' in the British crown.

7.11 How does the painting of the recapture of Lucknow depict the actions of the British Army during the Indian Mutiny? What impression was it meant to convey? What are its merits and shortcomings as a piece of historical evidence?

AT2/L7 AT3/L7

7.12 What was significant about the date of the speech by Richard Cobden (Source 7.D)?

7.13 Write a brief report saying what the sources and pictures on these pages tell you about British attitudes to India in the nineteenth century.

AT1C ■

The Suez Canal

A new stage in the expansion of the British Empire began in November 1875. The Conservative Prime Minister, Benjamin Disraeli, paid £4 million to buy the Khedive of Egypt's shares in the newly-opened Suez Canal (page 63). This gave Britain, the world's leading sea power, the largest shareholding in the Canal. The new route was very important to Britain since it cut many days off the long trip to India. But after the Khedive was overthrown by rebels in 1879, threats were made to the Europeans living in Egypt. When several were killed in a riot in Alexandria in 1882, people in Britain reacted angrily (Source 7.E).

The Liberal Prime Minister, W.E. Gladstone, did not share Disraeli's enthusiasm for the Empire, but had to take action. British warships shelled Alexandria and an army defeated the rebels at the battle of Tel-el-Kebir. They went on to occupy Egypt 'to protect the canal'. This action alarmed the other governments of Europe, jealous of Britain's empire. It led to the division of the rest of Africa into separate European colonies. This process was so rapid, it was called 'the scramble for Africa'.

Cartoon in Punch, *26 February 1876*

Source 7.E

'The British flag is being trailed still further in the dust.'

'We are the laughing-stock of Europe.'

'Every Englishman is ashamed.'

◀ *Dr Livingstone's steam launch disturbs an elephant on the Zambezi in 1858. This picture was painted by an artist who was with the expedition*

'The scramble for Africa'

In 1800 most of the interior of Africa was unknown to Europeans. It only became better known when adventurers and missionaries, such as Richard Burton and David Livingstone, explored it. Their accounts of hot, wet, tropical forests and a primitive way of life (in Victorian eyes) gave people few grounds for thinking that Africa would be of any great interest to European settlers.

In 1880, the map of European settlements in Africa still looked much the same as it had done in 1800. But by 1897, as you can see from the map, Africa had been divided into colonies. The fifteen nations attending a conference in Berlin in 1884–5 had agreed to divide Africa between them in a peaceful fashion. Territories would be regarded as being colonies if they were occupied. The 'scramble for Africa' had begun.

Britain founded colonies in Nigeria, the Gold Coast (Ghana), Gambia, Sierra Leone, Kenya and Uganda. As in India, local leaders continued to rule but with the advice of the resident British officials who could interfere if they felt it was necessary. This was called *indirect rule*. Roads, railways, schools, hospitals and public buildings were built and many Africans were converted to Christianity. Cash crops were planted for use in British industries, such as cacao (chocolate) and palm oil (soap and margarine). Lord Lugard, who later become Governor of Nigeria, explained the reasons in a book published in 1893 (Source 7.F).

Source 7.F By Lord Lugard in 1893

The 'scramble for Africa' by the nations of Europe was due to growing rivalry in trade. It is in order to encourage the growth of trade of this country and to find a market for our manufactures and surplus coal, that our statesmen and businessmen support the growth of the Empire.

There are some who say we have no right to be in Africa at all, that 'it belongs to the natives'. I hold that our right is the need to provide for our ever-growing population. We can do this either by opening new fields for emigration or by providing work and employment which the development of a colony entails. By selecting men of the right quality to control new territories, we can bring many advantages to Africa.

7.14 What was the point of the *Punch* cartoon? Write a long caption explaining what the cartoon tells us about Disraeli and the Suez Canal.
AT3/L5

7.15 How does the map illustrate what was meant by the 'scramble for Africa'?

7.16 What reasons did Lord Lugard say made it right to colonise Africa? Was it for Britain's benefit or for the welfare of the people of Africa?
AT1B/L5

7.17 What does Source 7.G tell you about the different attitudes of the British, the Boers and the Black Africans to the war in South Africa?
AT3/L5

South Africa

The only part of Africa where large numbers of Europeans had settled by 1800 was Cape Colony in South Africa. This had once been Dutch but was now British. The Dutch farmers, or Boers, used Blacks as slaves on their farms. When the British abolished slavery throughout their Empire in 1833, the Boers began a mass migration – 'The Great Trek'. They crossed the the Vaal river and set up the Transvaal as an independent republic.

The Boers did not get on well with the British and war broke out between the two sides in 1899. When it ended in 1902, the Boers acknowledged the British Crown in return for a promise of self-government.

You can see what many Black Africans thought of the Boer War in Source 7.G. This comes from a letter sent by the British commander defending Mafeking to the Boer general besieging the town. Solomon Tshekisho Plaatje, a Black South African who spoke English, Dutch, Xhosa, Tswana and Zulu, was working as an interpreter there. He quoted this letter in his diary.

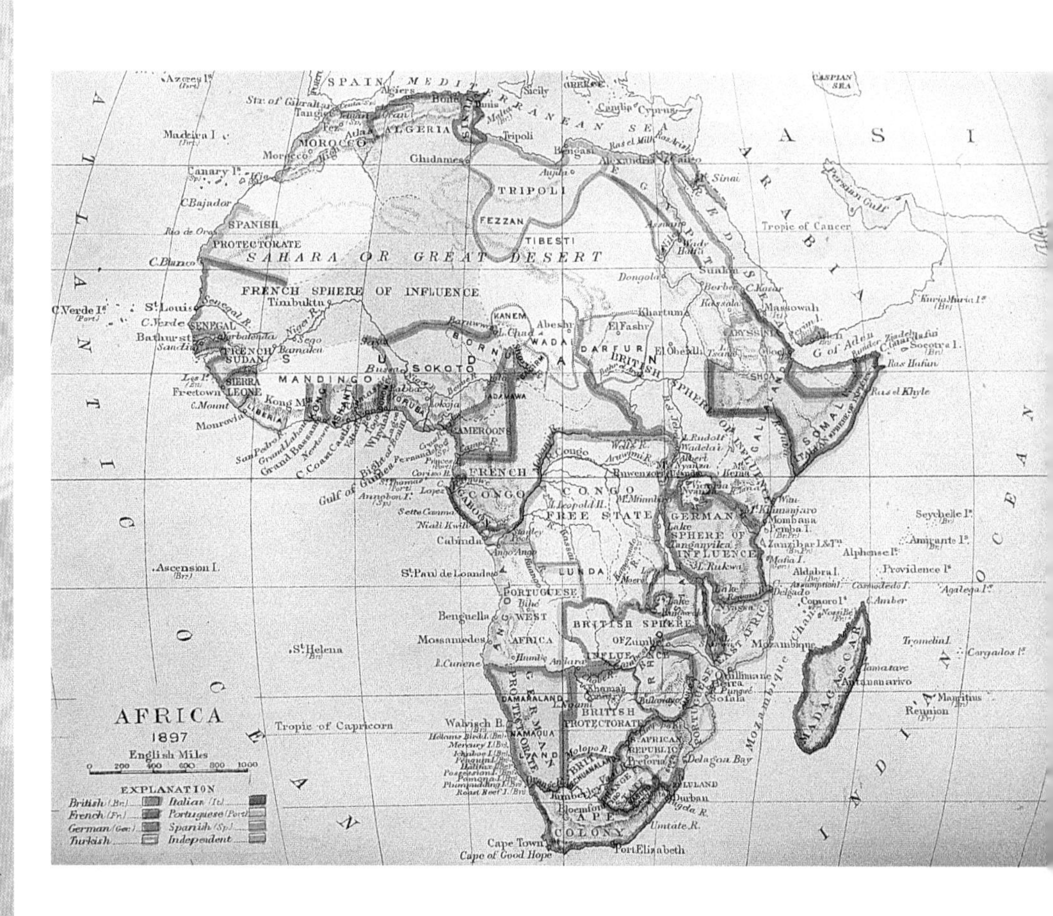

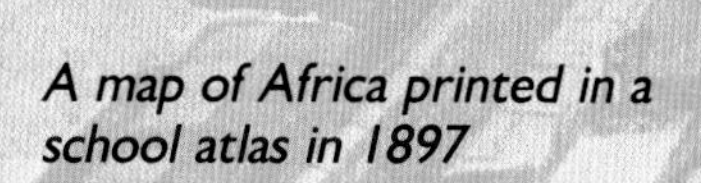

A map of Africa printed in a school atlas in 1897 ►

Source 7.G Letter from Colonel Baden-Powell to General Snyman

8 December 1899 *In my previous letter, I went out of my way, as one White man to another, to warn you that the natives are becoming extremely angry at your stealing their cattle, and the wanton burning of their Kraals* [villages]. *They argued that the war lay only between our two Nations, and that the quarrel had nothing to do with themselves, and they had remained neutral in consequence.*

Imperialism

In the late nineteenth century most people in Britain took pride in the Empire as a symbol of Britain's importance in the world. This attitude was called Imperialism. It was associated with patriotism – 'loyalty to the Queen' and 'doing one's duty for one's country'. When there were setbacks, such as the Zulu massacre of British soldiers at Isandhlwana (in 1879) or the death of General Gordon at Khartoum (in 1885), people shouted for revenge. Any insult to Britain had to be punished. This aggressive form of patriotism – my country right or wrong – was called Jingoism.

When uprisings were crushed with brute force, they were acclaimed. Lord Kitchener's victory at Omdurman in September 1898 was celebrated with wild rejoicing in Britain when 11 000 Muslim warriors mainly armed with spears had been killed for the loss of 50 British soldiers armed with guns.

Imperialism appealed to ordinary workers as well as to the upper and middle classes. They hoped the riches of the Empire could be used to improve their own way of life. They were thrilled by the exploits of explorers like Livingstone and Stanley. During the Boer War they flocked to the London music-halls to see newsreel films from the battle front, shown on the newly-invented cinématograph. When Mafeking was relieved in May 1900, they sang and danced in the streets.

Poets and painters (see pages 85–6) also took pride in the Empire. Rudyard Kipling said it was the duty of the White man to govern these countries in the interests of the 'natives' (Source 7.H). A Radical writer took a different view (Source 7.I).

7.18 What was 'the White Man's burden' according to Kipling? How was his poem ridiculed by the magazine *Truth*? How did the writer of that poem differ in his attitude to the British Empire? AT1C/L6

7.19 What is meant by Jingoism? How did it get its name? AT3/L4

7.20 Compare Source 7.J with Source 7.K. What do they tell us about imperialism? On which point did the two writers agree? How did they disagree? AT1C/L6 AT3/L6

7.21 What does the advertisement tell you about British attitudes to the Empire in 1900? What were the advertisers trying to do? AT3/L5

Source 7.H From a poem by Rudyard Kipling

Take up the White Man's burden –
Send forth the best ye breed –
Go bind your sons to exile
To serve your captives' need;

Source 7.I From a poem in the magazine *Truth*

Pile on the Brown Man's burden!
And if ye rouse his hate,
Meet his old-fashioned reasons
With Maxims – up to date.
With shells and Dum-Dum bullets
A hundred times make plain
The Brown Man's loss must never
Imply the White Man's gain.

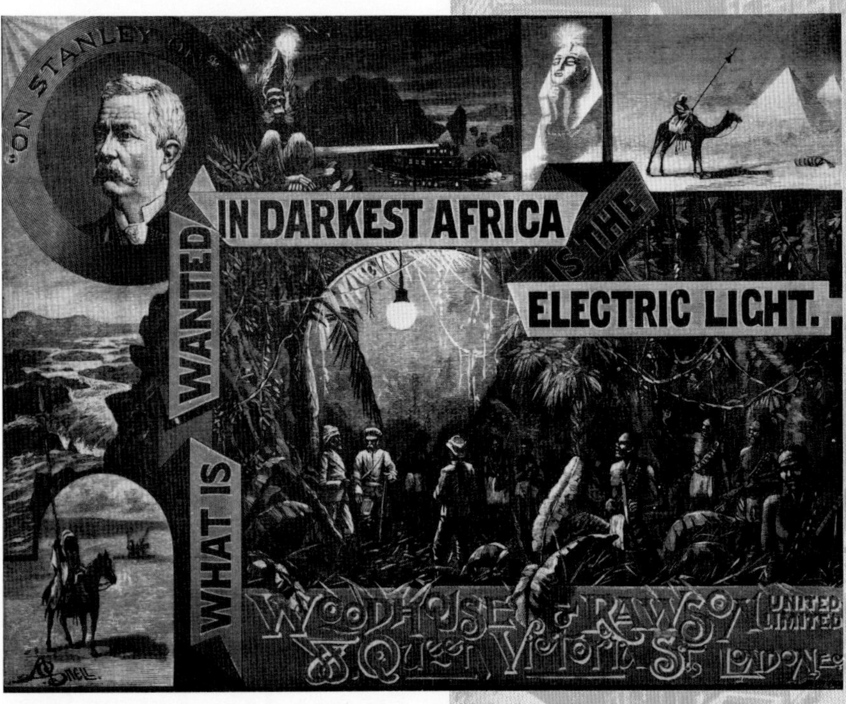

Advertisement from 1900

Sources 7.J to 7.M tell you what other people thought about Imperialism in the Victorian period.

Source 7.J Richard Cobden in 1849

People tell me I want to abandon our colonies. But I say, are you going to hold your colonies by the sword – by armies and ships of war? That is not a permanent hold upon them.

7.22 Make a list of the main arguments which were used to attack and defend Imperialism. AT1B/L6

Source 7.K Edward Dicey in 1877

Once this country comes to the conclusion that we have had enough of empire, then the days of our rule as a great power beyond the four seas are clearly numbered.

Wherever the Union Jack floats, there the English race rules. English laws prevail. English ideas are dominant. English speech holds the upper hand. England, like Rome, is the cornerstone of a great empire.

Source 7.L Music hall song in 1878

We don't want to fight, but, by jingo if we do, We've got the ships, we've got the men, we've got the money too.

Time Line

1757 Battle of Plassey
1759 Capture of Quebec
1770 Cook lands at Botany Bay
1776 American War of Independence
1807 Abolition of the slave trade
1833 Slavery abolished throughout the British Empire
1836 The Great Trek
1857 Indian Mutiny
1867 Canada becomes a dominion
1869 Suez Canal opened
1877 Queen Victoria becomes Empress of India
1898 Battle of Omdurman
1899 Boer War begins
1900 Relief of Mafeking

Ships in procession at the opening of the Suez Canal. It was built between 1859 and 1869 by the French engineer Ferdinand de Lesseps

Source 7.M By J.A. Hobson in 1902

What is the outcome of Imperialism? A great expenditure of public money upon ships, guns, military and naval equipment and stores. Large profits for manufacturers of weapons when a war occurs. More jobs for soldiers and sailors and diplomats. Every one of the steps of expansion of the Empire in Africa, Asia, and the Pacific has been accompanied by bloodshed.

Effects of Empire on Britain
The shipbuilding and iron and steel industries prospered. They built the ships needed by the Royal Navy and the shipping companies which served India, the Far East, Australasia and America.
The British coal industry sent millions of tonnes of coal to supply coaling stations across the world. They provided the fuel needed by merchant ships and the ships of the Royal Navy before the use of oil.
Many industries used raw materials produced by the colonies, such as Indian jute and cotton, Australian wool and Caribbean sugar.
Manufacturers exported their products to the colonies without fear of competition. The Australians complained they were buying woollen cloth from Britain made from Australian wool. Indians resented the importation of cotton cloth from Britain made from Indian cotton.
The colonies and dominions acted as a release valve for the rapidly expanding population of the British Isles. Emigration offered an outlet for the adventurous and the downtrodden.
The Empire offered young members of the ruling classes adventure and the chance to succeed as a district officer governing a small area.
Since Britain was almost always at war somewhere in the world, men who wanted an adventurous life could always serve in the army or the navy.
The Empire provided business people with the chance to invest money (capital) in profitable business projects, such as new railways, harbours and plantations.

8 Trade and the Empire

Trade with the Empire

Britain's trade with the rest of the world greatly increased between 1750 and 1900. This was due chiefly to the fact that the Industrial Revolution made Britain 'The Workshop of the World' (page 18). Moreover, the growth of the British Empire provided Britain with new sources of raw materials, such as cotton, wool, cocoa and palm oil. These were processed in Britain where they were used in industry, such as the manufacture of cotton textiles in Lancashire, woollens in Yorkshire, chocolate in Birmingham and soap on Merseyside. The colonies of the Empire also bought many British goods. India with its hot climate bought much of the output of cotton cloth from Lancashire. Nonetheless, trade with the colonies of the Empire only made up part of Britain's trade with the world in the nineteenth century – as you can see from the table of statistics in Source 8.A.

Source 8.A Value of British trade in 1900 (£s)

Europe	339 million	
America	211 million	
British Empire	231 million	
India	57 million	(Cotton, tea, jute)
Australia	46 million	(Wool, wheat, mutton)
The Far East	46 million	(Tea, silk, rubber, tin)
Canada	30 million	(Timber, wheat, metals)
Africa	28 million	(Wheat, wool, gold, diamonds)
New Zealand	18 million	(Lamb)
West Indies	6 million	(Sugar)

The Chartered Companies

Trade in the eighteenth century was handled by the merchants of the Chartered Companies. They had been granted royal charters giving them the sole right to trade in certain parts of the world. The Hudson's Bay Company, for instance, had the exclusive right to trade in Canada whilst the East India Company controlled trade with India and China. Huge fortunes were made by many of the merchants in these companies. They imported luxuries, such as silks, spices, coffee, cocoa, sugar and tea. As you have seen, the East India Company became so rich and powerful, it even formed its own private army and conquered much of India.

The slave trade

Some otherwise respectable and kindly merchants, however, made huge fortunes trading in slaves. Even this was organised by a Chartered Company – the Royal African Company. The slave traders had devised the very profitable Triangular Trade route. Ships set out from Liverpool or Bristol on the first leg of the journey, bound for West Africa carrying cheap trinkets, such as badges and buttons.

They traded with Arab and African slave traders in West Africa. The trinkets were exchanged for slaves captured in local wars. Yoked together in chains, they were loaded on to the slave ships for the six-

FOCUS

► *HOW and WHY did Britain's trade grow between 1750 and 1900?*

ATIA ■ ATIB ■ ATIC ■

Quayside on the Thames in 1756

8.1 Draw pie charts to show Britain's trade with (a) Europe, America and the British Empire as a whole, (b) the different parts of the Empire. AT1C/L5

8.2 Use Source 8.B and the picture to describe the conditions on board a slave ship. AT3/L4

8.3 Write a short description of the London dock scene above. How were heavy goods loaded and unloaded on to the ships? AT1C/L5

8.4 What did Parson Woodforde mean when he talked of gin having come 'by Moonshine'? What is surprising about this? What does it tell you about the customs regulations? AT1A/L6

8.5 Look at the pie charts showing British exports. Write notes saying what you notice about the changes between each of the dates shown. AT1A ■

Source 8.B
From *Atlas of the British Empire*, 1989

Male slaves were chained to prevent them attacking the crew. Little movement was possible and most had to lie in their own filth for the entire journey. An average of ten per cent of the slaves died on the voyage.

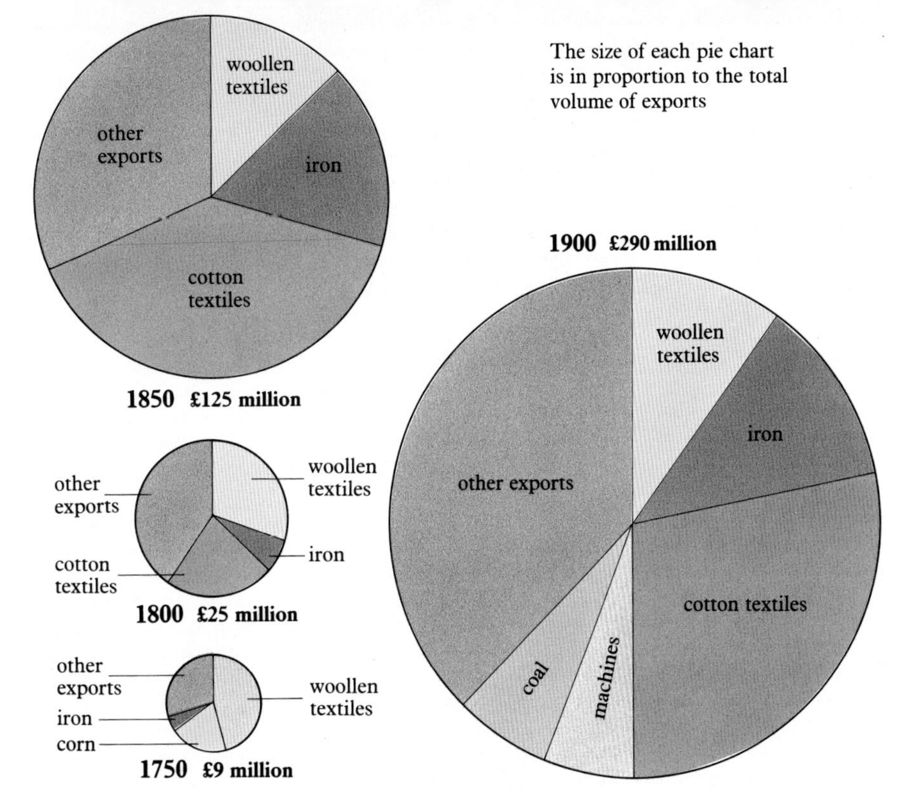

British exports from 1750 to 1900 ▶

week journey across the Atlantic. Little consideration was given for their comfort – as you can see from the picture. You can read how a modern writer described their journey in Source 8.B.

Once the slaves were sold, the proceeds were spent on luxury plantation products, such as sugar, rum, tobacco and cotton. They were carried back to Britain on the third and final leg of the trade route to Bristol or Liverpool. In this way a small investment in cheap manufactures paid eventually for a rich and valuable cargo which could be sold at a huge profit.

Conditions on board a slave ship

The slave trade collapsed when it was abolished in Britain in 1807. This was largely as a result of William Wilberforce's crusade in Parliament against the evils of slavery. But it was another 26 years before slavery itself was abolished (in 1833) in the places where it really mattered – throughout the colonies of the British Empire.

The Mercantilist System

As you can see from the pie charts, British trade grew at a phenomenal rate between 1750 and 1900. For the first hundred years of this period, however, trade was restricted by the British government. Heavy customs duties were charged on goods imported from abroad. This made them more expensive than similar products grown or made in Britain. This control of trade was called the Mercantilist System. Exports were encouraged by paying people to sell their goods abroad.

In doing this, the government hoped to expand the merchant navy, since its seamen could be recruited into the Royal Navy in time of war. The government also insisted that many goods from the colonies, such as tobacco and sugar, must be exported first to Britain. When these were later re-exported to Europe, the merchants made an extra profit.

Source 8.C
Extract from the diary written by James Woodforde, a Norfolk country parson

13 December 1794 *Busy all morning bottling two tubs of Gin, that came by Moonshine this-morning very early.*

These regulations were known as the Old Colonial System. They annoyed settlers in the colonies, especially those in North America. This was one of the reasons why the American colonists signed the Declaration of Independence in 1776 (page 57). In practice many of these trading regulations were hard to enforce and smuggling was common (Source 8.C).

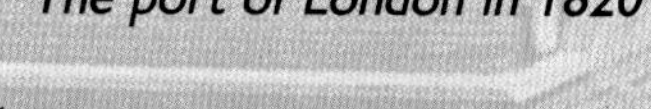

The port of London in 1820

◀ *This picture was produced for the souvenir edition of the* Illustrated London News *during Queen Victoria's Diamond Jubilee in 1897. It celebrated the fact that the Royal Navy had been master of the seas throughout her reign. The Victorians had little doubt that this was why Britain was the most important trading nation in the world*

8.6 Look at Source 8.D. What happened if the average price for British wheat was (a) £4 per quarter, (b) £6 per quarter, (c) £2 per quarter?

AT1B/L5

8.7 Which of the following is an example of Free Trade?

a) charging customs duties on wine and tobacco.

b) smugglers landing rum and tobacco in Cornwall.

c) abolishing the Corn Laws.

d) insisting that goods from the British Empire should be sent to Britain first before re-exporting them to Europe.

AT1B/L5

Source 8.D The Corn Law of 1815

- *Foreign corn may only be imported into the United Kingdom without payment of duty when the average prices of British corn are at or above these prices:*
- *Wheat at or above the price of eighty shillings* [£4] *a quarter* [about 200 kg. in weight].
- *Barley at or above the price of forty shillings* [£2] *per quarter.*
- *Whenever the average prices of British corn are below the prices stated, no foreign corn, or meal, or flour, shall be imported into the United Kingdom for home consumption.*

8.8 How was Free Trade the opposite of the Old Colonial System and Mercantilism? AT1C/L5

8.9 Why did Free Trade help manufacturers and factory workers in the towns but not farmers and the farmworkers they employed? AT1B ■

8.10 Look at the picture from *The Illustrated London News* celebrating Queen Victoria's Diamond Jubilee in 1897. Why was control of the seas of such importance to Britain at this time (see also Source 7.K on page 63). AT1B ■

Free trade

In 1776 Adam Smith wrote a book called *The Wealth of Nations.* This made a deep impression on a British politician, William Pitt, when he was Prime Minister. Adam Smith said trade between countries should be free of restrictions. He wanted Free Trade. This meant doing away with customs duties and any other restrictions on trade. The Government should not try to control what could or could not be imported into the country. He wanted free enterprise. Products should be sold at whatever price people were prepared to pay for them. Governments should leave trade alone. In time, the French phrase *laissez-faire* (meaning 'leave it alone') was used to describe this policy.

Pitt simplified the duties on foreign goods entering the country. In 1786 he made an agreement with France to lower duties on French wines in return for lower duties on British exports sent to France. However, the French Revolution of 1789 made the agreement unworkable.

In fact, the Napoleonic wars between 1799 and 1815 caused the amount of trade between Britain and Europe to fall off drastically. This was because the Emperor Napoleon tried to ban all trade between Europe and Britain. Imports of foreign corn fell and the price of British corn rose sharply. When the war ended, however, the Government took a backward step by passing the first of the Corn Laws (Source 8.D). They did this to protect the British farmer. It stopped cheaper foreign corn competing with British corn.

The immediate result of the Corn Law in 1815 was a rise in bread prices, since foreign wheat was no longer cheaper than British wheat. This came at a time when there was great distress and poverty amongst the working classes (see page 69). Opposition to the Corn Laws was one of the causes of the Peterloo Massacre (see page 70).

In 1839, the Anti-Corn Law League was formed to try to force the Government to repeal (cancel) the Corn Laws. Workmen and farmworkers complained that they kept bread prices higher than they need be. Manufacturers complained that the Corn Laws stopped foreigners selling corn to Britain to pay for British manufactures. However, not everyone agreed. Farmers and landowners said that repealing the Corn Laws would make them bankrupt, because the price of corn would fall.

Sir Robert Peel, the Tory Prime Minister, was convinced by now of the advantages of Free Trade, even though many members of his own party were farmers and landowners. In 1842 he lowered customs duties on many goods and in 1846 abolished the Corn Laws for good. In 1860 most of the remaining customs duties were abolished as well, except for those which were used to bring in taxes to pay for public spending, such as the duties on wine and tobacco.

From this time onwards until the 1930s, Britain traded freely with the rest of the world. The policy seemed to work. Britain's trade with the rest of the world expanded rapidly, as you can see from the pie charts on page 65. What is more, the farmers who had predicted a calamity if the Corn Laws were repealed enjoyed a period of great prosperity – the Golden Age of Agriculture.

Thirty years later, however, British agriculture began to slump when cheap corn from the American prairies was imported into Britain and wheat prices fell drastically.

9 Popular protest movements 1750~1850

FOCUS

► *HOW did people try to extend the right to vote between 1750 and 1850 and with WHAT results?* AT1B ■ AT1C ■
► *WHAT were the origins of the trade unions?* AT1B ■

The march organised by the Grand National Consolidated Trades Union to protest against the conviction of the Tolpuddle Martyrs in 1834

The Corresponding Societies

In 1750, despite the fact that Government decisions affected everyone, only a handful of well-to-do people could vote at an election to Parliament. When the rest of the population wanted to be heard, they could only do so by protesting in the street. Few workers were members of a trade union at that time since almost all worked at home or in small workshops.

However, the French Revolution in 1789 impressed rich and poor alike. If French workers could seize power, what stopped workers doing the same in Britain? Reform clubs, such as the London Corresponding Society, sprang up to discuss ways of gaining the right to vote. This reform movement alarmed the Government. They clamped down. They wanted no repetition of the French Revolution in Britain, and arrested some of the organisers. However, although the law courts found them innocent, the reform movement soon ran out of steam.

The first trade unions

At about the same time, workers in different industries were forming friendly societies and trade clubs. They met in pubs to discuss ways of improving working conditions (Source 9.A). Workers saved money with the societies in return for benefits, such as financial help when they were ill or unemployed. However, some societies went further than this. Their members took action to protect jobs, raise wages and improve working conditions.

This was why Parliament, still fearful of a working-class revolution, passed the Combination Acts in 1799 and 1800. These stopped workers *combining* together to force their employers to raise their wages. In other words, they banned trade unions.

9.1 What would we call the benefits provided by the Society of Woolcombers? Why were they necessary at that time? AT1C/L5

9.2 What value is a song, such as Source 9.B, as a source of information about the past? AT3/L7

9.3 Who was Ned Ludd? Why was the Luddite movement doomed to failure? What do people mean today when they call someone a Luddite? Does the introduction of new machines cause problems like this today? AT1A ■

9.4 How does Source 9.F help us to understand the problems of the first trade unions? AT3/L5

9.5 What do the sources and pictures tell you about the story of the Tolpuddle Martyrs? AT3/L6

Source 9.A Aims of the Society of Woolcombers in 1794

To enable the woolcomber to travel from place to place to seek for employment when work is scarce in his home area. To have relief when he is sick. If he should die to be buried by the club.

Source 9.B Luddite song

For in Derby it's true and in Nottingham too,
Poor men to the jail they've been taking;
They say that Ned Ludd, as I understood,
A thousand wide frames has been breaking.

The Luddites

Working-class anger increased as the use of steam power and machinery forced many people out of work at a time when bread prices were high (see page 67). In 1811 Nottinghamshire workers took action against the introduction of the wide stocking frame (Sources 9.B and 9.C).

Source 9.C From the Annual Register for 1811

On November 10th a number of weavers, assembling near Nottingham, began forcibly to enter houses in which were frames of this kind and destroyed them. The rioters took the name of Luddites and acted as if they were under the command of an imaginary Captain Ludd.

Tolpuddle Martyrs inn sign

The Luddite riots took a more serious turn when textile workers destroyed power looms and shearing frames in the North. A factory near Wigan was burned down and five handloom weavers were killed at Middleton. At Liversedge, near Leeds, two men died in a night attack on a mill and a manufacturer was murdered near Huddersfield. Other Luddites died on the gallows or were transported to Australia.

The Grand National Consolidated Trades Union

The strict laws against trade unions were relaxed in 1824–5. This enabled new trade unions to be formed, such as the Association of Colliers. Like the friendly societies and trade clubs, they were still local unions, not national trade unions as they are today. In February 1834, however, a number of unions got together to form the Grand National Consolidated Trades Union (the GNCTU). Almost immediately the new union faced a serious threat to its existence – the case of the Tolpuddle Martyrs.

Source 9.D *The Times*, 1 April 1834

The crime brought home to the prisoners did not justify the sentence.

The Tolpuddle Martyrs

It began when six farmworkers were transported to Australia after trying to start a trade union in the small Dorset village of Tolpuddle. They were not charged with joining a trade union, since this was legal. Instead, they were accused of swearing secret oaths, although most people were unaware that this was against the law. Their conviction caused widespread protests – as you can see in the pictures and in Sources 9.D to 9.F. The Tolpuddle Martyrs were later freed, although it was not until 1838 that they all returned to Britain.

Source 9.E *Standard*, 28 March 1834

Let those who have sinned in ignorance have the benefit of that ignorance. Let the six poor Dorsetshire fellows be restored to their cottages.

Source 9.F *Morning Post*, 29 March 1834

The Dorchester conspirators were, we admit, as far from being dangerous as it is possible for conspirators to be. The Trades Unions are, we have no doubt, the most dangerous institutions that were ever permitted to take root, under the shelter of the law, in any country.

Soon afterwards, the Grand National Consolidated Trades Union collapsed after the failure of a strike in Derby. At that time most workers were only too thankful to get a job. If they were sacked, they knew someone else would take their place.

The Peterloo Massacre

When Parliament passed the Corn Laws in 1815 (page 67), it caused widespread anger since the price of bread remained high. Many workers were unemployed. Riots broke out in London in 1815 and 1816 and the home of a Government minister was attacked. Since working people did not have the vote, the only way they could be heard was at a public meeting.

This is why a huge crowd of about 80 000 textile workers and their families met in St Peter's Fields, in Manchester, on Monday, 16 August 1819. They went there to hear the Radical speaker Henry 'Orator' Hunt tell them why Parliament should be reformed. But the meeting ended in tragedy. Thirteen people were killed and hundreds were wounded. You can read what happened in Sources 9.G to 9.L.

Source 9.G By a reporter in the *Courier*

Before 12 o'clock crowds began to assemble, each town or hamlet having a banner. Some wore a cap with 'Liberty' upon it. Each group, as they came through the streets, kept in military order, with sticks on their shoulders. Banners were painted 'UNITE AND BE FREE', 'DIE LIKE MEN, AND NOT BE SOLD LIKE SLAVES', 'UNITY AND FRATERNITY', 'STRENGTH AND LIBERTY'.

Source 9.I From a letter in the *Courier*

The meeting was addressed by several speakers in a menacing tone. The shouts seemed to split the very air and shake the ground. The constables [volunteer policemen for the day] *were tauntingly insulted wherever they stood. Sticks and hats always waving at every shout.*

About half-past one the Magistrates read the Riot Act. Immediately after, the platform was surrounded [by the soldiers]. *This move would have taken place without bloodshed had not the mob attacked the military and civil authorities with missiles. Consequently the cavalry charged in their own defence.*

◀ *This picture was dedicated 'To Henry Hunt and the female Reformers who suffered from the furious attack made on them by that brutal armed force, the Manchester and Cheshire Yeomanry Cavalry'*

Source 9.H By a reporter from *The Times*

A club of 156 female Reformers came from Oldham. They carried a white silk banner, inscribed 'ANNUAL PARLIAMENTS, UNIVERSAL SUFFRAGE, VOTE BY BALLOT'.

A posse of 300 or 400 constables marched into the field about 12 o'clock. Not the slightest insult was offered to them.

[Later] *The cavalry drew their swords and rode into the mob which gave way before them. Not a brickbat was thrown at them – not a pistol was fired during this period. All was quiet and orderly.*

9.6 How do the slogans explain the reasons for the demonstration? AT3/L6
9.7 How can you tell which sources were definitely written by eyewitnesses? AT3/L6

Source 9.J From a letter in the *Courier*

The principal part of them were stout men, with sticks or clubs; but there were a few female Reformers. They marched in regular order. The word 'Halt' was shouted and instantly obeyed.

After Hunt had spoken about ten minutes, the Cavalry rode up to the hustings and surrounded it. Instantly the mob attacked them with stones and sticks. The confusion then became dreadful. The mob threw stones at the military. The cavalry then charged amongst them and many were hurt with sabre cuts.

9.8 Which sources may have been biased for or against the demonstrators? Why is it important to know this? AT2/L6 AT3/L6

9.9 Is there any reliable evidence that the soldiers acted in self-defence? AT3/L6

9.10 Samuel Bamford (Source 9.L) wrote his account in 1842. How reliable is his evidence? How could he remember accurately events which took place on a single day twenty years earlier? How likely is it that anyone caught up in the Peterloo Massacre would ever forget it? AT3/L7

9.11 Compare the two pictures. What are the similarities and differences? Which do you think best depicts the Peterloo Massacre? Why? AT1C/L5

9.12 Which sources blamed the crowd for the violence? Which blamed the cavalry? Who do you blame? Write down what you think happened using the information in the pictures and in the written sources. AT3 ■

Source 9.K A witness giving evidence at the inquest on one of the victims

When I got to the end of Watson Street, I saw ten or twelve of the Yeomanry Cavalry and two of the Hussars cutting at the people, who were wedged close together. An officer of Hussars rode up to his own men, and knocking up their swords said, 'Damn you, what do you mean by this work?' He then called out to the Yeomanry, 'For shame, gentlemen, what are you about? The people cannot get away.'

Source 9.L Samuel Bamford, one of the organisers of the meeting, wrote this in 1842

The cavalry were received with a shout of good will. They shouted again, waving their sabres over their heads and then dashed forward and began cutting the people. 'Stand fast,' I said, 'they are riding upon us. Stand fast.' The cavalry were in confusion. Their sabres were used to cut a way through naked held-up hands, and defenceless heads. Chopped limbs and heads with gaping wounds were seen. Groans and cries mingled with the din of that horrid uproar. 'Ah! ah!' 'For shame! For shame!' was shouted. Then, 'Break! break! They are killing them in front and they cannot get away'.

Afterwards, Parliament passed the Six Acts to prevent similar protests in future. Illegal military training and the printing of anything which might encourage people to riot were banned. Magistrates were given the right to search people's homes for weapons. Newspapers were even taxed to make them too expensive for poor people to buy.

This picture was printed with the caption 'Dreadful scene at Manchester meeting of Reformers'

Election scene at Covent Garden in 1818. The temporary wooden platform was called the hustings. *This was where people voted. There was no secret ballot at that time. Everyone knew who you voted for – such as your landlord, your employer or your commanding officer. Candidates bribed voters to vote for them, since it was easy to make sure they did so when voting took place. Charles Greville claimed that £100 000 was used to bribe the voters at the Liverpool election in 1830*

9.13 What event explains John Croker's attitude to the Reform Bill in Source 9.O?
AT3/L4

Reform of Parliament

Before 1832 Parliament did not represent the people as a whole. Less than one person in 50 could vote. Each county sent two members to Parliament, no matter how small or how big it was. These county voters had to own land or a house worth at least £2 a year in rent. This meant that most ordinary people, such as farmworkers, could not vote. There were similar requirements in the towns. In almost all cases, only people who owned a certain amount of property could vote.

Then, as now, each MP represented an area of land called a *constituency.* You would have thought that each of these would have had roughly the same number of voters. This was not the case. Manchester, the third largest English city with about 200 000 people in 1831, did not have a single MP. This affected everyone, not just the poor. The richest mill-owners in Manchester were no more able to vote than their poorest workers. The need for reform was urgent now that many towns and cities were growing rapidly.

By contrast, Castle Rising, a small Norfolk village where only ten families lived, elected two Members of Parliament! A constituency like this was called a 'rotten borough'. There were 56 rotten boroughs in Britain in 1830, many of them in Cornwall.

The Reform riot in Bristol in 1831 (Source 9.N)

The Great Reform Bill

The need to draw up new constituencies was accompanied by demands that the right to vote should be given to many more people. The manufacturers of Manchester and Birmingham were just as keen as their workers to see these changes. So too were many Whig, or Liberal, members of Parliament. The demand for reform grew. A revolution in France in 1830 convinced the ruling Whig Government (page 79) that the time had come to reform the electoral system. They were opposed by the Tories who had a majority in the House of Lords. In these sources you can read what happened.

The Reformed House of Commons in 1833

9.14 Use the painting of the election in Covent Garden to write a detailed description of an election at the time of the Peterloo Massacre. AT3/L5

9.15 Look at Source 9.Q. What percentage of the population were electors in 1851 in (a) Arundel and Norwich, (b) Macclesfield and Bradford? What does this tell you about these towns? AT3/L5

9.16 Use Source 9.Q to say how and why election to Parliament was still undemocratic after 1832. AT3/L5

9.17 Why do you think Members of Parliament thought that only well- to-do people should have the right to vote in 1832? AT1C/L6

9.18 What did the Reform Bill of 1832 achieve? AT1B ■

Source 9.M From the diary written by Charles Greville

7 March 1831 *Nothing talked of, thought of, dreamed of, but Reform. Every creature one meets asks, What is said now? How will it go? What is the last news? What do you think? And so it is from morning till night, in the streets, in the clubs, and in private houses.*

Source 9.N From the diary written by Charles Greville

11 November 1831 *The riots in Bristol, for brutal ferocity and unprovoked violence, may compete with some of the worst scenes of the French Revolution. The spirit which produced these atrocities was inspired by Reform. It was a longing after havoc and destruction, which is at the heart of Reform in the mind of the mob.*

Source 9.O By John Croker, MP

11 November 1831 *There can be no longer any doubt that the Reform Bill is a stepping-stone to a republic. I find that those who some months ago laughed at my alarms are now at least as much frightened as I am.*

Source 9.P By Thomas Creevey, MP

5 June 1832 *Thank God! I was in at the triumph of our Bill. This is the third great event of my life at which I have been present – the Battle of Waterloo, the battle of Queen Caroline, and the battle of Earl Grey and the English nation for the Reform Bill.*

In the face of massive public protests the Tories in Parliament agreed to let the Bill through. The Whigs had told them the king would create enough new lords to outvote the Tories in the House of Lords if they continued to hold up the Reform Bill. So in June 1832 it became law.

Effects of the Reform Bill

The new law abolished the old rotten boroughs and gave their seats to the industrial cities. Nonetheless the allocation of seats was still unfair. Manchester with a population of 200 000 was represented by the same number of MPs as Bolton with only 22 000. You can see further examples in Source 9.Q.

Source 9.Q Representation in Parliament in 1851

	Population	Electors	MPs
Arundel	2 750	208	1
Macclesfield	39 000	1058	2
Norwich	68 200	5390	2
Bradford	104 000	2683	2
Liverpool	376 000	17 433	2

The rules controlling who could vote were also changed. Voters had to be men, over 21, and be the owners of property or tenants of a house paying a rent of at least £10 per year. This was a substantial sum of money for those days. As a result, no more than about 300 000 extra voters from the well-to-do middle classes gained the vote. The new Members of Parliament for the industrial towns were manufacturers, not workers. The working classes were no better off.

Chartist procession

The Chartists

The workers who had demonstrated in support of the Great Reform Bill of 1832 felt betrayed. The savage conviction of the Tolpuddle Martyrs (page 69) in March 1834 and the Poor Law Amendment Act (page 50) in the same year sparked off fresh anger. Working people felt they had only two choices if they were to improve their standards of living. Either they should follow the example of the French and start a revolution, or they should try to get people to represent them in Parliament and use their influence to bring in reforms. This is why three Radicals, Francis Place, William Lovett and John Roebuck, drew up the People's Charter (Source 9.R). They wanted to collect so many signatures, it would convince Parliament that everyone wanted reform.

The Chartist demonstration on Kennington Common on 10 April 1848

Source 9.R The Six Points of the People's Charter

1 A vote for every adult male – *over 21, of sound mind, who was not a criminal.*

2 A secret ballot – *to protect the voter, so his employer or landlord could not influence the way he voted.*

3 Annual parliaments – *to make sure Members of Parliament always supported the views of their constituents.*

4 No property qualification for MPs – *so that poor men could stand for Parliament as well as the rich.*

5 Payment of salary to Members of Parliament.

6 Constituencies of equal size – *so that every constituency had the same number of voters.*

Thousands of people signed the Charter. They saw it as a chance to put right many other wrongs. Although most wanted to gain their aims peacefully through Parliament, some supported violent action. This worried the Government. In 1839, a large group of Welsh miners, armed with clubs and other weapons, tried to seize Newport, but without success. Shots were exchanged with soldiers and the

9.19 Which of these six points have since been achieved? Which have not? Why? What other important changes have been made since then? AT1A/L5

9.20 Why do you think the Chartists demanded salaries for MPs?

9.21 Look at Source 9.Q on page 73. Draw up a new table as it might have looked had the Chartists' sixth demand been successful in 1848.

9.22 How can you tell the Government was afraid there might be an armed rebellion? Why did they refuse the Chartists' demands? AT3/L6

Punch *cartoon, 'Not so very unreasonable!!! Eh?', 15 April 1848*

9.23 What was the attitude of *Punch* to the Chartists and their Petition? AT1C/L6

9.24 Use Sources 9.S to 9.V and the pictures to write an account of the Chartist Demonstration on Monday, 10 April 1848. AT3/L6

Time Line

- **1789** French Revolution begins
- **1792** London Corresponding Society formed
- **1799–1800** Combination Acts passed
- **1811** Luddite riots
- **1819** Peterloo Massacre; Six Acts
- **1825** Repeal of Combination Acts
- **1831** Reform riot in Bristol
- **1832** Great Reform Bill passed
- **1834** Tolpuddle Martyrs; GNCTU founded
- **1837** Chartist movement started
- **1839** Newport uprising
- **1848** Last Chartist demonstration

ringleaders were arrested. In 1842 striking miners in Stoke-on-Trent listened to a Chartist speaker and went on to break into shops and attack coal mines that were still at work.

It is not surprising, therefore, that the Government looked on the Chartists as revolutionaries. However, the Chartist leaders were always careful to stay within the law. They submitted three petitions. The largest, the 1848 petition, was the last. You can see what happened, on Monday 10 April 1848, in these sources and in the pictures.

Source 9.S From the *Illustrated London News*, 15 April 1848

The van [a horse-drawn vehicle] *waiting for the delegates was inscribed on the right side with the motto, 'THE CHARTER. NO SURRENDER. LIBERTY IS WORTH LIVING FOR AND WORTH DYING FOR'. On the left side it read, 'THE VOICE OF THE PEOPLE IS THE VOICE OF GOD'. On the back was inscribed, 'WHO WOULD BE A SLAVE THAT COULD BE FREE? ONWARD, WE CONQUER; BACKWARD WE FALL'. Eight banners were fixed (four on each side) inscribed, 'THE CHARTER', 'NO VOTE, NO MUSKETS', 'VOTE BY BALLOT', 'ANNUAL PARLIAMENTS', 'UNIVERSAL SUFFRAGE', 'NO PROPERTY QUALIFICATION'.*

Source 9.T Letter from the Prime Minister to the Queen

The Kennington Common Meeting has proved a complete failure. About 12 000 or 15 000 persons met in good order. Feargus O'Connor was told that the meeting would not be prevented, but that no procession would be allowed to pass the bridges. He then addressed the crowd, advising them to disperse, and went off in a cab to the Home Office [where he handed over the petition with one or two of the other delegates].

Source 9.U From the diary of Charles Greville, a Government official

13 April 1848 *Monday passed off with surprising quiet. Enormous preparations were made, and a host of military, police, and special constables were ready if wanted. The Chartist movement was contemptible. Everybody was on the alert. Our office was fortified and all our guns were taken down to be used in defence of the building. However, at about twelve o'clock crowds came streaming along Whitehall, going northward, and it was announced that all was over.*

Source 9.V 'The Chartist Procession', *Punch*, 15 April 1848

If the signatures to the Petition are to be believed, Her Majesty would have been at an early hour wending her way towards Kennington Common with seventeen Dukes of Wellington at her side, and Sir Robert Peel.

After it failed to move the Government, Chartism faded away. Living standards and working conditions were improving and working people no longer felt quite the same anger. Nonetheless, the call for 'one man, one vote' continued even though it was no longer part of the package of measures proposed in the Charter.

10 Parliament and politics

Several of the benefits of joining this shipbuilding trade union are shown on the membership certificate, such as help when old, unemployed, sick, or injured in an accident

The New Model Unions

Trade unions in the early nineteenth century made little progress in their efforts to improve working conditions and raise wages. In the 1850s, however, a new and much more effective type of trade union was formed. However, it was only for skilled workers, such as the shoemakers, carpenters, joiners, bricklayers and iron workers. These were the New Model Unions. The first was the Amalgamated Society of Engineers which was founded in 1851. Like the other new unions, it had its main offices in London and employed paid officials to run its affairs. This was possible because the railway (from 1830), the electric telegraph (from 1838) and the penny post (from 1840) enabled national officials to keep in touch with their branch offices.

► ► *HOW did political parties, voting rights, women's rights and trade unions change between 1850 and 1900?*

ATIA ■ ATIB ■ ATIC ■

► *WHAT was the Irish Question and HOW did politicians hope to solve it?*

ATIB ■ ATIC ■

10.1 Why do you think the match girls and the dockers were so successful in gaining the sympathy of Londoners during their campaigns?

AT1C ■

10.2 Make a list of the words and phrases in Source 10.C which show the writer was strongly biased against the demonstrators. Is she a reliable witness? AT2 ■ AT3/L7

10.3 Write a paragraph to say what rights the working classes gained during the nineteenth century. In what ways were they still at a grave disadvantage compared with the middle and upper classes?

AT1A ■

Source 10A
By Annie Besant

We asked for money and it came pouring in. We gave the girls strike pay. We wrote articles and held public meetings. Mr Bradlaugh [a Radical MP] *asked questions in Parliament. We led a procession of the girls to the House of Commons. The girls behaved splendidly and stuck together throughout the strike.*

The London match girls in a protest march to Westminster ▼

Source 10.C
By Lady Monkswell – a right-wing Liberal

The subject which most commends interest just now is the battle of Trafalgar Square on Sunday 13 November. The so-called 'unemployed' and a crowd of roughs had taken possession of the space round Nelson's Column in Trafalgar Square since the middle of October. They had persistently slept there and held meetings assisted by the Socialists and the extreme Radicals. Sunday, 13 November arrived and some Radical and all the Socialist Clubs from all parts of the town set off, followed by the whole criminal population and vast numbers of sightseers, for Trafalgar Square.

The members of the new unions also earned higher than average wages as skilled workers. This meant they could afford to pay a high annual subscription in return for welfare benefits, such as sickness and unemployment pay. The union's officials talked to employers to try to settle disputes. When that failed, they called a strike.

Gradually, the different unions began to co-operate. This led in 1868 to the holding of an annual conference – the Trades Union Congress or TUC – to discuss trade union matters in general. The Government, meanwhile, was looking closely at the power of the trade unions. As a result, Gladstone's Liberal Government brought in the Trade Union Act of 1871 giving the unions some of the legal rights they wanted but making picketing illegal. This would have prevented them from taking effective strike action, but it was soon amended by Disraeli's Conservative Government.

Unions for the unskilled workers

For much of the nineteenth century unskilled workers had a raw deal. Their jobs were usually temporary. They could be sacked at a moment's notice, were paid very low wages and often worked in appalling conditions. It was a great triumph, then, when these unskilled manual workers won three great victories in the late 1880s.

The first was in 1888 when the young match girls of London went on strike. They were among the poorest paid workers in the city. A prominent woman writer called Annie Besant helped them organise their protest. She wrote a pamphlet – *White Slavery in London* – listing ways in which the girls were badly treated. The publicity the match girls got brought a tremendous response from the people of London (Source 10.A). The employers gave in and the girls got their pay rise and improved working conditions.

Source 10.B By Annie Besant

As the match girls tramped along the embankment in orderly array, 3 or 4 deep, they made a striking object-lesson for the careless well-to-do folk who gazed at them with puzzlement as they passed. Some very young, pale, thin, undersized, ragged, their very appearance evidence enough of hard labour unfit for childish bodies.

The second success came early in 1889 after the gas-workers demanded a reduction in the length of their shift from 12 hours to 8 hours for the same pay. Later the same year the London dockers went on strike for a wage rise from fivepence to sixpence an hour. They called it the 'dockers' tanner'. The strike was successful because three left-wing activists, Ben Tillett, John Burns and Tom Mann, combined forces to help them achieve this remarkable victory. Like the match girls a year earlier, they were greatly assisted by a sympathetic public. They even got a generous contribution of £30 000 from Australian trade unionists.

Efforts were made to form a political party which would stand up for the interests of the workers. This is why H.M. Hyndman founded the Social Democratic Federation in the early 1880s. The Victorian upper and middle classes were hostile (Source 10.C). They still feared the prospect of an English Revolution. Matters came to a head on 13 November 1887, when the Social Democratic Federation organised a demonstration in Trafalgar Square against rising unemployment. It was called 'Bloody Sunday' because two of the demonstrators were 'so injured they subsequently died, and a policeman was stabbed'.

Politics and problems in the United Kingdom

Wales

The Industrial Revolution revived the fortunes of the Welsh people. The South Wales coalfield became one of Britain's leading industrial regions. It was said that 'half the world ran its trains on the rails made in South Wales'. The growth of Welsh industry was also accompanied by industrial strife. Twenty people were killed in a riot at Merthyr Tydfil in 1831. Protesters dressed as 'Rebecca and her daughters' (Source 10.D) smashed turnpikes when tolls were raised in 1839–44.

The use of the Bible to support a riot was appropriate since Wales had responded with enthusiasm to John Wesley and the Methodist movement (page 48). The Nonconformist chapel, not the Anglican church, was now the centre of Welsh life. People took a growing pride in the Welsh language and its traditions. This Nonconformist, Welsh-speaking background helped to produce David Lloyd George, Britain's inspiring Prime Minister in the First World War (see page 113).

Scotland

The coalfields of Scotland, too, prospered during the Industrial Revolution. Glasgow became Britain's second largest city and the centre of the world's most important shipbuilding industry. But this was matched by tragedy in the Highlands where large numbers of crofters were cleared from the land (see Source 5.I on page 43). Like many poor Welsh farmers, they were forced to emigrate or move to the industrial towns.

Scotland was also a hive of industrial unrest and a centre of the trade union movement. A number of leading left-wing politicians grew up there, such as Keir Hardie, one of the founders of the Labour Party, and Ramsay MacDonald, the first Labour Prime Minister.

Ireland

In 1801 Ireland finally became part of the United Kingdom. But the union did not bring equality of opportunity as the Irish had hoped. Catholics were still barred from holding many official positions and from sitting as Members of Parliament at Westminster.

The King and many important Tory political leaders were opposed to the idea of changing this ban. It was only after an extensive campaign, run by Daniel O'Connell, that Parliament eventually passed the Catholic Emancipation Act in 1829. O'Connell later joined up with the Young Ireland Movement to campaign for repeal of the union with England. He and other Nationalists wanted an independent Ireland. However, O'Connell lost some of his support when he renounced the idea of using violence to achieve this end.

By contrast, the leaders of Young Ireland attempted an unsuccessful rebellion at Tipperary in 1848, during the Great Famine (page 41). Soon afterwards the Fenian Brotherhood (a forerunner of the IRA) was formed. It was financed by Irish emigrants to the United States, bitter about their treatment in Ireland. The Fenians made a number of attacks on the police and army in Britain in the 1860s.

In the 1870s many more people were demanding Home Rule for Ireland. Charles Stewart Parnell, an Irish MP, led the Irish Party in the House of Commons and a Land League was formed in Ireland to defend

Source 10.D From *Genesis 24:60*

And they blessed Rebecca, and said unto her . . . let thy seed [children] *possess the gate of those which hate them.*

Source 10.E Official report on Captain Boycott

On 22 September 1880, Captain Boycott's walls were thrown down, his cattle were driven off and scattered over the roads. He had no one to work for him, but had to do the work of the stables and farm himself. When he met people on the road they hooted and booed him, and spat across his feet as he went. No cause for this treatment of Captain Boycott has been suggested other than his collecting rents.

This picture shows a forced eviction from an Irish cottage. When it was printed on 15 January 1887, the Illustrated London News *explained that it had been drawn from a sketch by their special artist in County Kerry. The artist who drew the picture in the magazine, however, was Amedée Forestier. He lived and worked in London*

Source 10.F
From the *Guardian*, 4 September 1889

I visited the farmhouse from which Thomas Minogue was recently evicted. Every Galway man who now passes by that house hisses a curse through his teeth.

10.4 How can you tell that the artist sympathised with the Irish tenant farmers? Does this make the picture more or less valuable as a source of information about Ireland in the 1880s? AT2/L7 AT3/L7

10.5 Do you think this is a realistic picture of what actually happened? What difference does it make to know that Forestier drew the picture in his London studio instead of outside the cottage in Ireland? AT3/L7

10.6 What was the Irish Question? Why was it so difficult to solve? AT1C ■

10.7 What is meant by the word *boycott* today?

10.8 What were the main complaints of the Irish tenant farmers? Use these sources and the picture to write a short account of the land disputes in Ireland in the 1880s. AT3/L6

the rights of tenants against the agents (Source 10.E) of the landlords who often lived in England and never visited their properties. They were evicting farmers and putting up rents.

By 1880, the Liberal Prime Minister, W.E. Gladstone, was convinced that something had to be done. He got Parliament to pass a number of laws to protect the tenant farmers and eventually tried to bring in an Irish Home Rule Bill to let the Irish people govern themselves. But the Irish Protestants in Ulster were fearful of joining a Catholic Ireland. They wanted to stay inside the Union with the other countries making up the United Kingdom. The Home Rule Bill was defeated when a number of Liberals from Gladstone's own party (the Liberal Unionists) voted with the Conservatives and forced Gladstone out of office. By the end of the century, the Irish Question was still no nearer a solution.

The political parties

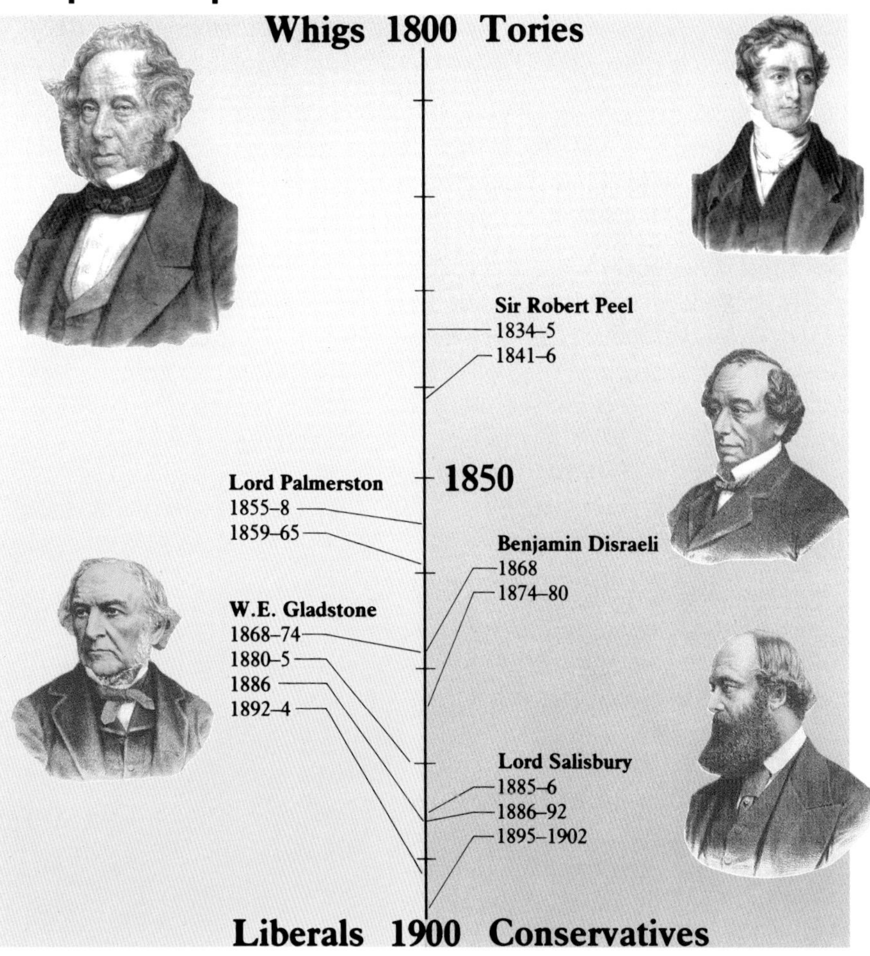

In the eighteenth and early nineteenth centuries the Whigs and Tories were the main political groups. In those days politicians often changed from one side to the other. Gladstone, for instance, started as a Tory before becoming a Liberal. But after the passing of the Great Reform Act in 1832, the two political parties we know today began to emerge.

Meanwhile, the position of the Crown also began to change during this period. When Queen Victoria came to the throne in 1837, the monarchy was very unpopular. When she died in 1901, millions mourned. By then it was firmly established that her role as Queen was that of Head of State. Government was left to her ministers, led by a Prime Minister who was the leader of the main political party in the House of Commons.

Extending the right to vote

The old Chartist demand to extend the right to vote to all adult males was renewed in 1865 when the National Reform League was founded. Popular demonstrations and a growing belief in democracy convinced Gladstone and other leading politicians that the time had come at last to give the working classes more say in how they were governed. However, it was the Conservative leader, Benjamin Disraeli, who actually brought in the Second Reform Bill in 1867. He gave the vote to working men in the towns who were over 21 and either a householder or else a lodger paying at least £10 a year in rent.

The new Bill did not apply to working men in the country. Nor, indeed, did it apply to women – not even to Disraeli's wife or Mrs Gladstone. Large numbers of working men in the towns were also disqualified from voting. They included lodgers who paid less than £10 a year in rent and any adult man who lived in the same home as his parent (the householder). This meant, for instance, that no one could vote in a house where a widow (the householder) lived with her five adult sons.

Nonetheless, the number of people entitled to vote doubled to about two million men. It was still far from being representative of the people of Britain as a whole, but it did give many workers in the towns a say in the choice of government.

Until this time, votes were still cast openly at the hustings, so employers and landlords could see how their employees and tenants voted. After 1872 this ceased to be a problem. Gladstone's Liberal Government brought in the Ballot Act. It enabled voters to cast their votes in secrecy. You can see the effect it had in the picture and in Source 10.G.

Source 10.G Report in *The Times*, 14 September 1872

Usually an election day here has been a day of great political tumult and uproar. But today, when the poll opened the principal streets of the town were almost as quiet as usual. At the polling booths, thirty-seven in number, there was very little crowding.

The Third Reform Bill of 1884 put right the wrong which had been done in 1867 to people living in the countryside. It extended the vote to all adult male householders in Britain and lodgers paying at least £10 a year in rent. The effect of this was to give the vote to farmworkers and miners living in pit villages.

Source 10.H

Effect of the Reform Bill of:	Percentage of adult males who could vote		
	England and Wales	Scotland	Ireland
1832	20%	12%	5%
1867	33%	33%	17%
1884	67%	60%	50%

10.9 Compare the election in Source 10.G with the picture on page 72. Draw a Time Line to show how ways of electing MPs changed in the course of 54 years. Were they sudden or gradual changes? AT1A/L5

10.10 Roughly how many adults in England and Wales were without the vote in 1900? Was it (a) one in six, (b) one in three, (c) two out of three?

10.11 Which of Frederick Ryland's arguments were based on prejudice and not on facts? AT1C/L6

10.12 Which of Emily Hall's arguments do you think Frederick Ryland would have had most difficulty in answering? AT1C ■

10.13 What was the point of each of the two *Punch* cartoons? How did Bernard Partridge, the cartoonist in 1905, differ in his attitude to women's voting rights to Sir John Tenniel, the cartoonist in 1870? AT1C ■

10.14 Look at Sources 9.G to 9.L on pages 70–1. What evidence is there that people campaigned for women's rights in 1819? AT3/L4

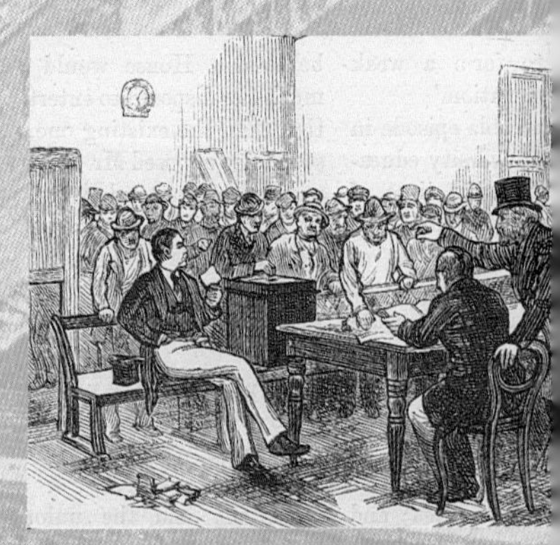

Working men casting their votes by secret ballot at the General Election of 1874

Votes for women

In 1867 and again in 1884, many people in Britain hoped the Government would extend the right to vote to women as well as to men. A small number of MPs worked without success in Parliament to try to persuade the Government to do this. They and their supporters were often ridiculed – as you can see in the *Punch* cartoon (below). Some of the arguments used on both sides are illustrated in Sources 10.I and 10.J.

Punch *cartoon, May 1905. Qualified Voter: 'Ah, you may pay rates an' taxes, an' you may 'ave responserbilities an' all; but when it comes to VOTIN', you must leave it to US MEN!'*

Source 10.I By Emily Hall in *Bibby's Quarterly*, 1898

If people have a right to a say in the making of the laws which all must obey, it is difficult to think of a reason why this right should belong to one sex and not to the other.

Their coachmen, their gardeners, the very labourers on the estate, have votes, while the mistress who employs and pays them is not considered competent to give this simple vote.

Source 10.J By Frederick Ryland in *The Girl's Own Paper, 1896*

The truth is that the intelligence of highly intelligent women is not political. Only a few will take an interest in politics steadily and continuously.

The factory girl class will be by far the most important class of women voters. Political power in many large cities will be chiefly in the hands of young, ill-educated, giddy, and often ill-conducted girls, living in lodgings.

In this Punch *cartoon from 1870 John Bull (with his back to the door) represents Britain as a whole. The cartoon was captioned* An Ugly Rush. *John Bull is saying 'Not if I know it!'* ▼

The new Houses of Parliament were built in the 1850s after the old House of Commons was burned down in 1834

Women's rights

One of the first British feminists to make her name was the writer Mary Wollstonecraft. In her book *Vindication of the Rights of Women*, published in 1792, she said women should be given equal rights with men. But no one listened to her. Women were badly treated at this time. Until 1870 a married woman could not even own property in her own name. It was her husband's. Before 1857 it was almost impossible for a woman to get a divorce, but the man could. After a marriage broke down it was the father, not the mother, who was given custody of the children.

The unfairness of these laws angered lawyers and judges as well as the unhappy victims. Slowly they were put right by Parliament. But even when the Marriage and Divorce Acts of 1857 and 1858 gave a woman the right to sue her husband for divorce, it was not on equal terms. He could sue her on the grounds of adultery alone. It was another 66 years before a woman was given the same right.

Queen Victoria had nine children, was happily married to Prince Albert until his early death in 1861, and symbolised the belief of the Victorian middle classes in the importance of family life. The woman's place in such a society was that of housewife and mother

Soap advertisement in a magazine in 1889. The attitude that a woman's place was in the home did not stop the upper and middle classes from employing working-class women as servants

10.15 'There were no women cabinet ministers, industrialists, professors or judges. It was a man's world.' Is this still true of Britain today? AT1A ■

10.16 How does the painting *The Dinner Hour* help us to know more about women at work in the nineteenth century? AT3/L5

10.17 Which of the different attitudes to women in the sources on these pages have you experienced yourself in recent weeks? AT1C ■

10.18 Use these sources and those on women's voting rights on pages 80–1 to write an account saying how women gained some rights during the nineteenth century but were still at a great disadvantage compared with men. AT1A/L5 AT1C/L6 AT3/L6

Working women

Throughout the eighteenth and nineteenth centuries most working-class women went out to work. It was only the well-to-do middle classes who thought a woman's place was in her own home. Neither the middle-class mother nor her daughters looked for a job. Most hoped to get married, manage their husband's household and raise children. It was considered their duty to do so. In 1870 a story in *The Graphic* even ended with a ludicrous warning (Source 10.K).

Source 10.K

Terrible was the punishment that awaited the vain and cruel Genevra. She was never married!

The philanthropist Lord Shaftesbury (see page 22) said it was wrong for women to do manual work. Speaking in Parliament in 1842, he supported his argument against women working in coal mines by quoting a Dr Sadler from Barnsley (Source 10.L).

Source 10.L
Women in the mines

I strongly disapprove of females being in pits. The female character is totally destroyed by it. Their habits and feelings are altogether different. They can neither carry out the duty of wives nor of mothers. I see the greatest difference in the homes of those colliers whose wives do not go into the pits.

Only a handful of enterprising women overcame these obstacles, such as the social reformers Octavia Hill and Florence Nightingale, the writers Mrs Gaskell and the Brontë sisters, and performers such as the actress Ellen Terry and the opera star Jenny Lind. Yet however talented, these women were unable to enter politics, had no vote, and could not become Members of Parliament. Until the second half of the nineteenth century they could not even go to university. It was only through persistence that Elizabeth Garret Anderson was able to qualify as a doctor. By 1900 there were still only 260 women doctors in Britain and 20 women dentists. There were no women cabinet ministers, industrialists, professors or judges. It was a man's world.

Only in the 1880s and 1890s did a number of middle-class women find employment. They got jobs as telephonists, as teachers, as office workers using the newly-invented typewriter and as shop assistants in the new department stores. But there was a catch – as a woman reporter found out in 1881 (Source 10.M).

Prejudice against working women was also revealed by a headmistress in 1895 when she recalled the comments she had heard during her career (Source 10.N).

Source 10.M Working women in 1881

The Government is evidently of the opinion that married women should find quite sufficient to occupy them in their home duties and that the task of providing an income should rest solely with the husband. Directly a lady clerk marries she is compelled to resign her situation. Only single women are eligible for appointment.

Source 10.N

'Girls will be turned into boys if they attend the college'.

'I have not learned fractions. My governess told me they were not necessary for girls'.

'My dear lady, if my daughters were going to be bankers it would be very well to teach arithmetic as you do, but really there is no need'.

'It is all very well for my daughter to read Shakespeare, but don't you think it is more important for her to be able to sit down at a piano and amuse her friends?'

Nowhere was this prejudice better seen than in the case of women doctors. In 1870 Queen Victoria told Gladstone she thought it was 'an awful idea' to allow 'young girls and young men to enter the dissecting room together'. Gladstone, the Liberal, agreed with her. He said it was a 'repulsive subject'!

The Dinner Hour. *Women mill workers outside a textile mill in Wigan in Lancashire in 1874*

Time Line

- **1851** First New Model Union
- **1865** National Reform League formed
- **1867** Second Parliamentary Reform Act
- **1867** Fenian uprising in Ireland
- **1868** First meeting of TUC
- **1871** Trade Union Act
- **1872** Secret Ballot Act
- **1879** Land League formed in Ireland
- **1884** Third Parliamentary Reform Act
- **1887** 'Bloody Sunday' demonstration
- **1888** Match girls' strike
- **1889** Dockers' strike
- **1893** Independent Labour Party formed

11 Culture in the Industrial Revolution

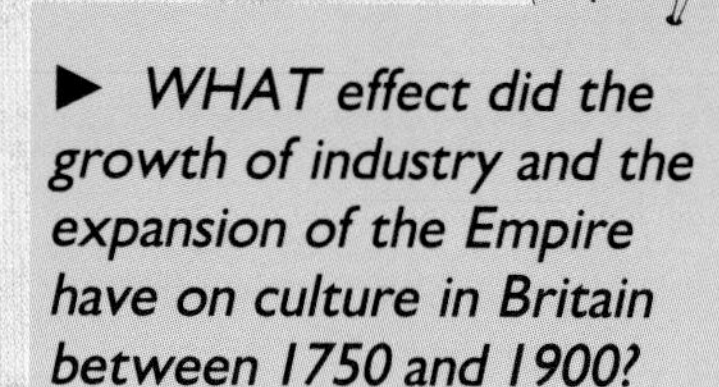

▶ *WHAT effect did the growth of industry and the expansion of the Empire have on culture in Britain between 1750 and 1900?*

ATIA ■ ATIB ■ ATIC ■

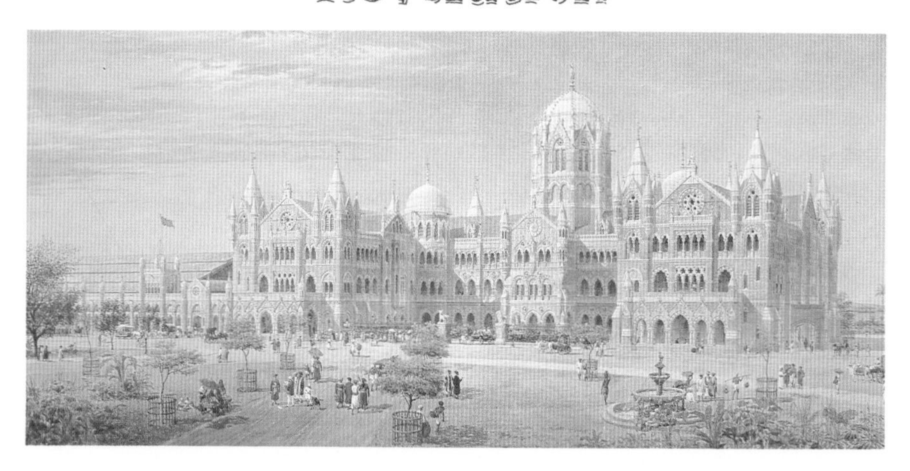

◀ *This huge railway station in Bombay was the terminus of the Great Indian Peninsular Railway*

Even a Victorian tombstone can resemble a Gothic church, like this monument to the heroine Grace Darling at Bamburgh in Northumberland

The effect of the Industrial Revolution

In the eighteenth century only the rich had been able to enjoy the arts. Great artists and musicians were employed by wealthy patrons. Architects designed great mansions. Artists painted portraits for wealthy families.

However, the rapid growth in population and the increasing prosperity of the middle classes as a result of the Industrial Revolution and the expansion of the British Empire, gave architects, artists, writers and musicians new and different ways of earning a living. As you have seen, however, this prosperity was bought at a terrible price – the development of a huge underclass of very poor people working long hours in gloomy, deafening mills and living in squalid, unhealthy homes.

Architecture

As the towns expanded and the slums multiplied, however, thousands of churches, factories, railway stations, town halls and other public buildings were needed. Architects followed two main styles in planning their designs. In the eighteenth century, they built churches and stately homes in the Classical style. This means they were designed to look like the buildings of ancient Greece or Rome. They often had tall, round columns at the front and a large triangular feature (called a *pediment*) on top – as you can see in the photograph of the Bury St Edmunds Corn Exchange. These designs were also used in the Victorian period for public buildings. Town halls like this were built to impress, such as Leeds Town Hall on page 45. The Classical design was used to show the wealth, power and greatness of the city.

When it came to building a church, chapel or cathedral, however, many Victorian architects felt that the Classical architecture of a Greek or Roman temple was unsuitable for a Christian place of worship. Instead, they copied the medieval Gothic style of architecture. Large windows with pointed arches, buttresses and spires made many Victorian churches look as if they had been built in the thirteenth and fourteenth centuries. Only the smoothness and newness of the stone tells us these churches are less than 150 years old. Gothic architecture was also used for the design of other buildings as well, such as museums, railway stations and even houses.

11.1 What style of building was followed by the architect who designed Bombay Railway Station (above)? What does it tell you about the British in India? What did it tell the Indian people? ATIC ■

11.2 How can you tell that the artist John Everett Millais used Rupert Potter's photograph when painting his portrait of Gladstone? AT3/L6 AT1C/L5

11.3 Is a photograph likely to be more, or less, reliable as an historical source than a painting or drawing by an artist? AT3/L7

11.4 What do the paintings on these pages tell you about everyday life in the Victorian period? AT3/L6

11.5 What story do you think the artist Abraham Solomon was telling in the paintings *Departure – Third Class* and *Return – First Class* on page 33? AT1C/L5

Art

At the start of the nineteenth century many artists, such as John Constable and J.M.W. Turner, painted in the Romantic style. This means a way of painting in which artists made the scenes they depicted look idealistic and perfect rather than completely natural or as they really were. Romantic pictures owed a lot to the artist's imagination.

Art changed when painters faced a serious challenge in the middle of the nineteenth century. This came from photography, a product of the Industrial Revolution. When Louis Daguerre showed off his new way of taking photographs in Paris in 1839, a French artist forecast that 'From today painting is dead'.

In fact, painting flourished. Some artists, like John Everett Millais, used photographs to help them catch a likeness in the studio. Others tried to outdo the photographers by painting very realistic, detailed pictures like the painting below of the Victorian family. Artists had one great advantage – they could paint in colour.

Many artists painted everyday scenes in factories (page 83), weddings, scenes in school, advertising hoardings (page 86) and other pictures portraying everyday life. Some used these methods to draw attention to a particular social problem, such as Sir Luke Fildes when he painted the queue of vagrants outside a workhouse (page 50). Paintings like these are called *genre* pictures. Many Victorian artists used them to give either a warning to wrong-doers or an uplifting message!

Many artists benefited from the improvements in printing brought about by the Industrial Revolution (Source 11.A). They designed greetings cards, Christmas cards and pictorial advertisements. They drew the illustrations for books and magazines, such as *Punch*, *The Illustrated London News* and *The Graphic*. You can see some of these illustrations in this book. Artists also painted pictures for the enjoyment of ordinary people who bought cheap prints and engravings to hang in their homes. They chose subjects which they knew would appeal, such as Sir Edwin Landseer when he painted his famous picture of a stag in the Scottish Highlands – *Monarch of the Glen*. Paintings glorifying military conquests and the British Empire were also popular, such as *The Relief of Lucknow* (on page 59).

People went to see these paintings on display at the Royal Academy and at the National Gallery in London. New public art galleries were built in many of the great industrial towns as well. Wealthy industrialists gave money and paintings to support them. This is why many towns have art galleries today, with good collections of Victorian paintings.

Photograph of the Liberal Prime Minister W.E. Gladstone taken by Rupert Potter (father of the authoress Beatrix Potter)

Portrait of Gladstone by the painter John Everett Millais

Source 11.A From the magazine *Art Union*, 1 March 1848

Inventions and discoveries have brought about a wonderful change in tastes and habits. Large-scale reproduction of the copies of a work of art is a way of increasing the fame of the artists, from the applause of a few amateurs, to the honest appreciation of some thousands, and perhaps millions of his countrymen.

Victorian Corn Exchange in Bury St Edmunds in Suffolk

A middle-class family painted in 1867

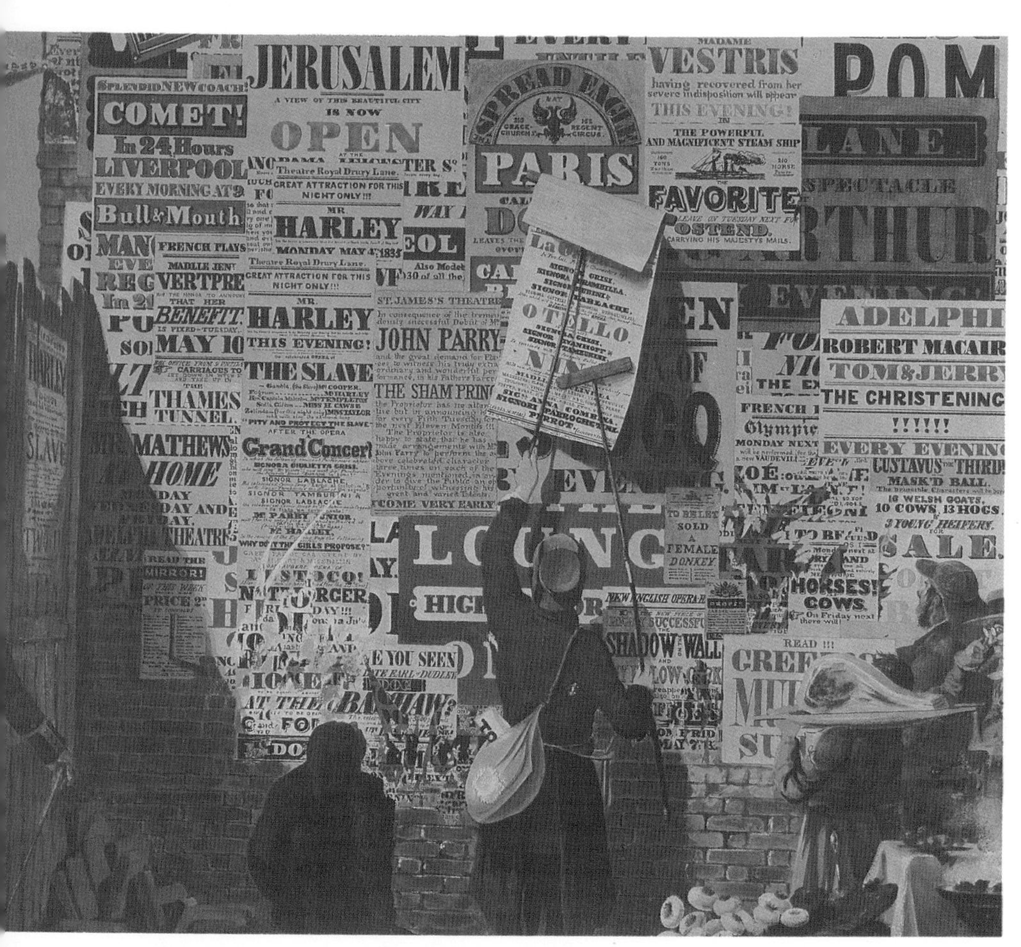

Billposters on a wall in London in 1835

Writing

Writers, too, were affected by the Industrial Revolution and by the growth of the Empire. Rudyard Kipling wrote poems and stories about the lands and peoples of the British Empire (Sources 11.B to 11.E).

Source 11.B By Rudyard Kipling

Asia is not going to be civilised after the methods of the West. There is too much Asia and she is too old.

Source 11.C By Rudyard Kipling

The 'eathen in 'is blindness bows down to wood and stone;
'E don't obey no orders unless they is 'is own;
'E keeps 'is side-arms awful: 'e leaves 'em all about,
An' then comes up the Regiment an' pokes the 'eathen out.

Problems affecting poor people, such as child workers in factories and the workhouse system, were the subject of novels by many writers. Mrs Gaskell wrote about working conditions in the cotton industry and the rise of the Chartists in her novel *Mary Barton* (Source 2.F on page 13). Charles Dickens, regarded by some as Britain's finest novelist, gave many of his novels an industrial setting. In the novel *Dombey and Son* he wrote about the coming of the railway (Source 4.K on page 34). In *Hard Times* he described the imaginary industrial town of Coketown shortly after visiting Preston in Lancashire (Source 11.F).

Popular culture

The eighteenth and nineteenth centuries also saw the rise and growth

11.6 Look at the picture on the left. What does it tell you about London in the early nineteenth century? AT3/L5

11.7 Why do you think Kipling wrote some poems (Sources 11.C and 11.E) as if they had been written by a private soldier? AT1C/L6

11.8 Why did Kipling think India could never be turned into a replica of Britain?

11.9 What value is Source 11.F as a source of information about the factory towns of the Industrial Revolution? AT3/L5

11.10 Source 11.F comes from a novel. Does this make any difference to its value? AT2/L7 AT3/L7

11.11 What does the cover of the sheet music for *The Early Closing Movement* tell you about London in 1860?

11.12 What evidence is there from the picture of the Great International Exhibition that artists and manufacturers had been working together (Source 11.A)? AT1C/L5

Source 11.D By Rudyard Kipling

Oh, East is East, and West is West, and never the twain shall meet.

Source 11.E A warrior in the Sudan – by Rudyard Kipling

You're a pore benighted 'eathen but a first-class fightin' man.

Cover of the sheet music to a song called The Early Closing Movement *published in about 1860*

Charles Dickens

Source 11.F 'Coketown' from *Hard Times* by Charles Dickens

It had a black canal in it, and a river that ran purple with ill-smelling dye, and vast piles of buildings full of windows where there was a rattling and a trembling all day long, and where the piston of the steam-engine worked monotonously up and down...

The whole town seemed to be frying in oil. There was a stifling smell of hot oil everywhere. The steam-engines shone with it, the dresses of the hands were soiled with it, the mills throughout their many storeys oozed and trickled it.

Ornamental fountain in the main hall at the Great International Exhibition of 1862

of popular culture. This is the name given to music, art and literature which appeals to a large number of ordinary people rather than to just a few. In the nineteenth century it covered a wide range of different types of entertainment and leisure activity.

The growing middle classes had more money to spend. They bought books, paintings, and went to concerts, the theatre and the music-hall. They sang popular hymns and the latest songs. Many had pianos in their homes and played from sheet music, such as *The Early Closing Movement* (above). Like many Victorian paintings and the melodramas at the theatres, songs often had a moral lesson to tell, such as the story of a fallen woman or the reform of a drunkard.

People read popular detective stories. The Sherlock Holmes stories, for instance, were published in the 1890s in *The Strand Magazine*. Romantic novels in three volumes and horror stories, such as Mary Shelley's *Frankenstein*, were also popular. When story-tellers like Charles Dickens and Thomas Hardy wrote their novels, they often appeared first of all in weekly instalments in a popular magazine. Daily newspapers and weekly and monthly magazines flourished. W.H. Smith even opened a railway bookstall in 1848 with the idea that people would want something to read on long train journeys.

Interest in sport also grew. The FA Cup, Test Matches against Australia at cricket, Rugby Union, Rugby League, lawn tennis at Wimbledon and many other games and sports first became popular between about 1870 and 1900. These had also been made possible by the Industrial Revolution. The rapid growth of population and the increasing prosperity of working people meant that more people were able to spend money on leisure. By 1900, hundreds of thousands of workers went to watch 'the match' on Saturday afternoons after finishing work at lunch-time. They went on day excursions and holidays to the seaside. Hundreds of thousands of ordinary people flocked to see the Great Exhibition in 1851 and its successor, the Great International Exhibition of 1862.

Britain and the Great War 1914-18

12 How the war started

FOCUS

▶ *WHAT were the causes of the First World War?*
ATIB ■

Young Britons rushing to volunteer at the start of the war in August 1914

'The blackest Bank Holiday'

On Saturday, 1 August 1914, R.D. Blumenfeld, the editor of the *Daily Express*, had been playing cricket. That evening he wrote down in his diary the disturbing news which had spoiled the game (Source 12.A).

Source 12.A Saturday, 1 August

After the match we learned that Germany had declared war on Russia and had marched into Luxembourg, thus breaking her treaty agreements. If this country [the UK] *does not stand up for Right and Honour she will be for ever damned.*

On Sunday, the Reverend Andrew Clark (see also page 100) heard the same news on his way to the station to preach at a church service in the Berkshire village of Hagbourne. On the spur of the moment he decided to warn the congregation: 'I mentioned the grave news and spoke for a little on the impending war, and the sacrifices it would call for'.

Both Clark and Blumenfeld assumed that Germany's actions could only mean that Britain, too, might soon be involved in the war. However, the Prime Minister, Herbert Asquith, was not so sure. He wrote in his diary that Britain was under no 'obligation of any kind' to give military help to France or Russia. But he did say it would be 'against British interests' if France were defeated. Next day there was more bad news – as you can see from the diary of the writer Vera Brittain in Source 12.B (see also page 98).

Source 12.B By Vera Brittain (aged 20)

Monday August 3rd *Yesterday the Germans attacked France without declaring war. . . . They also broke a treaty in occupying neutral Luxembourg. . . . The great fear now is that our bungling Government will declare England's neutrality. If we were to refuse to help our friend France, we should be guilty of the grossest treachery*

12.1 How do we know the outbreak of war caught everyone by surprise? AT3/L3

12.2 Why did the writers of Sources 12.A and 12.B think Britain had a duty to go to war? AT1C ■

12.3 Use the Sources to say how people in Britain and Germany differed in the way they greeted the outbreak of war. What similarities were there? AT1B/L5 AT3/L6

12.4 What evidence is there that stories of people welcoming the outbreak of war may not give a true picture of what they really felt? AT2/L5

12.5 What difference would it make if you only used Sources 12.C and 12.E to answer question 12.3? AT2/L6 AT3/L6

Source 12.C
1 August: in Berlin, capital of Germany

Up and down the wide road of Unter den Linden crowds paced incessantly by day and night singing the German war songs. The unending crowds went past, excited at the prospect of war, because they had never known it.

Source 12.E
4 August: in London, capital of the UK

Piccadilly Hotel. Was awakened by loud noises. Great crowds are parading the streets, rejoicing in the anticipation of war. I cannot sleep. They are going mad. Have they no imagination? Can they not realise what war really means – what it means to women as well as men?

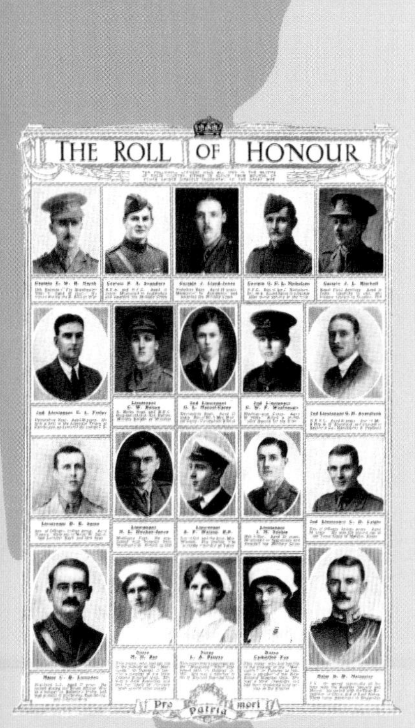
THE ROLL OF HONOUR

Pro patria mori

Each week, newspapers and magazines printed long lists of soldiers, and sometimes nurses, who had died as a result of enemy action

Cheering crowds in Berlin

. . . I should think this must be the blackest Bank Holiday within memory. Pandemonium reigned in the town. What with holiday-trippers, people struggling for papers, trying to lay in stores of food and dismayed that the price of everything had gone up, there was confusion everywhere. . . . The papers are full of stories of tourists in hopeless plights trying to get back to England.

War!

As you can see from the photographs and from these sources, when war did break out, many people throughout Europe greeted the news with delight, although some had their doubts.

Source 12.D 2 August: in Neumagen, a small German town

The women were mostly snuffling and gulping. And the men, the singers of the night before, with drawn faces and forced smiles, were trying to seek comfort from their long drooping pipes and envying those who need not rejoin their barracks till Tuesday. I have never seen a sight more miserable.

Source 12.F 5 August: in Buxton, a small English town

The town was quite quiet when we went down, though groups of people were standing about talking. Several Territorials [part-time soldiers] *and one or two Reservists were going off by train this morning and there was a small crowd on the station seeing them off.*

Sacrifice

Few people then or now could have begun to imagine the full extent of the sacrifices which Andrew Clark mentioned in his sermon. Most thought it would be over by Christmas. They were wrong. It lasted $4\frac{1}{4}$ years. In Britain alone, over seven million soldiers fought in the War. About three-quarters of a million of these were killed or died from wounds. Another one and a half million were wounded, many of them maimed for life. Few families in Britain or the Commonwealth were untouched by the war. Most people mourned the loss of a son, brother, father or uncle. Diaries and letters from these years are filled with tragic stories.

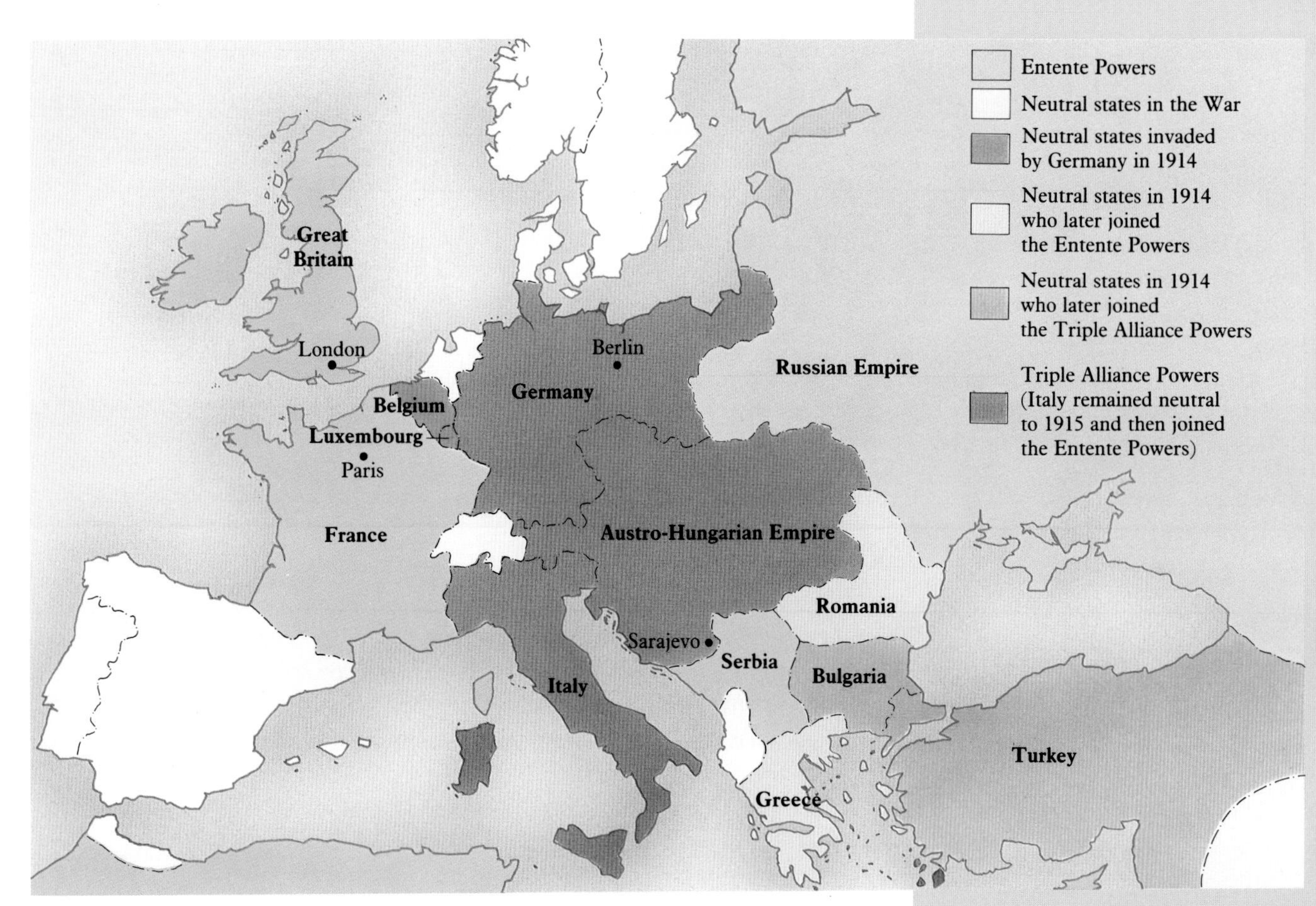

Map of Europe in 1914

Causes of the war

Evelyn, Princess Blücher, an Englishwoman who had married a German nobleman and was living in Berlin, saw the war from the German side. She had her own explanation of why it started (Source 12.G).

Source 12.G

Berlin, August 9 1914 *Exactly what was the real cause of the war no one seems to know. Neither the people here nor there* [in Britain] *wished for war. It is said in England that Germany provoked the war, and here they emphatically deny it. To me it seems that Europe was thirsting for war, and that the armies and navies were no longer to be restrained.*

In fact, some of the causes of the war went back over forty years. In 1871, France had had to give Germany two of her provinces – Alsace and Lorraine – after losing the Franco-Prussian War in 1871. This was bitterly resented by the French people. They vowed to get them back one day.

This is why both countries formed alliances with other powers as protection in case the other side attacked first. Germany linked up with the Austro-Hungarian Empire and later with Italy to form the Triple Alliance. France and Russia, in turn, formed an alliance against them. Britain remained apart from the others at first but later became more friendly to France (and Russia) and more hostile to Germany. The agreement with France was called the *Entente Cordiale.*

The German Kaiser annoyed Britain by supporting the Boers in the South African War in 1899–1902 (page 61) and by making it clear he

The German Kaiser (Emperor), Wilhelm II, was Queen Victoria's grandson

12.6 What did the Princess Blücher think was the main cause of the war? AT3/L3
12.7 Which countries do you think were called the *Entente* Powers?
12.8 Look at the map of Europe in 1914. Compare it with a modern map. How has Central Europe changed?
AT1A ■

wanted Germany to become the leading power in Europe. He told the *Daily Telegraph* in 1908 that Germany needed a strong navy because she had a 'growing empire' (Source 12.H).

Source 12.H

Germany is a young and growing empire. Her worldwide trade is rapidly expanding. Germany must have a powerful fleet to protect that commerce and her interests in even the most distant seas.

Making a gun for a Dreadnought *battleship at Woolwich Arsenal in London*

As you have already seen (on pages 56–63), however, most of the world's surface had already been claimed by the other great powers. A 'growing' German Empire could only come about after war with another European power, such as Britain or France.

The Arms Race

By 1914 Germany was the leading industrial power in Europe (see Source 17.G on page 120). This was deeply resented in Britain, once the 'Workshop of the World' (page 18). Britain even tried to ban the import of goods made in Germany in order to stop the influx.

What is more, Germany used her industrial strength to build a strong North Sea fleet to rival the Royal Navy. People in Britain took exception to this. Why did the Kaiser need a navy if he wasn't intending to go to war? The British reply to this threat was to build a new super-battleship called the *Dreadnought* in 1906. The Germans, not to be outdone, built their own *Dreadnoughts*. By 1909, Britain had eight and Germany seven. The Royal Navy wanted more. By 1914, it had 29 and the German Navy had 17. Racing each other to build up stocks of weapons like this is called an 'arms race'.

British battleships off Torbay in 1907

Other countries did the same, building up stocks of guns and ammunition. But this only made war more likely since the armies and navies of Europe were keen to test out their weapons and their conscript armies. France, Russia, Austria and Germany (but not Britain) made all their young men train in the army for a period after leaving school. This was called Conscription. Afterwards, as civilians, they were put on the Reserve List. This meant they could be called up (mobilised) at a moment's notice.

The Schlieffen Plan

As a result of the arms race, Germany had the most powerful army and the second most powerful navy in Europe by 1914. The German High Command had already worked out how to win the war when it came. They assumed they would have to fight on two fronts. The French would attack from the west and the Russians from the east. Ten years before the start of the war, Count Alfred von Schlieffen, a leading general, said the only way that Germany could beat them both was to defeat France first and then deal with Russia on her own. He worked out that it would take the Russians at least six weeks to move their troops to the German border. That gave the German army enough time to defeat the French – but only if they attacked them where they least expected it. This was through neutral Belgium (as you can see from the map on page 94).

There was only one snag. Belgium was a neutral country. Britain (and other nations) had pledged to protect her right to be neutral. Would Britain enter the war, with all its consequences, just to fulfil a promise made on a piece of paper?

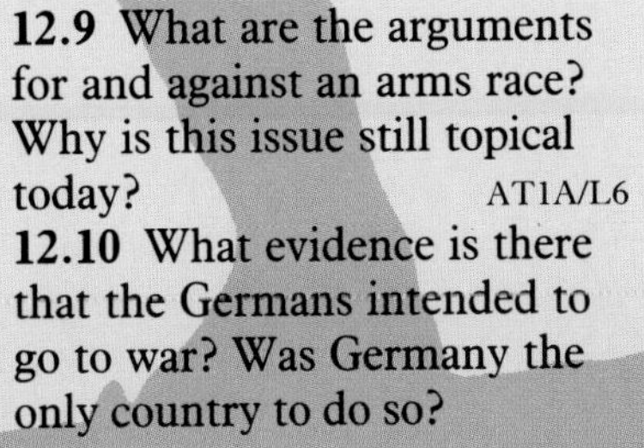

12.9 What are the arguments for and against an arms race? Why is this issue still topical today? AT1A/L6

12.10 What evidence is there that the Germans intended to go to war? Was Germany the only country to do so? AT1C/L5

Sarajevo

As you can imagine, with all these preparations for war, only a spark was needed before fighting broke out. The spark was expected in the Balkans – the area occupied today by Croatia, Serbia, Bosnia and Herzegovina. Russia and the Austro-Hungarian Empire were great rivals there. Many of the Slav peoples living under the Austrian flag wanted links with their fellow Slavs in Russia and not with the German-speaking Austrians. When Serbia became the leading power in the region, the danger increased.

Patriotic Serbs plotted to overthrow the Austrians. Their chance came on Sunday, 28 June 1914, when the Archduke Franz Ferdinand, heir to the Austro-Hungarian Empire, went on a visit to Sarajevo, capital of Bosnia and Herzegovina. He and his wife were assassinated. R.D. Blumenfeld made a note in his diary (Source 12.I).

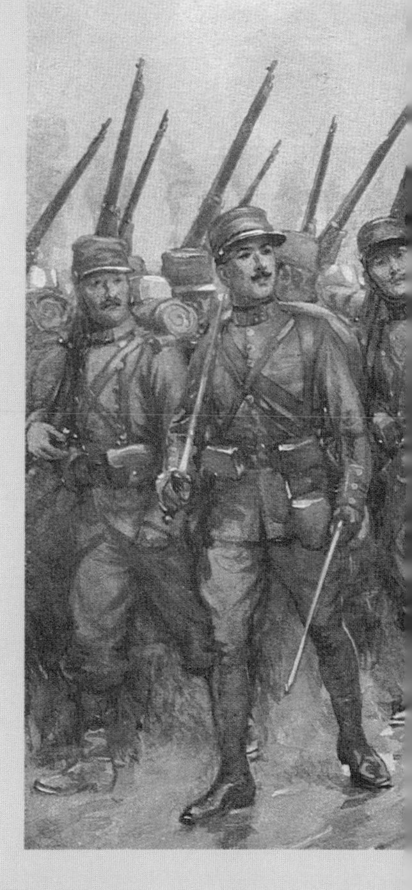

◀ *The Austrian Archduke Franz Ferdinand and his wife leaving the Town Hall in Sarajevo, moments before their assassination on 28 June 1914*

Source 12.I

H.G.Wells came over to tea. While we were talking, news came that Austria's Crown Prince and his wife have been assassinated by a Serbian. That will mean war. Wells says it will mean more than that. It will set the world alight. I don't see why the world should fight over the act of a lunatic.

The 'lunatic' was a Serb called Gavril Princip. The news of the assassination shocked the world. But the Austrian ambassador to Serbia reported a different reaction in Belgrade, the Serbian capital (Source 12.J).

Source 12.J

The accounts of eyewitnesses say that people fell into one another's arms in delight. Remarks were heard, such as 'It serves them right, we have been expecting this for a long time.'

The Austrians were outraged. After all, the heir to their throne had been killed. They believed the Serbian government was behind the plot and should be punished. But how? If Austria declared war on Serbia, Russia would come to her aid. Could they rely on Germany to fulfil her obligation under the Triple Alliance? They got their answer on 5 July. Yes! Germany would support Austria. 'It is now or never,' said the Kaiser. 'Deal with the Serbs. Straight away.' The Czar of Russia was unlikely to intervene. If he did, 'Germany will stand at Austria's side'.

12.11 Draw a Time Line like the one on page 111 to show the most important events which led up to the start of the war. AT1A ■

12.12 Look at Sources 12.A, 12.I, 12.L, and 12.M. How did R.D. Blumenfeld's attitude to the war change between 28 June and 5 August? AT1C/L6

12.13 How do you account for these changes in attitude and that of other people at that time? AT1C/L7

12.14 Draw up a table listing, (a) the long-term, (b) the short-term causes of the First World War. AT1B/L5

12.15 Which do you think were the most important causes? AT1B/L6

12.16 How were the different causes connected to one another? AT1B/L7

French and Belgian soldiers in August 1914

German troops advancing into Belgium in 1914

On 23 July 1914 the Austrians sent a fierce list of demands to Serbia, knowing it would not be accepted. When the Serbs rejected it, Austria declared war (on 28 July 1914). The Czar assumed at once that the Austrian action was aimed at Russia as well as Serbia. He mobilised Russia's armies immediately so they would be ready if Germany declared war.

Germany demanded that they be withdrawn at once and asked France (Russia's ally) for an immediate assurance she would not intervene in the west. When no such reassurances had been given, the Kaiser ordered that Germany's armies be mobilised as well.

On 1 August, he declared war on Russia and sent troops into neutral Luxembourg. France mobilised at once. The Kaiser declared war on France on 3 August and German troops invaded neutral Belgium in accordance with the Schlieffen Plan.

As you can see from Sources 12.A, 12.B and 12.K, there was now a strong feeling in Britain that it was her duty to declare war on Germany as well.

Source 12.K From *The Times*, Sunday, 2 August

In the first place, we must stand by our friends. The Empire has no written undertakings which say it must intervene. But it has an obligation of honour. In the second place, we have a vital interest in seeing that France is not overwhelmed by Germany. In the third place, the Empire stands for civilized relations between peoples and the utmost regard for the spirit of international law.

On 4 August 1914, Britain declared war, to the great satisfaction of R.D. Blumenfeld (Source 12.L).

Source 12.L

At midnight Great Britain declared war on Germany. We are in it! How long?

The following day, Wednesday 5 August 1914, his newspaper, the *Daily Express*, carried a banner headline (Source 12.M).

Source 12.M

England Expects That Every Man Will Do His Duty

Italy, the third partner in the Triple Alliance, disappointed Austria and Germany by staying neutral at first. She later joined the *Entente* Powers in the hope of gaining colonies and part of the Austro-Hungarian Empire after the war. Other countries who became involved included Turkey (in November 1914) and Bulgaria (in 1915) who joined Germany and Austria-Hungary. Japan (in 1914), China (in 1917) and the United States (in 1917), however, all joined Britain and her Allies.

13 How the war was fought

► *HOW was the war fought before it developed into trench warfare?*
ATIC ■
► *WHICH other countries fought in the war?* ATIC ■
► *HOW was the war fought at sea and in the air?*
ATIC ■

The German invasion of France

In August 1914, the German armies swept into Belgium to carry out the Schlieffen Plan. Things started to go wrong when the Belgian army held them up at Liège. This gave enough time for a small British force, led by General French, to cross the Channel. It also gave the much larger French armies time to prepare as well.

The German armies quickly closed in on Paris, but the German General von Kluck made a serious mistake. Instead of going round Paris as planned (see the map), he moved his troops across towards the north-east of Paris. It gave the French commander, Marshal Joffre, the chance to counter-attack. He drove the German armies back at the Battle of the River Marne in September. The Schlieffen Plan had failed. France had not been knocked out of the war in six weeks. Both sides dug trenches and as you can see from the map, the Western Front (the front line between the two sides) hardly altered in the next four years.

Meanwhile, the Russians in the east moved their forces much more rapidly than Schlieffen had thought possible. When they advanced into East Prussia, the Germans had to send reinforcements there instead of

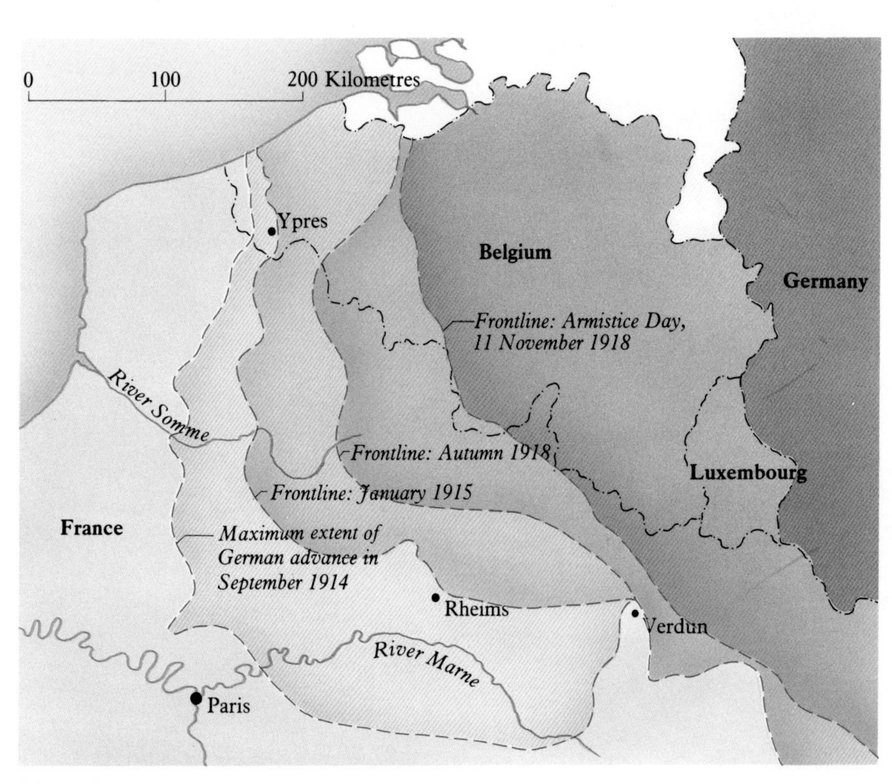

Map of the Western Front in 1914–18

to France. Germany's worst fears had been realised. She was fighting a war on two fronts against the combined armies of France, Russia and Britain. The Princess Blücher wrote about these fears in her Diary (Source 13.A).

Source 13.A

Berlin, October 12 1914 *It is being whispered here that this defeat on the Marne may prove the decisive turning of the war, and the greatest misfortune for Germany, in spite of her successes everywhere else.*

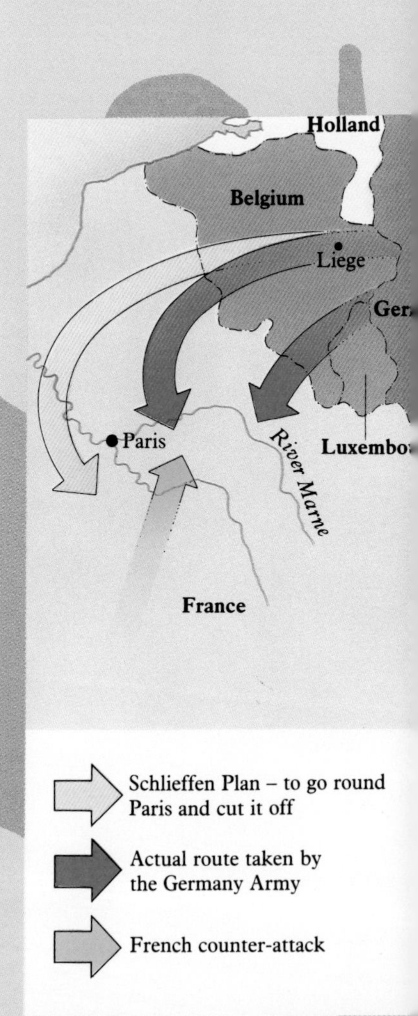

The German invasion of France

'Bravo Belgium!' Cartoon in Punch, *12 August 1914*

13.1 What was the point of the *Punch* cartoon? How do you know the artist was biased against the Germans? AT2/L5
13.2 What is the value of this cartoon to someone writing about the First World War? AT3/L5
13.3 Why did the Schlieffen Plan fail? AT1B ■
13.4 What does the map of the Western Front tell you about the course of the war? AT3/L5
13.5 Use Source 13.B and the picture to explain why the average expectation of life of a pilot on the Western Front was only two weeks. AT3/L4
13.6 How do we know that the scene shown in the painting of the dogfight may differ from what actually took place? AT2/L5

Source 13.B By a British pilot in 1917

When twenty or thirty planes were engaged, there was always a grave risk of collision. Machines would hurtle by, intent on their private battles, missing each other by feet. Such fighting demanded iron nerves, lightning reactions, snap decisions, a cool head, and eyes like a bluebottle, for it all took place at high speed and was three-dimensional.

Fighting on other fronts

The Russian success in attacking the Germans first was not kept up for long. They suffered a major defeat at the Battle of Tannenberg at the end of August. When Turkey entered the war on 4 November 1914, she cut Russia off from supplies from the West. Allied ships could no longer sail through the Dardanelles, the narrow stretch of water leading to Russia's Black Sea coast. This was one reason why Britain sent an invasion force to Turkey in April 1915. They landed at Gallipoli but met tough resistance from the Turkish army and had to withdraw after suffering heavy losses. There was fighting, too, on other fronts, such as in northern Italy, in the Balkans and in the Middle East. But the war was won and lost in the trenches on the Western Front (as you will see on pages 102–111).

The war in the air

The First World War was the first major conflict in which the aeroplane was used as a weapon of war. At first, Britain's aeroplanes were flown and serviced by men of the Royal Flying Corps, a branch of the army. It was not until 1 April, 1918, that the Royal Air Force (RAF) was formed. By then it was becoming clear that in future air power would be important in war – as you can see from the section on the Zeppelins (pages 118–19). In 1914, the RFC had 63 aeroplanes. In 1918, the RAF had 22 000.

In 1914–18, however, the main use for aeroplanes was in making 'reconnaisance flights'. At great risk, pilots flew over enemy lines, took photographs, and provided information about enemy troop movements and the position of heavy guns and trench defences. There were dogfights when German aeroplanes tried to shoot them down (Source 13.B). Pilots who could manoeuvre their planes effectively while chasing the enemy became air aces, like the German pilot Baron Manfred von Richthofen. He shot down eighty Allied planes in two years before he was killed in action in 1918.

A dogfight between British and German aeroplanes

This picture of a German U-boat attacking a British warship was published in 1915 in a German book about the war called Die Grosse Zeit *('The Great Time')*

The war at sea

Britain's expensive *Dreadnought* battleships spent most of the war on patrol in the North Sea. There were a number of minor skirmishes between the two navies but only one main battle. This was the Battle of Jutland. It was fought in May 1916 about 60 kilometres off the coast of Denmark. The Germans treated it as a great victory because their losses were only 2500 dead and 11 warships to Britain's 6000 dead and 14 warships. But the British claimed victory because the German warships had retreated to their harbour at Kiel. They stayed there for the rest of the war. The Royal Navy was still the mistress of the seas. British warships prevented merchant ships bringing food and supplies to German ports. As a consequence, there were serious food shortages. These caused widespread discontent and near-starvation. They helped to bring about the Kaiser's downfall in November 1918 (page 124).

The British had a more pressing problem to face. Their *Dreadnoughts* seemed powerless to deal with the menace of the German U-boats (submarines). It was a shock when, very early on in the war, a single U-boat sank three British cruisers off the coast of Holland with the loss of 1600 lives. German U-boats continued to menace Allied shipping – as you can see in Source 13.C.

The ocean liner Lusitania *was sunk by a German U-boat in 1915*

Source 13.C
By a German U-boat commander

The steamer appeared to be close to us and looked colossal. The death-bringing shot was a true one, and the torpedo ran towards the doomed ship at high speed. I could follow its course exactly by the streak of bubbles which was left in its wake. A frightful explosion followed. From all the hatchways a storming, despairing mass of men were fighting their way on deck: grimy stokers, officers, soldiers, grooms, cooks. They all rushed, ran, screamed for boats, tore and thrust one another from the ladders leading down to them, fought for the life-belts and jostled one another on the sloping deck.

Then a second explosion, followed by the escape of white hissing steam from the hatchways. I could not bear the sight any longer, and I lowered the periscope and dived deep.

13.7 Who won (a) the Battle of Jutland, (b) the U-boat war? AT1B ■

13.8 Source 13.C and the picture of the German U-boat attack on a British warship are German, not British, sources of information. Does this make any difference to their value in history? AT2■ AT3 ■

13.9 Write an account of the war at sea. Explain its importance to both sides in the conflict. AT1C/L5

13.10 In what different ways did naval warfare change during the First World War? AT1A/L5

German U-boats sank as many as one ship in every 20 in 1916. Famous people, such as the War Minister Lord Kitchener, the American multi-millionaire Alfred Vanderbilt and the Spanish composer Enrique Granados, were drowned when their ships were torpedoed. Most of these sinkings took place in the waters close to the British Isles. The worst was in May 1915 when the huge Cunard ocean liner *Lusitania* was sunk off the coast of Ireland, killing 128 US citizens among the 1400 people who were drowned. Another 500 were saved. Many Americans wanted the USA to declare war on Germany at once but US President Woodrow Wilson calmed them down. He didn't think America was ready to enter the war yet. In any case, the Germans had promised to restrict the activities of their submarines in future.

In 1917, however, the Germans decided to use their submarines to wage all-out war in the North Atlantic. The sinking rate shot up to one ship in every four. The Kaiser hoped to make Britain agree to a peace settlement by starving the British people of food and essential supplies rather than by defeating her armies on the battlefield. In doing this, however, the German U-boats also sank many American ships trading with Britain. They knew this might well bring the United States into the war, but took the risk. This was a serious mistake. The United States declared war in April 1917. Her vast resources of men, materials and cash were much greater than those available to Germany and the Austro-Hungarian Empire. It was only a matter of time before America's immense power would triumph.

Nonetheless, the losses from the renewed U-boat attacks were so great, there were serious shortages of food in Britain (as you can see on pages 116–17). The British Government had to bring in rationing. Luckily, the convoy system (see the picture below), was introduced at the insistence of the new Prime Minister, David Lloyd George. It was a great success. In 1918 only one ship in every 300 was sunk.

An American convoy bringing troops to France in 1918. It worked like this. Warships surrounded and protected merchant ships bringing troops, passengers and goods to Britain and Europe. If a German U-boat fired a torpedo, the warships knew immediately where to concentrate their attack. They used depth charges (underwater bombs) to destroy the U-boats below

14 Your Country Needs You

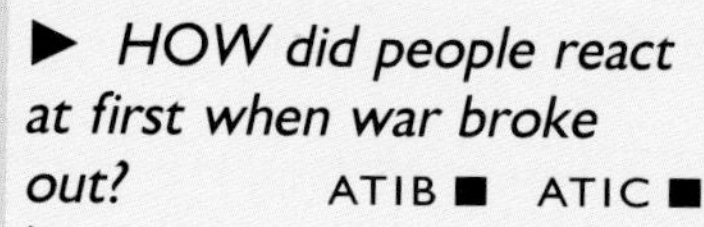

► *HOW did people react at first when war broke out?* ATIB ■ ATIC ■
► *HOW were young men persuaded to volunteer for the army?* ATIC ■

Kitchener's New Army

In August 1914, many people thought the war would be over by Christmas. Lord Kitchener, the War Minister, did not. He was convinced it would last several years. He called for 100 000 volunteers. Within four weeks over half a million young men had joined up to form Kitchener's New Army.

Why did they do it? Most of the volunteers who joined as junior officers came from the public schools and universities. Many had served in the cadet corps at school. Some volunteered for an obvious reason: they were unemployed. The army gave them a paid job at last. A journalist queuing up outside a recruiting office was told 'Make way for us lads without jobs'.

Lord Kitchener

Patriotism, duty and honour

The composer Sir Arthur Bliss, who with his brother was one of the young officers recruited in August 1914, said they did so in a 'spirit of devotion and self-sacrifice'. They were The First Hundred Thousand, later called The Lost Generation because so few of them survived the war. These young officers had been taught that it was their duty to obey the King and serve Britain. It was a matter of honour to volunteer. Three weeks before war broke out, the Headmaster of Uppingham School had even told his pupils 'If a man cannot be useful to his country, he is better dead'.

Edward Brittain was one of those pupils. He had just left school. According to his sister Vera, he was furious when his father refused to let him join the army (Source 14.A). In the end he got his wish and gained a commission as an officer in November 1914. Like his two closest friends at school, he paid the penalty for his patriotism. He was killed in action in 1918.

Many of the volunteers genuinely believed they were fighting for God as well as the King – even though Germany and Austria were also Christian countries and there was no reason to suppose that the Almighty favoured one side rather than the other. Lieutenant Engall told his parents he was going into battle 'with His name on my lips' and said he 'could not wish for a finer death . . . doing my duty to my God, my Country, and my King'. He was killed. The poet Rupert Brooke (who died on active service on his way to Gallipoli in 1915) wrote the poem 'Now, God be thanked' (Source 14.B). It summed up the attitude of many young men who, like those in the photographs on pages 88–9, welcomed the outbreak of war.

Source 14.B

Now, God be thanked Who has matched us with His hour,
And caught our youth, and wakened us from sleeping,
With hand made sure, clear eye, and sharpened power,
To turn, as swimmers into cleanness leaping,
Glad from a world grown old and cold and weary,
Leave the sick hearts that honour could not move,
And half-men, and their dirty songs and dreary,
And all the little emptiness of love!

Source 14.A

Friday August 7th
E[Edward] said that Daddy, not being a public school man or having had any training [i.e. in the officer cadets] *could not possibly understand the impossibility of his remaining in inglorious safety while others, scarcely older than he, were offering their all.*

Wednesday September 7th *After dinner we all discussed again Daddy's refusal to let Edward go into the Army & the unmanliness of it, especially after we read in The Times of a mother who said to her hesitating son 'My boy I don't want you to go, but if I were you I should!'.*

Oh! It's a lovely war!

The young men who still held back from volunteering were told what fun they would have if they joined up. Popular stars of the Music Halls sang all the latest songs (Source 14.C), such as 'Oh, we don't want to lose you, but we think you ought to go'. With flags, patriotic music from the orchestra and clapping from the audience, they urged the young men present to come up on stage and volunteer for the army there and then. This attitude, that going to war could be fun, was also put over by the press. Jokes about the trenches and cartoons (below) may have helped to sway the young men who were still hesitating.

In the end, however, many volunteered simply because their friends were doing so as well. They went along with the crowd. In many cases they were able to form special army units, such as the Accrington Pals. Being together with friends from their town gave them strength in a terrible situation. But it had its drawbacks. When some of these units were wiped out, the effect on the home community was devastating.

This drawing, Two Crosses, *was published in* The Graphic *in 1917*

14.1 Why do you think the 'pointing finger' recruitment poster became so famous? AT1B/L4

14.2 Which words and phrases in Source 14.A tell us why many young men felt it was their duty to volunteer? AT1C/L6 AT3/L6

14.3 What can the pictures *Two Crosses* and *The Incorrigibles* tell you about attitudes to the war? AT1C/L6 AT3/L6

14.4 Why did Rupert Brooke welcome the war? AT1C/L6

Source 14.C Popular songs of the First World War

'Oh! it's a lovely war'

'Your King and Country want you'

'When the war is over, Mother dear'

'Good-by-ee'

'Over there'

'I'll make a man of you'

'Oh Boy! When you're home on leave'

'It's a long way to Tipperary'

'Belgium put the kibosh on the Kaiser'

'Pack up your troubles in your old kit bag'

This cartoon, The Incorrigibles, *was published in the humorous magazine* Punch *on 7 October 1914. [*Incorrigible *means someone who won't learn]* ▼

THE INCORRIGIBLES.

New Arrival at the Front. "WHAT'S THE PROGRAMME?"

Old Hand. "WELL, YOU LAY DOWN IN THIS WATER, AND YOU GET PEPPERED ALL DAY AND NIGHT, AND YOU HAVE THE TIME OF YOUR LIFE!"

New Arrival. "SOUNDS LIKE A BIT OF ALL RIGHT. I'M ON IT!"

Persuading the unwilling

Despite the enthusiastic rush to volunteer in August 1914, there were still millions of young men in civilian clothes that autumn. This is why the Government plastered Britain with recruitment posters. Recruitment meetings were held. Other types of pressure were also used – as you can see from the posters and sources on these pages. Source 14.D is from the diary of the Reverend Andrew Clark, vicar of a small Essex village.

Source 14.D

Sunday, 30 August *The Rector of Fairstead preached a horrifying sermon on the horrible scenes of the battlefield and told all the young men to join the army. He had a big Union Jack hung in front of the pulpit.*

Tuesday, 1 September *Village lads are not very pleased at pressure put by the Squire to compel his two footmen to enlist.*

Tuesday, 15 September *There is a great village feeling against lads who are of age and physique to enlist and who have not done so.*

Monday, 19 October *Mr Caldwell told me that Mr Stoddart had approached some of the farm lads telling them they ought to enlist. They met him with the counter-threat that they were waiting for the farmers' sons of the district to show them the example.*

Sunday, 9 May 1915 *The resentment of farm labourers at being badgered to enlist is shown by the fact that every recruiting poster from the Rectory to Lyons Hall has been torn down; torn into shreds; and cast away.*

Some employers told their employees to join up or face dismissal. Some offered financial rewards (Source 14.E). Groups of women also put pressure on the 'slackers' as they were called. Some joined the Active Service League. The members of this organisation agreed to do their utmost to get the young men they knew to volunteer. They promised not to be seen in their company if they failed to do their duty. Some even presented the 'slackers' they saw with four white feathers – the mark of cowardice.

The rich and well-to-do were also asked to use their influence. A newspaper advertisement in December 1914 asked them to sacrifice their personal convenience for the country's need. 'Have you a man digging your garden who should be digging trenches?' they were asked. 'Ask your men to enlist today.'

In fact, there were many good reasons why even the most patriotic of young men could be seen out of uniform. Many worked in jobs which were vital to the country. A very high percentage, as many as four in every ten working-class recruits, were found to be unfit for service. Some were not tall enough or failed to meet the standard chest measurement (34 inches – 86 centimetres) laid down as the minimum requirement at the start of the war.

Conscription

Conscription was not introduced into Britain until January 1916. Many people had wanted it earlier. In 1914, farm workers in Essex said: 'If so many men are needed by the country, let the country say all *must* go.'. Under the new regulations, all men aged between 18 and 41 had to serve in the armed forces whether they liked it or not. Those who

14.5 How did the recruitment posters on these pages and on page 99 put pressure on men to join the army? Which of these posters appealed to (a) their patriotism, (b) their desire to protect their homes and families, (c) their sense of duty to their country? Which were designed to make the 'slackers' feel guilty? AT1C ■

14.6 In your opinion, was the official and unofficial wartime recruitment campaign fair or unjust? Would you have volunteered, or encouraged someone else to volunteer? Give your reasons. AT1C ■

14.7 How useful are these posters and sources as evidence of people's attitudes to the war? What else would you want to know? AT2/L6 AT3/L6

14.8 Use the extracts in Source 14.D to show some of the ways in which people's attitudes to war could differ. AT3/L6

Source 14.E Advice from a West End clothing store

We think it is absolutely necessary for every single man between 19 and 30 to answer his country's call. We shall be pleased to pay half his present salary to any of our present employees while serving and will keep his situation open to him.

refused to do so on the grounds that their conscience would not allow them to kill other people were called *conscientious objectors*. Popular opinion, the Government and the Army tried to bully them into submitting. A handful of men still refused – even when they were court-martialled and sentenced to death (although this was later reduced to a sentence of imprisonment). One of these men was Robert Mennell, a Quaker (Source 14.F).

Source 14.F By Robert Mennell, conscientious objector

I learnt that the only people from whom I was to expect sympathy were the soldiers and not the civilians. While I was waiting in the guard-room, five men were bustled into the room.

'What are you in here for, mate?'

I said: 'I am a Quaker, and I refused to join the army, because I think that war is murder.'

'Murder?' he whispered. 'Murder? It's bloody *murder!'*

Many conscientious objectors served in France as non-combatants. These were men who did not actually fight but served at the front in another capacity, such as doing the job of a stretcher-bearer. Their work was often every bit as hazardous as that of the front-line soldier.

15 On the Western Front

Dusty road near Arras drawn by an Army Captain in 1918

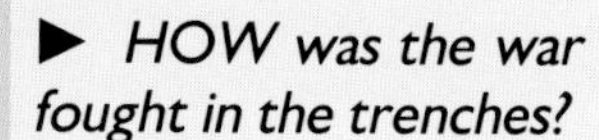

FOCUS

▶ *HOW was the war fought in the trenches?* ATIC ■

▶ *HOW and WHY did technology change warfare in 1914–18?* ATIA ■ ATIB ■ ATIC ■

▶ *HOW and WHY was the Battle of the Somme fought and with what consequences?* ATIB ■ ATIC ■

Life in the trenches

After 1914 (page 94), the war on the Western Front became one of trench warfare. As you can see from the painting, the battlefields of Flanders (Belgium) and northern France were low-lying and mainly featureless. The troops had no choice. They had to dig long trenches to give themselves the shelter and protection they needed. There were often two or more front-line trenches, one behind the other, connected to each other and to reserve trenches further back by a network of communication trenches. One soldier said going to and from the trenches was 'a hundred times worse than being in them.' It often meant an arduous march carrying heavy kit, waist deep in mud (Source 15.A).

Source 15.A From a poem by Wilfred Owen

Bent double, like old beggars under sacks,
Knock-kneed, coughing like hags, we cursed through sludge,
Till on the haunting flares we turned our backs
And towards our distant rest began to trudge.
Men marched asleep. Many had lost their boots
But limped on, blood-shod. All went lame; all blind;
Drunk with fatigue.

Living in a trench

Some of the most vivid accounts of trench warfare were written by soldier poets like Wilfred Owen (Sources 15.A and 15.G). Owen was killed in action in 1918 only days before the war ended. Artists volunteered, too, and like the brothers John (page 104) and Paul Nash (page 114), and the German painter Otto Dix (page 115), depicted the war in their paintings. From diaries, letters and memoirs (recollections of the past) we get a striking and often horrific impression of what it was like to live and fight in the trenches. But, according to the writer of Source 15.D, since most of these eyewitness accounts were written by men who came from comfortable homes, can we be sure their views were shared by everyone?

One thing is certain – all complained about the mud. Heavy rain turned the ground into a swamp of pools and thick sludge (pages 114–15). Fog and mist, however, were welcome (Source 15.U on page 110). Living conditions were primitive. Soldiers often had to shave in cold, muddy water. Vermin such as rats and lice were an everyday experience. Photographs show soldiers having a rare bath in a farm cart lined with an oilcloth, using water heated in biscuit tins. Outside, a steam-powered baking machine disinfects their bedclothes and uniforms.

15.1 What do you think about the views expressed in Source 15.D? How and why does it differ from the others? Is it possible to say whether the writer is right or wrong? AT2 ■ AT3 ■

15.2 Is there any reason to wonder if any of these extracts and pictures do, or do not, give a fair or accurate picture of life in the trenches and on the Western Front? AT2 ■ AT3 ■

15.3 Use these pictures and sources to write an account of life in the trenches in the First World War. ATIC ■ AT3 ■

A donkey brings supplies up to the French frontline in 1916 using a communication trench

Source 15.B By Lieutenant-Colonel Rowland Feilding

December 14, 1916 *We stay in the front line eight days and nights; then go out for the same period. The men are practically without rest. They are wet through much of the time. They are shelled. They work all night and every night, and a good part of each day, digging and filling sandbags, and repairing the trench. The temperature is icy. They have not even a blanket. The last two days it has been snowing. They cannot move more than a few feet from their posts. Except when they are actually digging, they cannot keep themselves warm by exercise. When they try to sleep, they freeze. The curious thing is that all seem so much more contented than the people at home* [see Source 17.K on page 121]. *Everybody laughs at everything here. It is the only way.*

Source 15.C By [ex-Sergeant] Otto Dix, a German artist

Lice, rats, barbed wire entanglements, fleas, grenades, bombs, caves, corpses, blood, drink, mice, cats, gases, cannons, filth, bullets, machine-guns, fire, steel. That's what war is! Nothing but the devil's work!

Source 15.D From *The Great War* (1979), by Correlli Barnett

Middle-class writers were later to paint a dismal picture of existence in the trenches... Yet to the majority of soldiers, being peasants or farm labourers or industrial workers from city slums, actual living conditions in and behind the line on quiet sectors were little if any worse than in peacetime. Certainly many British working-class soldiers enjoyed a better diet, better medical care and better welfare than they had as civilians.

Source 15.E By Major Arthur Borton

4 July 1916 *Am in a very comfortable dugout with heaps of head cover. But the mud is awful. Have had two days of torrential rain which has flooded everything. And the rats are a caution. I didn't believe there were so many in the country. Black as well as brown.*

Source 15.F By Private Frank Richards

We were also getting a ration of coke and charcoal. We scrounged buckets from the village, and by stabbing holes in them converted them into fire-buckets. Rations were also more plentiful and we were getting more bully beef [in cans] *and jam than we could eat, also plenty of biscuits. But the bread ration was still small. We were always short of that. Each man was his own cook. It was not until the following September* [1915] *that hot tea and cooked food were sent up to the trenches. A man who had plenty of tea and sugar, a tin of milk, bread and some candles was looked upon as a millionaire.*

Operating on a man in a trench. Trench warfare gave the world four new diseases. Trench foot made feet swell up and become painful. It was caused by long exposure to cold and damp. Trench mouth gave a soldier very painful, swollen gums. Trench fever was an infectious disease caused by lice crawling over the body. Shell shock or battle fatigue was thought to be cowardice at first. Some soldiers suffering from it were even executed for leaving the battlefield. Later, doctors realised it was really a new type of nervous illness brought on by a very frightening experience, such as a shell exploding nearby ▼

Painting by the artist John Nash entitled Over the top

Going over the top

As you can imagine, it was much easier to defend the trenches than it was to attack them. In order to attack, soldiers had to 'go over the top' of the trench, knowing that the Germans would start firing immediately. Wilfred Owen described the reaction of soldiers to the news of such an attack: 'Over the top to-morrer; boys, we're for it. First wave we are, first ruddy wave; that's tore it!'

German machine-gun nest pictured by a German artist in 1915

The soldiers went over in several 'waves', one line at a time. Then, for a distance of several hundred yards, weighed down with equipment weighing about 30kg (220 rounds of ammunition, helmet, wire cutters, spade, hand grenades) and food for the day, they had to walk or run forwards across No Man's Land. This was the name given to the waste ground separating the Allied front-line trenches from the German trenches on the other side. Shelling by both sides made this a mass of deep craters. There were also barbed wire entanglements to get through. These were put up at night, under cover of darkness, by wiring parties from both sides. Troops in the second and third waves had an extra hazard to avoid – piles of corpses (their dead comrades)

15.4 Imagine you are serving in the trenches in 1916. Write down your feelings on being told 'to go over the top'.
AT1C/L6

15.5 Look at the pictures and sources on these pages and on pages 102–3. Which illustrations and which sources would you use to give the most realistic picture of what it was like to fight in the trenches in the First World War?
AT2/L6 AT3/L6

15.6 Compare the paintings on pages 103–4, 108–9 and 114–15. How did the artists differ in the way they depicted the war in the trenches?
AT2/L7

15.7 Does the impression they give agree or disagree with the written sources? AT2/L7

15.8 What were the effects of a gas attack? AT1B/L4

15.9 What is the value of the poem quoted in Source 15.G as a source of information about the use of poison gas?
AT3/L5

15.10 Does it make any difference that this source is a poem instead of a simple written description? AT2 ■

German soldiers with gas-masks

and badly wounded soldiers lying on the ground. All the while, of course, enemy machine guns and rifles raked the ground with murderous fire. The German Maxim machine guns could fire 600 rounds of ammunition a minute and were said to have caused ninety per cent of the casualties on the first day of the Battle of the Somme. In addition, the German heavy guns pounded No Man's Land with shells.

The impossibility of capturing the enemy front line without suffering very heavy losses did not stop the generals far behind the front line (page 109) from repeatedly ordering such attacks. Most of them agreed with the French General Foch that 'to make war means always attacking.' They were slow to change their way of thinking.

Poison gas

Both sides tried to find weapons to help them break the deadlock. The Kaiser was the first to try chemical warfare. On 22 April 1915, German soldiers wearing gas-masks released the greenish-yellow fumes of chlorine gas into the air at Ypres in Flanders. It choked thousands of British soldiers and caused 5000 casualties (Source 15.G). The Allies retaliated by issuing gas-masks and firing their own gas shells. Two years later, German scientists perfected a yet more terrible weapon. This was mustard gas. Gas-masks could not stop it from blistering the skin.

Source 15.G From a poem by Wilfred Owen

Gas! GAS! Quick boys! – An ecstasy of fumbling,
Fitting the clumsy helmets just in time;
But someone still was yelling out and stumbling
And flound'ring like a man in fire or lime . . .
Dim, through the misty panes and thick green light,
As under a green sea, I saw him drowning.
In all my dreams, before my helpless sight,
He plunges at me, guttering, choking, drowning.

. . . watch the white eyes writhing in his face,
His hanging face, like a devil's sick of sin;
. . . hear, at every jolt, the blood
Come gargling from the froth-corrupted lungs.

Verdun

On 21 February 1916, the Germans attacked the great French fortress town of Verdun in a year-long battle which exhausted both armies. The French defended bravely with the slogan 'They shall not pass'. The Germans attacked again and again but were unable to break through. Nonetheless, the French were under great pressure. If the German armies had been able to break through at Verdun, they might have won the war. This is why the British agreed to launch a joint attack with other French units along the valley of the Somme. The aim was to relieve Verdun since the Germans would have to withdraw troops to reinforce the Somme 200km away.

The British and Empire volunteers – Kitchener's Army (see page 98) – prepared to take part for the first time in a major battle. Compared with the German Army, with its highly competent regular officers and NCOs, the volunteer soldiers were poorly trained and lacked experience under gunfire. Nonetheless, they were full of courage. It was not their fault they were mown down in their thousands on that fateful day – 1 July 1916.

The first day of the Battle of the Somme

The 'Big Push', as it was called, began at 7.30 a.m., on 1 July 1916. The British guns (see picture below) had shelled the German positions for a week and destroyed many of their frontline trenches. But they didn't wipe out the German army, as the British soldiers were led to believe. German dugouts, 10 to 12 metres deep, gave protection against the heaviest bombardment. You can see what happened in Source 15.H. British accounts of the battle all make grim reading (Sources 15.I and 15.J).

Source 15.I From the novel *Gommecourt* by Daniel George of the Queen's Westminster Rifles

1 July 1916 *On the fourth morning at 7.30, dazed by the shelling which had begun at dawn, warm and sleepy with rum, Horden stumbled forward blindly across No Man's Land. It seemed to him that he was alone in a pelting storm of machine-gun bullets, shell fragments, and clods of earth. Alone, because the other men were like figures on a cinema screen – an old film that flickered violently. Some of them stopped and fell down slowly. The fact that they had been killed did not penetrate to his mind. They were unreal to him. His mind was numbed by noise, the smoke, the dust – unable to understand anything but the need to hurry frantically on, on, on, out of the storm. They must go on. On, on! They dared not stop.*

Source 15.J By a Sergeant in the 1st Somerset Regiment

1 July 1916 *Punctually at 7.30 a.m. the attack was launched. The 1st Rifle Brigade advanced in perfect order and the same applied to all troops, left and right, as far as the eye could see. Everything was working smoothly, not a shot being fired. The first line had nearly reached the German front line, when all at once machine-guns opened up all along our front with a murderous fire, and we were caught in the open, with no shelter. Men were falling like ninepins.*

The invention of dynamite and high explosives gave the guns on the Western Front a much longer range than the guns in previous wars. Camouflaged to avoid detection from the air, they pounded away at the enemy trenches with thousands of shells

Source 15.H By a German officer at the Somme

At 7.30 a.m. the hurricane of shells ceased as suddenly as it had begun. Our men at once clambered up the steep shafts leading from the dugouts and ran singly or in groups to the nearest shell craters. The machine-guns were pulled out of the dugouts and hurriedly placed in position. Lines of infantry were seen moving forward from the British trenches. They came on at a steady easy pace as if expecting to find nothing alive in our front trenches. When the leading British line was within a hundred yards, the rattle of machine-gun and rifle broke out along the whole line of shell holes. The advance rapidly crumbled under this hail of shells and bullets. All along the line men could be seen throwing up their arms and collapsing, never to move again.

British soldiers preparing to attack at 7.30 a.m. on 1 July 1916. This picture in The Sphere *(5 August 1916) was drawn 'from a sketch and a close personal description by an eyewitness of the actual scene'*

15.11 Why did the British suffer such huge losses on the first day of the Battle of the Somme? AT1B ■

15.12 About 4000 officers and 140 000 soldiers (other ranks) took part in the attack on the German lines on 1 July 1916. Draw a bar chart to show the effect the huge losses listed in Source 15.K had on Kitchener's Army. AT3/L5

15.13 Draw pie charts to prove that the facts in Source 15.L are incorrect. AT3/L5

15.14 What difference would it make to the way you viewed the Battle of the Somme if you took it for granted that the figures quoted in Source 15.L were accurate? AT2/L6

15.15 In what ways does the German account in Source 15.H agree or disagree with the British account in Source 15.J? AT3/L6

15.16 Source 15.I is taken from a novel. How does this make a difference to its value as a source of information about the Battle of the Somme? AT2/L6

15.17 Use the sources and pictures to write your own account of the first day of the Battle of the Somme. AT3/L6

We were relieved about 11 p.m. and ordered to go back. How I escaped I do not know. I tripped over dead bodies, fell headlong into shell holes. My clothes were torn to ribbons by barbed wire. I tumbled back into our trenches alone.

[Next day] *We were roused at 7 a.m. for roll call. No officer who went into action (there were 26) was present, 17 were killed, 1 captured and 8 wounded. All Warrant Officers were killed, 7 sergeants survived, 438 other ranks were killed, wounded or missing.*

Source 15.K British casualties: 1 July 1916

	Dead	Wounded	Missing	Taken prisoner	Total
Officers	993	1 367	96	12	2468
Other Ranks	18 247	34 156	2056	573	55 032
Total	19 240	35 523	2152	585	57 500

Source 15.L From a history published in 1988

The British had 60 000 casualties; 60 per cent were officers, 40 per cent other ranks.

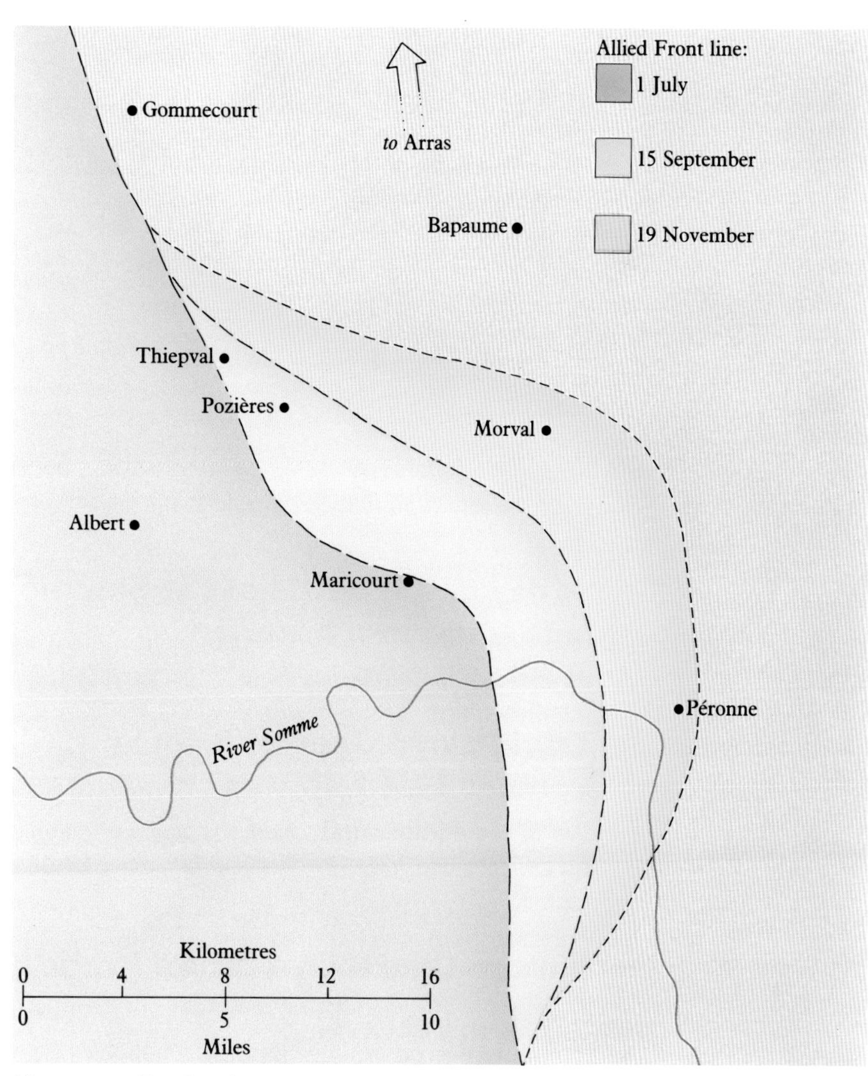

Map of the Battle of the Somme

Disaster or victory?

Source 15.M From the *Guinness Book of Records*

The battle with the greatest recorded number of military casualties [dead, wounded, missing] *was the First Battle of the Somme, France from 1 July to 19 Nov 1916, with 1 043 896 – Allied 623 907 (of which 419 654 were British) and 419,989 German.*

Despite the scale of the British losses on 1 July, the Battle of the Somme was far from over. It lasted, off and on, for another five months and ended with the loss of hundreds of thousands of men. The battle had been planned to take the pressure off Verdun but the French were already beginning to fight back there. The Germans had taken up a defensive position along the Somme, so there was no reason to expect a major attack. Nonetheless, the British Commander-in-Chief, Field Marshal Sir Douglas Haig, continued to attack. You can see the extent of his achievement in the map on page 107. Some thought the battle a disaster. Haig thought it a victory (Source 15.N).

The London Territorials during the attack on Pozières in mid-July

Source 15.O First day of the Battle of the Somme – by Correlli Barnett, a modern historian

A catastrophe without parallel in British history.

Source 15.P By David Lloyd George, Prime Minister from December 1916 onwards

It is claimed that the battle of the Somme destroyed the old German Army by killing off its best officers and men. It killed off far more of our best and of the French best.

Source 15.Q By Winston Churchill, a future Prime Minister

The battlefields of the Somme were the graveyards of Kitchener's Army.

Source 15.N By Sir Douglas Haig

By the third week in November the three main objects with which we had commenced our offensive had already been achieved. Verdun had been relieved. The main German forces had been held on the Western Front. The enemy's strength had been very considerably worn down. Any one of these three results is in itself sufficient to justify the Somme battle. The attainment of all three of them affords ample compensation for the splendid efforts of our troops and for the sacrifices made by ourselves and our Allies.

Montreuil in 1918

Field Marshal Sir Douglas Haig, the British Commander-in-Chief

15.18 Look at the map on page 107. How much ground did the Allied forces recapture during the Battle of the Somme? How many men were killed or wounded for each metre of ground gained?
AT1A ■

15.19 Did the three reasons given by Haig in Source 15.N justify the huge losses on the Somme? AT1B ■

15.20 Haig could have ordered a stop to the battle after the first day's horrendous losses. Instead, he continued to press forward, regardless, for another twenty weeks. Why?
AT1B ■ AT1C ■

15.21 A writer called Max Hoffman said 'The English soldiers fight like lions . . . but they are lions led by donkeys'. What did he mean by this? Was it a fair comment on the Battle of the Somme? AT2/L7

15.22 Is it fair to compare the battlefield in the painting on the right with Haig's headquarters at Montreuil (shown in the centre picture and described in Source 15.R)? AT1C/L7 AT2/L7

Field Marshal Haig

The Battle of the Somme, like the other battles of the war, was controlled by Field Marshal Sir Douglas Haig from his headquarters in the walled town of Montreuil, about 50 kilometres from the front line. The Prime Minister, David Lloyd George, met him here in September 1917 and later wrote, 'Nowhere was there a more ecstatic belief in his imaginary victories than at the chateau and village where the Field Marshal and his staff were quartered'. In 1920, a war correspondent, Philip Gibbs, called it 'this city of Beautiful Nonsense' (Source 15.R). Field Marshal Montgomery, who commanded British forces at El Alamein from a tank (page 151), had his own criticism to make about the way the war was run when he wrote about it in 1968 (Source 15.S).

It was from Montreuil that Haig ordered the disastrous Passchendaele campaign in 1917, a year after the Somme, when another 250 000 British soldiers were killed, wounded or missing. The poet Siegfried Sassoon wrote 'I died in hell (They called it Passchendaele)'. It was from Montreuil, too, that in 1918 Haig ordered the British Army to fight with its back to the wall and told them 'each one of us must fight on to the end' (Source 18.A on page 124).

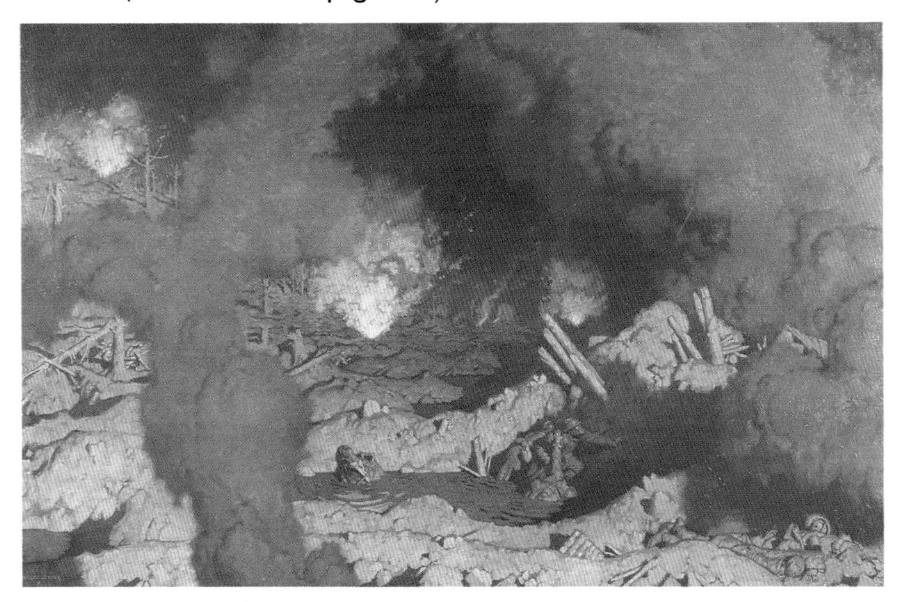

The French painter Georges Leroux called this painting L'Enfer *('Hell')*

Source 15.R Life at Haig's GHQ at Montreuil

Often one saw the Commander-in-Chief starting for an afternoon ride with an escort of Lancers. A pretty sight, with fluttering pennons [small flags] *on all their lances and horses groomed to the last hair. It was prettier than the real thing beyond the Somme, where dead bodies lay in upheaved earth among ruins and slaughtered trees. War at Montreuil was quite a pleasant occupation for elderly generals who liked their little stroll after lunch, and for young Regular officers, released from the painful necessity of dying for their country.*

Source 15.S By Field Marshal Montgomery (in 1968)

A remarkable, and disgraceful, fact is that a high proportion of senior officers were ignorant of the conditions in which the soldiers were fighting. It was normal for orders to be given that attacks were to be delivered regardless of loss – often for several days in succession.

The invention of the tank

As you can appreciate, the Allies badly needed a super-weapon which would enable them to break through the German defences. Scientists and engineers worked hard on a number of inventions to try to give the Allies an edge over the Germans. The most effective weapon they devised, the tank, went on to become the principal land weapon used in war for the rest of the twentieth century. It was invented in Britain in 1915 as a landship and based on the way in which a caterpillar track could be used to climb over obstacles. The test tank, codenamed Mother, was first put through its paces in February 1916. The Army was impressed and ordered 100.

The tank gave the soldiers inside the protection they needed when advancing towards the enemy lines. It was first used on 15 September 1916 during the Battle of the Somme (Source 15.T). Unfortunately, the first tanks often broke down and were unreliable. In any case, there were too few of them at first to achieve success.

Source 15.T

Out for first time. Strange sensation. Worse than being in a submarine. At first unable to see anything, but imagined a lot. Suddenly we gave a terrible lurch. Lookout said we were astride an enemy trench. 'Give them hell', was the order. We gave them it. Our guns raked and swept trenches right and left. Got a peep at frightened Huns. It was grimly humorous. They tried to bolt like scared rabbits, but were shot down in bunches before getting to their burrows. Machine guns brought forward. Started vicious rattle on our 'hide'. Not the least impression was made.

When tanks were assembled in sufficient numbers, they proved to be a battle winner. This was largely due to the efforts of a small number of senior officers who had faith in the idea. They were led by an outstanding Australian General, Sir John Monash, who said that the infantry should be given machine-guns, tanks and aeroplanes to protect them when going over the top. They should not be exposed, unprotected, to 'merciless machine-gun fire', he said.

Breakthrough at last

On 8 August 1918, the dreams of a breakthrough came true at last. Over 400 British tanks, supported by 800 aeroplanes armed with machine-guns, broke through the German ranks at Amiens and ruptured the German front line for good (Source 15.U). This time, the generals had already learned their lesson. The build-up of forces was concealed from the enemy. There was no preliminary bombardment – the usual signal that an attack was due. What is more, they were blessed with good luck. On the morning of the attack, as you can see from Source 15.U, the battlefield was covered in thick mist.

Source 15.U Tank Driver Bacon at Amiens in 1918

We learned that the moment for attack was to be 4.20a.m. Gosh, it was quiet. There was a fine mist which cloaked all movement. Very quietly the order was passed along for men to get into their places for action. Now the silence was painful.

'Get ready', said the officer. Crash! Hell was let loose. The noise was

Camouflaged tank in 1918

Tanks being loaded on to a steamer for France

Life inside a tank could be 'a veritable hell' according to Tank Driver Arthur Jenkin . Machine guns caused metal splinters to prick the gunners' faces while 'the noise of the engine, the intense heat, exhaust petrol fumes, and nauseous vapour from the guns made an inferno that no outside observer would have thought possible to exist within those steel plates'

15.23 Look at Sources 15.T and 15.U. Make a list of the advantages which the tanks had over infantry in the First World War. What were the disadvantages? AT1B/L5

15.24 How did the tank change modern warfare. How did it help to win the war? AT1B ■

15.25 Look at the map of the Western Front on page 94. What was the furthest distance penetrated by German forces into enemy territory during the fighting on the Western Front? How far had the Allied armies advanced into German territory by the end of the war in 1918? AT1A ■

Time Line

1914
June Archduke Ferdinand assassinated at Sarajevo
August War declared; Russians defeated at Tannenberg
September Battle of the Marne
October Turkey enters the war

1915
March Battle of Neuve Chapelle
April Germans use poison gas; Italy enters the war; Gallipoli landings
May *Lusitania* sunk
September Bulgaria enters the war

1916
February Battle of Verdun begins
May Battle of Jutland
July Battle of the Somme begins

1917
January German U-boat campaign stepped up
April Convoy system introduced; America enters the war
June Battle of Passchendaele begins

1918
August Tanks lead Allied breakthrough at Amiens

like that of a colony of giants slamming iron doors as fast as they could go. Thousands of screaming shells raced overhead and swamped the German trenches.

I drove immediately towards the sound of the nearest German machine-gun. The tank crushed the German wire defences like so much paper, and left a clear pathway through which the infantry followed. The mist was still dense and it was most uncanny driving at speed towards an invisible objective. I had only my compass to guide me.

Another German machine-gun was now firing very close to us, so I swung round and made straight for it. Suddenly I noticed a brick wall but just charged straight through. I opened my window and peered out. Gosh, we were inside a church, and had routed a machine-gun nest! I drove out.

Then the mist lifted. Goodness – what a sight met our eyes! The enemy had retreated all along the line. We pushed on. The attack that day yielded 10 000 prisoners, 200 guns, and 7½ miles of enemy territory. The Allies never ceased to advance until Germany sought the Armistice which ended the war.

British tanks crashing through a German fortification

16 Changes in attitudes to the war

▶ *HOW and WHY were censorship and propaganda used to change people's attitudes to the war?* ATIB ■ ATIC ■

▶ *HOW and WHY did attitudes to the war change?* ATIA ■ ATIB ■

Wartime propaganda

At the start of the war, censorship, advertising and propaganda were used to ensure that people were given powerful reasons why everyone should do their bit for the war effort. Newspapers spread abuse, rumours, lies and half-truths about the 'Huns', 'Boche' or 'Germ-huns'. The invading German soldiers were accused of various atrocities, such as beheading Belgian children or raping French nuns (Source 16.A). The effect of this propaganda lasted until after the war (Source 16.B).

Source 16.A Headlines in the *Daily Sketch*, 9 January 1915

The Huns would do the same if ever they came to England

Wild beasts fighting under the German flag

Can you still hang back? It may be your sister next

Germany's black page of shame

Slaughter, Outrage, Pillage And Arson Shown in Official Report

Neither sex or age spared

The Bavarian's Ferocity Against Hapless Civilians

3000 Belgians killed

Inhabitants shot like rats

Fate of women and girls

Slaughter of wounded

Priests tortured

Village priest flogged

Source 16.B From *Croydon and the Great War* (1920)

Without doubt the World War was the greatest crime in history. The length and magnitude of Germany's preparation for war, her inhuman brutality, her innummerable and in many cases indescribable cruelties to old men, women and children, prisoners and wounded, her diabolical inventions of air-warfare, and of the still more infamous submarine warfare, and the wholesale use of poison gases, made up together an immense villainy too bad for description.

Spies were seen everywhere. A car's headlights were said to have helped Zeppelins find their targets. People with German names or accents were insulted and sometimes persecuted. Butchers gave British names to the German sausages they sold. The music of Beethoven and Wagner was banned from some concert halls. It was rumoured that a British Admiral, Prince Louis of Battenberg, had been sent to the Tower as a spy. He later changed his name to Mountbatten (*berg* being

Edith Cavell's monument in Norwich

16.1 Use the sources to explain the arguments used for and against censorship in 1914–18. ATIB/L5

16.2 Why did one of the headlines in Source 16.A ask 'Can you still hang back?' What was the newspaper trying to do? ATIC/L6

16.3 How does 'The many faces of the Kaiser' illustrate what is meant by propaganda? AT3/L5 ATIC/L6 AT2/L6

16.4 How do you think a German writer might reply to Source 16.B? AT2 ■

16.5 How and why was the tragedy of Edith Cavell's death used for Allied propaganda? What effect do you think this news had on the Americans who were still neutral in the war? AT2/L5

Source 16.C By a war correspondent

While we were at St Omer, Sir John French permitted an old army friend to visit Sir Douglas Haig's sector of the line. The visitor wrote an account of what he saw in a London paper without submitting it first to the official censor in France. To show he had been on the spot, he indicated some landmarks. A day or two later the enemy gave that part of the line a very accurate shelling.

Source 16.D By David Lloyd George

If people really knew, the war would be stopped tomorrow. But of course they don't know and can't know. The correspondents don't write and the censorship would not pass the truth.

Source 16.E

20 May 1915 *There is a bitter feeling in the village that details of the charge of Essex Yeomanry are being officially held back, because they would show that the men were thrown away by the incompetence of the superior officers.*

Source 16.F

10 September 1917 *Driver Deacon was at Loos. He says that soldiers who were there are not supposed to tell what happened. We advanced 2000 yards and were then driven back 3000 yards. Our casualties were three times as many as was allowed to appear in the newspapers.*

'The many faces of the Kaiser'

German for 'mountain'). Even the King changed the Royal Family name – from Saxe-Coburg-Gotha to Windsor.

When the Germans executed Nurse Edith Cavell as a spy in October 1915, they gave the Allies a devastating piece of propaganda. It was rumoured that a German officer had had to shoot her with a revolver because the firing squad refused to fire. Newspapers and magazines denounced the Germans as fiends. In fact, the Allies were guilty of crimes just as bad. According to the writer Phillip Knightley, 'The French had already shot one woman for exactly the same offence'.

Censorship

The Government also used censorship to control what people were allowed to know about the war. Newspapers and soldiers' letters were read and censored (parts taken out) if they contained anything which might affect recruitment to the army or be helpful to the enemy (Source 16.C). Censorship also helped the army and the press to claim victories and conceal heavy losses. They thought that to do otherwise might cause a public outcry. This was the view of the Prime Minister, David Lloyd George (Source 16.D). As a result, people found it hard to know who or what to believe. They knew they couldn't believe everything they read in the newspapers.

Lloyd George underestimated the British people. They knew the casualty lists were terrible. The Reverend Andrew Clark, a patriotic supporter of the war effort, thought the Government was 'treating the people of Great Britain as if they were incompetent children'. Concealment of the facts made the local people think the worst (Source 16.E). Tales told by soldiers on leave only confirmed his suspicions (Source 16.F).

Disenchantment

Some people, such as the war poets (Sources 16.G and 16.H), did protest against the war. The writer and thinker Bertrand Russell, a pacifist, was harassed when he led the Non-Conscription Movement. Russell helped the soldier-poet Siegfried Sassoon when he wrote to *The Times* in July 1917 while still in the army (Source 16.H).

Instead of being court-martialled, however, Sassoon was told he was suffering from shell-shock and sent to a hospital near Edinburgh. Similar protests were made in Parliament (Source 16.I). A growing number of people wanted to discuss peace with Germany. This was opposed by the army and by many politicians. They wanted to destroy German power for good – even if this meant losing many more thousands of British lives – which it did.

Source 16.G By Arthur Graeme West (killed in 1917)

God! how I hate you, you young cheerful men,
Whose pious poetry blossoms on your graves
As soon as you are in them. . .
Hark how one chants –
'Oh happy to have lived these epic days' –
'These epic days!' And he'd been to France,
And seen the trenches, glimpsed the huddled dead
In the periscope, hung on the rusty wire.

Source 16.H By Siegfried Sassoon in 1917

I am making this statement as an act of wilful defiance of military authority because I believe that the War is being deliberately prolonged by those who have the power to end it. This War, on which I entered as a war of defence and liberation, has now become a war of aggression and conquest. I have seen and endured the sufferings of the troops, and I can no longer be a party to prolong these sufferings which I believe to be evil and unjust.

Paul Nash volunteered in 1914, fought in Flanders and was wounded in 1917. He painted this picture of the battlefield at Passchendaele, The Menin Road, *when he returned to France as an official British war artist. He said, 'I am a messenger who will bring back word from the men who are fighting to those who want the war to go on for ever. It will have a bitter truth and may it burn their lousy souls'*

Source 16.I
By Richard Lambert MP: November 1917

Peace has got to come some time or other. Every day that passes means so many of our own gallant men killed or mutilated or injured in some way or other. This House [of Commons] *ought to take every chance to try to do something to bring this horrible War to a close.*

16.6 Compare Source 16.G with Rupert Brooke's poem on page 98. What do they tell you about the way attitudes changed during the war? AT1A ■ AT1C ■

16.7 How could a war film like *All Quiet on the Western Front* give a misleading impression of what really happened during the First World War? AT2/L5

16.8 What different impressions of the war do Sources 16.G and 16.H give compared with Source 16.B? AT2/L6

16.9 What do the two paintings show? Which do you think is the more effective picture? Which picture would you use if you wanted to persuade someone to become a pacifist? AT2/L6

16.10 What evidence is there that these paintings accurately portray the battlefields of the war? AT2/L7

16.11 What reasons did Paul Nash and Otto Dix give for painting the pictures shown here? Were they trying to depict the war as it was, or were they trying to change people's attitudes to the war? Does this make any difference to the value of these pictures as sources of information? AT1C/L7 AT2/L7 AT3/L7

16.12 How far can a film or novel give an accurate or complete account of the war in the trenches? AT2/L7

The painter Otto Dix volunteered in 1914 and fought in the German Army at the Battle of the Somme in 1916. He whiled away the boring moments in the trenches by drawing sketches on postcards. He said he painted The War *in 1928–32 because 'people were already beginning to forget what unspeakable suffering the war had brought with it'*

By 1917, as you can see, many people had become disenchanted with the war. How strong this feeling was in the country as a whole we shall never know. There are many bitter accounts and paintings which show how terrible the fighting was. But most were written or painted *after* the war. Many of the fiercest criticisms were made in 1929–30 when people hoped the newly-founded League of Nations (page 130) would succeed in stopping all wars in future. They knew then the full extent of the casualties suffered in 1914–18. Strong feelings against the futility of war grew when the American feature film *All Quiet on the Western Front* was shown in 1930. It was based on a novel by a German writer called Erich Maria Remarque. It tells the story of a group of young Germans who volunteer with enthusiasm in 1914 and then, after appalling suffering in the trenches, lose faith that what they are doing is right. One writer said the film 'fixed in millions of minds the popular image of what it was like in the trenches'.

17 The Home Front

► *HOW and WHY did the war change the everyday life and work of people living at home?*

ATIA ■ ATIB ■ ATIC ■

► *WHAT measures did the government take to fight the war and HOW and WHY did this affect people at home?*

ATIA ■ ATIB ■ ATIC ■

► *HOW and WHY did the position of women change during the Great War?*

ATIA ■ ATIB ■ ATIC ■

Effect on life at home

The war affected everyday life in many different ways. The cost of many goods more than doubled in the space of only four years. Goods which cost £3 in August 1914 cost £7 in November 1918. At first people felt guilty at enjoying themselves in wartime but soon the strain of the war gave a boost to entertainments, such as the cinema (Source 17.A), restaurants and theatres (Source 17.E on page 119) and seaside holidays (Source 17.B). Critics, however, claimed that many of the pleasure-seekers were people spending the profits they made from the war and not soldiers relaxing while on leave.

Source 17.A Newspaper report in 1917

Every picture-palace is crowded night after night. Some people visit different halls three or four times a week.

◄ *Not surprisingly, children's comics and also toys and games were affected by the war – as you can see from this advert in 1916*

A wartime family photograph taken in about 1917

Source 17.B *The Times* in 1915

From Hastings to Bognor the hotels and lodging houses are full. There are bands playing, and singers singing, the theatres and cinematographs are doing well, and every place has its little troupes of Funs or Drolls or Merries, giving open-air entertainments. At Brighton and everywhere else the crowd is quiet, all except the children. Mother, seeing them happy, is content to write to their father, who is maybe somewhere over the water, or in London, taking no holiday this year.

Food shortages

The success of German U-boats in harassing and sinking merchant ships caused serious food shortages in Britain especially in 1917–18 (Source

17.1 Draw a graph to show the unemployment figures in Source 17.D. How did they change during the war? AT1A ■

17.2 Why do you think the manufacturers of Zambrene (below) advertised their weatherproof trench-coats in this way? Did it give an accurate or misleading impression of trench warfare? AT2/L5

17.3 Draw up a table like the one on page 18 to show some of the different effects on everyday life during the First World War. AT1B/L5

17.4 What does the poster *Don't Waste Bread!* tell us about the war in 1917? AT3/L5

17.5 Why did the Government control pub opening times and put the clocks forward? How could this help the war effort? AT1B ■

17.6 Why was rationing introduced? AT1B/L5

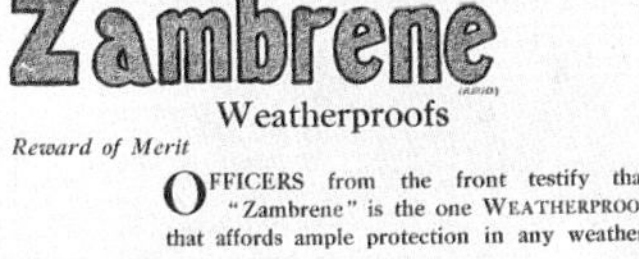

17.C). This is why the King led an 'Eat Less Bread' campaign in 1917 calling on people 'To reduce the consumption of bread by at least one-fourth'. Sugar was first to be rationed (in 1917), followed early in 1918 by meat, butter, margarine, coal, electricity and gas. General rationing came into force in June 1918.

Source 17.C From *How We Lived Then* by Mrs Peel (1929)

Bakers were forbidden to bake any but Government regulation bread made from various ingredients, including barley, rice, maize, beans, oatmeal and potato. Milk was the first item to be controlled, and sugar the first for which ration cards were issued. By now so great were discomfort and ill-feeling caused by the food queues and the suspicion that the rich were obtaining more than their fair share of eatables, that the demand for compulsory rations became more and more insistent.

Increasing output

Many people drowned their sorrows in alcohol. This led Lloyd George to call drink 'our greatest enemy' and the Bishop of London to say that 'the men who drank at home were murdering the men in the trenches'. The King decided to set an example. He gave up alcoholic liquor himself and drank barley water instead. To make certain the campaign against drinking worked, the Government controlled the times when public houses could open. Another permanent change to everyday life came on 21 May 1916 when British Summertime was introduced for the first time. The clocks were put forward an hour. Both these measures were designed to increase the output of the war industries.

Improvements in health

You might have thought that rationing and the concentration on the war effort would have meant that people's health suffered. Instead, the infant mortality rates – the number of babies in every thousand dying before the age of one – actually improved. In the six years before the war, the average rate was 112 babies in every 1000. In the six years from 1914 to 1919, the death rate fell to 98 in every 1000.

The reason for this improvement in health was due mainly to the fact that people were better off during the war than they had been in the years immediately before. The families of men in the services were paid allowances. The government made up the income of thousands of people whose wages dropped because of the war. The wages of the poorest workers, such as farm workers and labourers in engineering works, increased by more than inflation during the war years. The problem of unemployment disappeared (Source 17.D). Above all, the widespread employment of women and older children during the war meant that two or more wages went into many homes where before there had only been one or none.

Source 17.D

	Before the war			During the war		
Percentage of people unemployed	1908–9 7.8%	1910–11 3.9%	1912–13 2.7%	1914–15 2.2%	1916–17 0.6%	1918–19 1.6%

An Allied raid on a German munitions factory in 1918. Wartime paintings like this were mainly wishful thinking. Air raids had little effect on the course of the war

Air-raids

For the first time in world history, people at home experienced the danger of being fired on, even though they were many hundreds of kilometres behind the front line. The first such attack came from the sea, not the air. On 16 December 1914, German warships in the North Sea shelled a number of ports, including Scarborough, Whitby and West Hartlepool. They killed over 100 people. Civilians were shocked to be in the firing line. A month later, on 19 January 1915, a huge airship powered by engines dropped bombs on the Norfolk ports of Great Yarmouth and King's Lynn. Airships like this were called Zeppelins after their German inventor, Count von Zeppelin. The biggest was 225 metres long, 28 metres high, 24 metres wide and could travel at 100 kph (62 mph).

There were just over one hundred air-raids on Britain. They caused some damage and killed about 1500 people. Most of these raids were in Kent, London and East Anglia, although the Germans also bombed places as far afield as Tyneside and the coast of Cumbria. At the end of the war, they were using four-engined bombers capable of dropping bombs weighing a tonne. By then, however, the newly-formed Royal Air Force (page 95) had built a line of fighter airfields to protect London. Special balloons, called barrage ballons, flew in the sky to make it difficult for enemy aircraft to come in low. Anti-aircraft guns ringed the city as a further line of defence.

The last Zeppelin raid, on 19 October 1917, was undertaken by about eleven airships, five of which were lost. The raids reminded people at home that a terrible war was being fought. It helped to back up the propaganda campaign against the enemy. People experienced for themselves the danger of being under fire – as you can see from the account in Source 17.E. This was written by a young man called James Wickham who was working at that time at the Gaiety Theatre. In other parts of London, onlookers watched with mixed feelings when the raiders were themselves shot down (Source 17.F).

17.7 What things do you think you would have noticed most about Britain during the First World War? AT1C/L4
17.8 What were London's main defences against a Zeppelin attack? AT3/L4
17.9 Use Source 17.E to explain why people were enjoying London's night life at a time when men were dying in the trenches less than 150 miles away. AT3/L5
17.10 Use the sources and the pictures to say what differences there were in people's attitudes to the German Zeppelin crews who raided Britain. AT1C/L6 AT3/L6

A Zeppelin shot down in 1915 ▶

Part of the wreckage of the Zeppelin which crashed at Theberton in Suffolk in 1917

Memorial at Theberton in Suffolk

Source 17.E Air raid on 13 October 1915

Restaurants were crowded. From behind the heavily curtained windows of the big hotels there came the sounds of merry-making. The popping of champagne corks. The beat of dance music. Heady laughter. There were toasts, farewells, tears, promises, kisses. War! Tonight – Blighty [the soldier's name for Britain]. *Tomorrow – who cared? London had everything in the way of pleasure to offer her sons on leave. Theatres were flourishing. At the Gaiety Theatre we had been playing every night to packed houses.*

Almost impossible to realise the horrors of the trenches in France. Had it not been for the khaki everywhere, the war would have seemed even more remote. In the shadowy streets, vendors cried their wares by the feeble light of oil lamps. A barrel organ fumbled with the melody of the moment – 'Keep the Home Fires Burning'.

A beam of light swung across the sky. And then others. Some people glanced upwards uneasily. They did not know that three hours earlier an urgent message had been flashed from France to the War Office that five Zeppelins were approaching the East Coast.

As I went out of the stage door I met Billy, the errand boy. I stopped for a moment to light a cigarette. 'They say the Zepps are on their way, the swine,' I remarked. There was the sudden crackle of anti-aircraft gunfire and then the dreadful sound – a sound like no other on earth. It was the mournful wail of a descending bomb. I instinctively knew it was coming directly where we stood. I was not wrong. It exploded three yards from where we were standing. It flung me against the wall. I asked for Billy but he had been blown to pieces. I could hear screams and the dull thud of more bombs.

Source 17.F

I ran out on to the balcony and saw something which looked like a large silver cigar away to my left, and I realised that it was a Zeppelin. Almost immediately it burst into flames and the sky turned red. Then came the sound of cheering. We were cheering whilst men, who were after all very bravely doing what they thought it their duty to do, were being burned to death.

Industry in wartime

When war broke out in 1914, Britain was no longer 'The Workshop of the World' (page 18). Germany had already overtaken her in a number of important industries (Source 17.G). This left Britain at a great disadvantage, such as in producing drugs to treat the wounded and in making nitrates for high explosives. The German chemical industry was much more advanced. That is why they were able to use poison gas in 1915 (page 105). An even bigger problem in Britain was getting people to work in factories and on farms to take the place of the men who had left their jobs to join the Army. You can see how this problem was solved on page 122.

Source 17.G Industrial production at the start of the war

	United Kingdom	Germany
Coal	292 million tonnes	277 million tonnes
Pig iron	10.4 million tonnes	16.8 million tonnes
Steel	7.8 million tonnes	17.6 million tonnes
Sulphuric acid	1.1 million tonnes	1.7 million tonnes

Government in wartime

When war began in 1914, the Liberal Prime Minister, Herbert Asquith, was leader of a government which had been in power for $8^1/_2$ years. Later he agreed to form a Coalition Government with the other political parties. One of the most successful members of the new government was David Lloyd George, Minister of Munitions. His no-nonsense approach increased output from 23 million shells in 1915 to 172 million in 1917. By 1916, he could boast that production of machine-guns had gone up 14 times, heavy guns by 22 times and high explosives by 66 times. He did this by increasing the number of munitions factories from 1000 in 1915 to 4250 a year later. He also banned strikes in industries making munitions and directed labour (took people away from one factory and made them work in another).

After a Government crisis in December 1916, Asquith was forced to resign and Lloyd George took his place with the support of the Conservatives and some members of the Labour and Liberal Parties.

17.11 What measures taken by the Government in the First World War reduced the freedom of the people? AT1A/L5

17.12 Were these necessary in order to fight the war? AT1C ■

17.13 Why did people object to DORA? What type of power did it give the Government? AT1B ■

17.14 How and why did the First World War change politics in Britain? AT1A ■ AT1B ■

17.15 Does it make any difference when you read these sources to know that Sources 17.H, 17.I and 17.J were written in 1938 by two historians who sympathised with the workers, not the government, and that Source 17.K was written in 1916 by a Colonel serving in the trenches? AT1C/L7 AT2/L7 AT3/L7

17.16 Draw a bar chart to show the statistics in Source 17.G. Explain what the chart shows. AT1C/L5

◀ *The manufacture of shells played a part in changing the government. Early on in the war, the generals complained they were short of ammunition. This row was one of the reasons why a Coalition Government from all the main political parties was formed in the Spring of 1915*

Source 17.H

There were very few things which could not, under DORA, be regarded as spreading false news or taking action likely to discourage recruiting. Any discussion of the way in which the war came that did not cast the whole blame on Germany was liable to come under the second category.

Source 17.I

The searching of homes by force now became a regular feature of police procedure. Letters were opened and read.

Source 17.J

In addition to DORA, the Military Service Acts were used to break or prevent strikes. Tramway-men, printers, farm labourers and jute-workers within six months of March 1916 found strikes either prevented or broken by a threat of calling up the discontented workers.

Working in an aircraft factory

Asquith's Liberals became the new Opposition Party. The Liberal Party, split in two, never recovered from this blow. After the war, Labour became the main opposition party to the Conservatives.

Government controls

As soon as war began, the British Government brought in laws to make it easier to control the country. They took charge of the railways and used the Defence of the Realm Act (DORA) to take action against anyone helping the enemy (Source 17.H). Later on DORA and other actions (Source 17.I) were sometimes used, unjustly, to curb the activities of people with grievances about the way in which the war was being run. For instance, a Londoner was fined £100 for saying 'We shall see the Germans in the Mile End Road yet'. People were fined for giving out pacifist leaflets. The publication of a Conservative daily newspaper, *The Globe*, was stopped because it criticised Lord Kitchener (the War Minister). Trade unionists complained when workers exempted from military service (because their work was essential to the war effort) were threatened with conscription if they went on strike (Source 17.J).

Pay day at a WAAC barracks during the First World War. With over six million men and women serving in the armed forces, the wages bill alone cost the country a huge amount of money.

Source 17.K

It makes me feel sick. Those fellow-countrymen earning huge wages, yet for ever clamouring for more; striking, or threatening to strike; while the country is engaged upon this murderous struggle.

Finding money for the war

The war had a disastrous effect on Britain's trade. Factories which had exported goods now made shells, guns, vehicles and uniforms for the army. Yet they still needed many raw materials from abroad. To pay for these, and to help pay the enormous cost of running the war (about £6 million pounds a day – £60 billion a year in today's money), the Government borrowed very large sums of money from America. Income tax was also raised to a very high level and people were encouraged to put their money into a special savings scheme called War Loan.

Many women joined the armed services, like these wireless operators in the Women's Royal Naval Service (WRNS). Some joined the Women's Army Auxiliary Corps or WAAC (see picture on page 121). Others joined the Women's Royal Air Force (WRAF). Women did not fight in the war, but many served in France as drivers or nurses in areas close to the trenches

Members of the Women's Land Army load a cart with roots to feed cattle. Farming in 1914–18 was very hard work since there were few tractors and machines at that time

Women at war

In 1914, most women in Britain did not have paid work. Nor did they have the vote, despite the violent protests of suffragettes before the war. Mrs Emmeline Pankhurst, their leader, told them 'What is the use of fighting for a vote if we have not got a country to vote in?' Despite a Government appeal to women to sign on for war work in March 1915, some employers and trade unions were reluctant to see women working in factories or on the land. This is why 40 000 women marched through London in July 1915 under the slogan 'WE DESERVE THE RIGHT TO SERVE'.

Source 17.L

Employment of women	1914	1915	1916	1917	1918
Making munitions	200 000	250 000	500 000	800 000	950 000
Working in transport	18 000				117 000

The employment of women increased rapidly in 1916 when the conscription of male workers gave employers little choice. By 1918 it was common to see women doing jobs previously done only by men (Sources 17.L and 17.M). Their farm work was particularly important. The Germans hoped to use their U-boats (page 97) to end the war by starving Britain of food. It was vital to grow as much food as possible. The Food Production Campaign helped to increase the amount of crops grown. Farmers were paid to plough up new fields. They were greatly helped by the 16 000 women who joined the Women's Land Army.

Some trade unionists objected to women doing the work of skilled or semi-skilled men. Women didn't get the same pay as men, even when they did the same work. Male workers were afraid employers would use this as an excuse to lower their wages as well. Trade unions which had fought for the rights of the skilled male worker were reluctant to let unskilled female workers do the same jobs. They called this 'dilution of labour'.

A factory worker operating a machine

Source 17.M Report on 'Woman's work in wartime' in 1918

She has discarded her petticoats. There are girls at the wheels of half the cars that pass. If you go by train, women will handle your luggage. If you choose bus or tram, the conductress in her smart uniform has long been a familiar figure in our streets.

17.17 Draw a graph to show the changes in the employment of women between 1914 and 1918 (Source 17.L). Why were there problems because of these changes? AT1A ■

17.18 In what different ways, and why, did the war change the attitudes of people in Britain to the society in which they lived? AT1A/L5 AT1B/L5
17.19 How does Source 17.O illustrate some of these changes? AT3/L5
17.20 What did women gain as a result of their war effort? AT1A ■ AT1B ■
17.21 What are the advantages and disadvantages of using the type of historical evidence shown in Source 17.O? AT2/L7 AT3/L7

Time Line

1914
August Outbreak of war; DORA
December North Sea ports shelled

1915
January First Zeppelin raid
March Appeal to women to work in munitions factories
May Coalition Government
July Women's protest march

1916
January Conscription introduced
May Daylight Saving Act
July Battle of the Somme begins
December Asquith resigns; Lloyd George becomes Prime Minister

1917
February Food shortages as Germany steps up U-boat campaign
September Sugar rationing

1918
January Women given the vote
November Armistice declared

In 1915, Vera Brittain (page 88) responded to posters like this and volunteered to become a VAD – a Voluntary Aid Detachment nurse

A fashionable young woman in about 1916

Changes to society

In February 1918, as a reward for their war effort, women over 30 were given the vote and now had the right to be elected to Parliament as an MP. This was unfair to the younger women who had done much of the work, since the same Act of Parliament gave men the vote at 21. Worse was to come when the men returned and many women lost their jobs.

By the end of the war, however, the position of women had changed in a number of other ways (Source 17.N). They had much greater freedom than in 1914. Short hair was the fashion. The full-length skirt was on the way out. By 1926 hemlines were nearing the knees. It was no longer unusual for middle-class women to go into public houses and dance halls on their own or to smoke cigarettes in public.

Source 17.N From *The Graphic*: December 1919

The woman who lives alone in a flat is today no more remarked than the woman who lives with fifty others in a hostel. The factory girl who plays football is no more singular than the professional woman who writes and smokes cigarettes in a women's club. Women workers have their own trades unions and societies.

In 1914 it had been common for women to work in domestic service as maids, cooks or housekeepers. After the war there was a shortage of servants. In 1990, an old lady in Yorkshire recalled her days as a maid in a big house in 1917–18 (Source 17.O).

Source 17.O From a tape-recording in 1990

It were a shilling [5p] *a day. When sugar were rationed they took it! We had to have treacle. Cook gave in to them. She gave them our sugar! And he were a manager at local mill!*

After 1918 the lady in Source 17.0 left domestic service for good. Like thousands of others, she was no longer prepared to work as a servant. Men from the city slums who fought in the squalor of the trenches next to officers from the richest homes soon discovered that they were just as good as people they had thought of as their betters before the war. Their votes helped the Labour Party form a government in 1924.

18 Peace

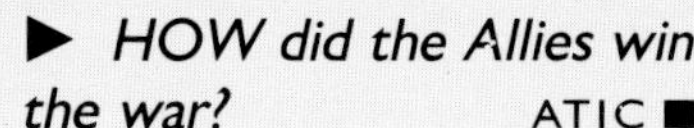

▶ *HOW did the Allies win the war?* ATIC ■
▶ *WHAT did the war cost in terms of human life and HOW was it remembered?* ATIC ■

Victory

In 1917, the Communist Revolution in Russia led to a peace agreement with Germany. Now German soldiers from the Russian Front could be used against the Allies in France. Since American troops (see page 97) had not yet arrived in large enough numbers to reinforce the Allied lines, the Kaiser made one last effort to win the war. The German Spring Offensive began on 21 March 1918. It was so successful, it pushed the Allies back to the river Marne once more. Field Marshal Haig told his men not to give an inch (Source 18.A). They were to fight to the death.

Source 18.A

Every position must be held to the last man. There must be no retirement. With our backs to the wall and believing in the justice of our cause, each one of us must fight on to the end.

The British Army obeyed. They and the French held firm and the Allies recovered. The German armies were now exhausted. They gave way before a fresh Allied onslaught in July and August, aided by tanks. After the Battle of Amiens (page 110) on 8 August 1918, the German commander, General Erich von Ludendorff knew the Germans were beaten. He called it 'Germany's Black Day' and said 'The war must be ended'. At home in Germany, there was widespread unrest. Socialists marched through the streets. On 9 November 1918, the Kaiser abdicated and the Germans agreed to an armistice (ceasefire). This was signed in a railway carriage at Compiègne near Paris. Two days later, at the eleventh hour, of the eleventh day, of the eleventh month, the armistice came into being. The war was over.

These pictures of a corporal (top) and an officer (below) were published in the Christmas 1918 edition of The Sphere *magazine*

War cemetery near the battlefield at Passchendaele in Flanders

In Memoriam

About a third of all the soldiers who had left Britain for France had been killed, died of wounds, or injured. Many of the dead were buried in the war cemeteries of Flanders and Northern France. The bodies of many other soldiers were never identified, such as those blown to pieces by shells or buried in the mud.

A heavy gun forms part of the Royal Artillery war memorial in London

18.1 How and why did the Allies win the war? AT1B ■

18.2 Look at the two pictures from *The Sphere* magazine. How have the officer and the corporal been portrayed? What impression of Britain in November 1918 do you get from these pictures? What do the pictures tell you about the magazine's attitude to the war? AT1C ■ AT2 ■

18.3 What do the war memorials tell you about the different ways in which people wanted to remember the soldiers who had fallen in battle? Which do you think are the most appropriate? AT2 ■

The Cenotaph in Whitehall

These simple wooden crosses from the battlefield displayed on a wall in Salisbury Cathedral are dedicated to the memory of the son and son-in-law of the Archdeacon of Sarum

The men who volunteered in 1914 are commemorated in this war memorial at Newcastle upon Tyne ►

In 1920, the remains of a single soldier, the Unknown Warrior, representing all who had died, was given a State Funeral at Westminster Abbey attended by the most important people in the land (Source 18.B). That same day the King dedicated the Cenotaph in Whitehall to the memory of all who had died. Then came two minutes of silence. A huge crowd stood motionless as Big Ben tolled eleven. Ever since, a similar ceremony accompanied by lines from Laurence Binyon's poem 'For the Fallen' (Source 18.C), has been held on Remembrance Day each November. Five years earlier, John McCrae, a Canadian army doctor, had written a famous poem which gave Remembrance Day a special meaning (Source 18.D).

Source 18.B Inscription on the Grave of the Unknown Warrior in Westminster Abbey

BENEATH THIS STONE RESTS THE BODY
OF A BRITISH WARRIOR
UNKNOWN BY NAME OR RANK
BROUGHT FROM FRANCE TO LIE AMONG
THE MOST ILLUSTRIOUS OF THE LAND
AND BURIED HERE ON ARMISTICE DAY
11 NOV: 1920.

Source 18.C By Laurence Binyon

They shall not grow old, as we that are left grow old:
Age shall not weary them, nor the years condemn.
At the going down of the sun and in the morning
We will remember them.

Source 18.D By John McCrae (who died in 1918)

In Flanders fields the poppies blow
Between the crosses, row on row,
That mark our place . . .

We are the Dead. Short days ago
We lived, felt dawn, saw sunset glow,
Loved and were loved, and now we lie
In Flanders fields.

The extent of the casualties suffered by different towns, villages and communities can be seen today in thousands of war memorials across the country. In Croydon alone, 2500 of the 25 000 men from the town who served in the war had died. The Essex village of Great Leighs, with a population of only 614 people, lost 19 of its young men. Many families lost two or more sons. Those who had volunteered first suffered the most.

The era of the Second World War

19 The search for a lasting Peace

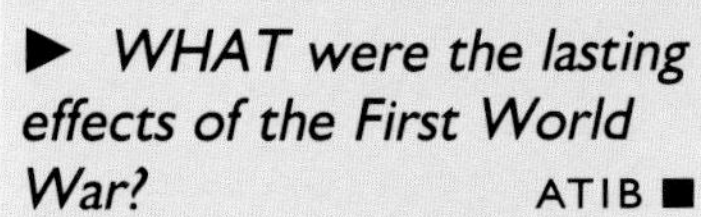

▶ *WHAT were the lasting effects of the First World War?* ATIB ■
▶ *HOW did the Treaty of Versailles change Europe and sow the seeds of a second war?* ATIA ■ ATIB ■
▶ *WHAT peace efforts were made in the 1920s?* ATIC ■

The Paris Peace Treaties

As you can see from Source 19.A, the end of the Great War gave people the feeling that a new and brighter future lay ahead. As we know now, of course, they were wrong in thinking there would 'never again' be news of the ending of a world war. The Great War was soon renamed the First World War to distinguish it from the even greater war which began only 21 years later in 1939. One writer called this 'the final battle of the Great War' because the Treaty of Versailles, which brought the war with Germany to an end in 1919, was one of the causes of the Second World War.

The Treaty of Versailles was signed near Paris on 28 June 1919. It came at the end of a long and bitter debate among the Allies. The Treaty was largely drawn up by the four leading Allied powers – Britain, France, Italy and the United States. Germany was not consulted, nor were the other defeated countries – Austria, Hungary, Turkey and Bulgaria – when they signed separate peace treaties in Paris. Even Russia, one of the three great Allied powers in 1914, was not consulted about the Treaty. The Russian Revolutions of 1917 had overthrown the Czar and put a Communist government in power, led by Lenin (page 128).

The French, who had suffered most, wanted revenge and compensation for the damage done to their country. They and the people of Belgium faced a colossal task in trying to rebuild their towns and villages. Over a quarter of a million buildings had been destroyed in the fighting. About 25 000 square kilometres of battlefield had to be restored to farmland or forest. By contrast, the Americans, who fought for little more than a year and suffered least, wanted a just and lasting peace. The British wanted an agreement which would satisfy the desire of the people of Britain to punish the enemy, but without causing Germany to turn to Communism, as Russia had done.

In the end the peace settlement satisfied no one. Italy and Japan failed to gain the territories they thought they deserved for their efforts during the war. The Germans, ruled now by a Socialist President, had to suffer for a war started by the Kaiser. Many politicians in Britain and France later recognised that an injustice had been done to Germany at Versailles. When they failed to insist that the terms of the Treaty (Source 19.B) be followed by Germany exactly as written, they sent the wrong signals to Hitler. He tore up the Treaty, clause by clause.

Other treaties were signed in Paris with Austria, Hungary, Bulgaria and Turkey. These also affected the map of Europe and the world. The old Austro-Hungarian Empire had by now collapsed and new countries –

Source 19.A From the *Daily Mirror*, 12 November 1918

The greatest, gladdest, most wonderful day in British history. A new chapter of the world's history is beginning. There never again will be such news.

19.1 If you had been living in Germany in 1919, which parts of the Treaty of Versailles would you have resented most? AT1B/L6

19.2 Look at the map of Europe in 1919. Compare it with the map on page 90. How did Europe change in the five years between 1914 and 1919? AT1A ■

19.3 Write a paragraph to explain which you think were the most important changes. AT1B/L6

19.4 David Lloyd George said in 1919, 'We shall have to fight another war all over again in 25 years, at three times the cost'. How did he see the Treaty? What made him take this attitude? AT1C ■

The two German delegates (on the near side of the table) sign the Treaty of Versailles. The three Allied leaders on the other side are US President Woodrow Wilson, French Prime Minister Georges Clemenceau and British Prime Minister David Lloyd George. ▶

Austria, Czechoslovakia, Hungary and Yugoslavia – had taken its place. New boundaries meant that large numbers of German-speaking peoples were transferred to neighbouring countries as part of the peace settlement. For example, German-speaking lands in Bohemia and Moravia went to Czechoslovakia.

German territory awarded to neighbouring countries

Austro-Hungarian Empire until 1918

Areas where a vote was taken on whether or not to be part of Germany

Parts of the Russian Empire which had become independent after the Bolshevik Revolution

The map of Europe in 1919

Source 19.B The Treaty of Versailles

Germany to lose about one tenth of her territory in Europe (see the map above).
Germany to lose all her overseas colonies. These were to be governed by different nations as mandates of the League of Nations.
Severe restrictions on the German Army, Navy and Air Force. • *Conscription forbidden* • *Army to have no more than 100 000 men* • *No German soldiers allowed in the Rhineland (bordering France)* • *Navy to have no more than 15 000 sailors and 36 warships* • *No German submarines* • *No German air force*
Germany not to form a union (Anschluss) with German-speaking Austria.
Germany to admit responsibility for starting the war. To pay reparations of $32 billion dollars (worth over £200 billion today) to the Allies in compensation.
All the nations signing the Treaty to join a League of Nations to be set up in Geneva (Switzerland) to settle world problems in future (page 130).

Russian painting of Lenin speaking to factory workers in St Petersburg

Source 19.C Effects of the First World War

- *It sowed the seeds of the Second World War. Bitter resentment at the terms of the Paris Peace Treaties was used by Hitler to sweep the Nazi Party into power in Germany (page 135). It also helped Mussolini to gain power in a disappointed Italy (page 129) and helped militarism grow in Japan, which had expected to gain territory as a reward for fighting on the Allied side.*

- *Opposition to the war and to bread and fuel shortages led to a revolution in Russia in March 1917. Eight months later, Lenin founded the world's first Communist State. Everyone was now equal. But many died in the civil war which followed. Western Powers, such as Britain, France and the USA, sent troops (unsuccessfully) to help Lenin's opponents.*

- *Four powerful empires disappeared. The Czar of **Russia** was overthrown in March 1917. The Kaiser abdicated and **Germany** became a republic in November 1918. The **Austro-Hungarian Empire** split up into separate countries in 1918. The **Ottoman Empire** (Turkey) became a republic in 1923.*

- *Women made a great leap forward during the war. Their work for the war effort gave them the vote in Britain (page 123). They were more independent. Many more had full-time jobs (page 120). The loss of millions of young men meant there were many widows and one-parent families. The birth rate fell. Many more women had to take on the role of head of the household.*

- *Horror at the appalling loss of life in the war (8 million dead – see page 89) made many British and French politicians determined to avoid war at any price in the future.*

- *The war weakened the UK as a trading nation. British manufacturers involved in the war effort lost export markets to Japan and the United States. Large loans to pay for the war had to be repaid to the United States. The post-war decline in trade and industry led to a General Strike in 1926 and widespread unemployment.*

- *The League of Nations was formed (see page 130)*

The rise of Communism

The collapse of the great empires meant that new governments took their place. Some were democracies, where the leaders were elected. Others, like Russia, became dictatorships where only one political party was allowed and one man became leader of the country.

The Russian Empire later became the Soviet Union. Lenin ruled it as a dictator with the aid of the secret police. Only the Communist Party was allowed. Within three years of his death in 1924, Josef Stalin ('Man

Communism and Fascism

- Both put the State first. Individuals had to give way to the State.
- Neither allowed people to oppose them. Both banned other political parties.
- Both killed and imprisoned their enemies. The Fascists put them in concentration camps, the Communists sent them to labour camps.
- Both used secret police. Hitler had the Gestapo, Mussolini had OVRA, Stalin had the NKVD.
- Both used education, propaganda and fear of punishment to make people believe in their ideas.
- Fascists were nationalists. They used compulsory military training (for men), uniforms, flags and parades to make people proud and ready to die for their country in war.

19.5 Look at the painting of Lenin. What effect do you think scenes like this had on politicians in Europe after the Great War? How does it portray Lenin?
AT1C/L6 AT2/L5

19.6 Compare the picture of Mussolini with the wartime picture of the Kaiser on page 113. Make a list of the differences and similarities between the two pictures. What do they tell you about the use of propaganda at that time?
AT3/L6

19.7 Why did the landowners, farmers and shopkeepers support Mussolini?
AT1B ■

- Communists also used conscription to defend the State against its enemies. They wanted to spread Communism abroad by revolution rather than by war.
- In the Communist State, the People owned and the Government controlled all the land and property.

  In the Fascist State, industry, land and businesses were privately owned but controlled by the Government.
- Fascists banned trade unions. Communists controlled them. Both banned strikes.
- Both started public building works, such as new roads and dams, to end unemployment.
- Communists said all people were equal. Most Fascists were racists. They thought other peoples – Jews, Slavs and Blacks – to be inferior races.

Propaganda painting of Mussolini. As you can see, his face has been merged with pictures of fascist building projects in Italy

of Steel') took his place. Stalin began a series of drastic reforms. He turned the Soviet Union from a vast land of peasant farms into a powerful industrial nation. Everything was run by the State or by groups of people (collectives) working for the good of the State. In the process, millions of Russians were killed, died of starvation, or were sent to labour camps in Siberia.

Communist parties were soon formed in many countries. They were helped by the Comintern (Communist International) which Lenin set up in Moscow. He made no secret of the fact that he wanted Communism to spread to other countries as well. Since this meant revolution, Communist Parties in many countries were banned.

The rise of Fascism

In Italy, widespread unemployment after the war led to industrial unrest. Many workers joined the Communist Party. Sharply rising prices, strikes and fear of Communism made Italians despair. The country's weak system of government and the fact that Italy was not given one of Germany's overseas colonies made people angry. This is why Benito Mussolini founded the Italian Fascist Party. His followers called him Il Duce ('The Leader'). In October 1922, Mussolini seized power and set up a one-party Fascist government in Italy with himself as dictator. Trade unions were banned and his Communist and Socialist opponents sent to concentration camps. He transformed Italy by electrifying the railways, building fast motor roads (*autostrada*), draining marshland, encouraging farmers and building hospitals, schools and dams.

Hatred of Communism led other European countries to take similar action, as in Nazi Germany. People with wealth and power, as well as peasant farmers and small shopkeepers, supported dictators who safeguarded their property, such as Pilsudski in Poland, Franco in Spain, Salazar in Portugal and Horthy in Hungary. Governments like this are called Totalitarian. They exercise total control over the people. You can see what it was like to live in a state like this in Chapter 20.

The Great Depression

The conflict between Communism and Fascism was heightened during the period of high unemployment known as the Great Depression (Source 19.D). Factories shut down, banks closed and millions of people were thrown out of work.

Source 19.D Unemployment in Britain

1927	1928	1929	1930	1931	1932	1933	1934	1935
10.6%	11.2%	11.0%	14.6%	21.5%	22.5%	21.3%	17.7%	16.4%

The miseries of the Depression helped both Communists and Fascists to gain recruits. Sir Oswald Mosley's British Union of Fascists were anti-Semitic (prejudiced against the Jewish people). They wanted a government which would put Britain first, help industry and agriculture grow by spending money on new projects and banning trade unions. Similar parties were formed in other countries, such as the *Croix de Feu* (Cross of Fire), *Jeunesses Patriotes* (Young Patriots) and *Francistes* (*France Fascistes*) in France, the Iron Guard in Romania and the Arrow Cross in Hungary.

The League of Nations

The horrors of the First World War convinced many politicians that future disputes should be settled by discussion, not by war. All the countries signing the Paris Peace Treaties agreed to form a League of Nations (Source 19.E).

The League of Nations was the idea of the American President, Woodrow Wilson. However, the US Senate refused to allow America to join. They did not want to send American troops to fight in another war in Europe. The nations who did sign the Treaty agreed to obey a number of rules (Source 19.F).

Source 19.F The League of Nations

All the member-states agreed to:

- *co-operate more with each other*
- *work for peace between all nations*
- *obey international laws*
- *respect each other's boundaries*
- *reduce armaments (such as tanks, warplanes, warships, weapons and ammunition)*
- *protect each other's independence*
- *take action if another member was attacked*
- *settle disputes with each other peacefully through the League*
- *set up and accept the decisions of the Court of International Justice*
- *treat any country going to war in defiance of the League as a common enemy*
- *stop all trade and, if necessary, take military action against any country attacking a member-state.*

Each member of the League had one vote, whatever its size. The Assembly, which met once a year, decided the general policy of the League. The Council, a committee of four permanent members (UK,

This election poster helped the Labour Party to make a big impact in the 1920s. They formed a government for the first time in 1924 and again in 1929

19.8 Use the statistics in Source 19.D to draw a graph showing the effect of the Great Depression on Britain. AT1A/L3

19.9 How did the Labour Party use the Great War to put over their policies? AT3/L5

Source 19.E From *The Graphic*, 27 November 1920

The first session of the League of Nations at Geneva constitutes a great landmark in the history of the world. As yet it is incomplete. The United States is not represented, though it summoned the delegates to the present gathering. And Germany, Austria, Bulgaria and Turkey, of course, are as yet outside, while Russia in the shackles of Bolshevism, also has no voice in the discussions.

19.10 How does Source 19.E show that prospects for the League of Nations were not good? AT3/L5

France, Italy and Japan) and four other nations, decided the day-to-day problems. Germany became the fifth permanent member of the Council when she joined the League in 1926. When Hitler left the League in 1933, Germany's place was taken by the Soviet Union.

Even though the League failed to stop the Second World War, it did provide a place where countries could discuss common problems. There had been nothing like it before. It dealt successfully with the problem of what to do with refugees after the war. It supervised the way the former German and Turkish colonies were governed. It helped to solve a number of disputes between nations, such as a frontier dispute between Iraq and Turkey over an oilfield in 1924. Through the International Labour Organisation it helped to improve working conditions, pensions and wages throughout the world. The Health Organisation helped to combat the spread of epidemic diseases.

After 1930, however, the League of Nations seemed powerless to stop the big powers when they broke the rules. No decisive action was taken in 1931, for instance, when Japan invaded Manchuria. The League never recovered when Italy was allowed to march into Abyssinia (later Ethiopia), a member-state entitled, therefore, to the protection of the League. You can see what happened on page 141. The other nations refused to use force against Italy.

In addition to the work of the League, a number of peace conferences were held in the 1920s and 1930s to try to get a general agreement on disarmament (reducing stockpiles of weapons) and to get governments to pledge they would never go to war. One of the first of these was held at Locarno in 1925 (page 134). In 1928, over 60 countries signed the Kellogg-Briand Pact renouncing war (Source 19.G). However, each nation still had the right to defend itself against aggression. The American representative, Frank B. Kellogg, said that the Pact did not stop nations defending themselves if attacked.

19.11 Look at the cartoon strip. How did the German cartoonist view the Manchurian Crisis of 1931? What do the pictures tell you about his attitude to the League of Nations? AT1C/L6

19.12 Most wars begin with both sides claiming the other attacked first. Write one or two sentences to say what difference the Kellogg-Briand Pact might make in such a situation. AT1B ■

Source 19.G
From *The Times*, 28 August 1928

Short and simple as were the proceedings, the ceremony was most impressive, and those who were present will not easily forget the occasion when the representatives of the greatest Powers of the modern world 'solemnly declared', in the names of their peoples, that they condemned going to war to solve international disputes.

German cartoon depicting Japan invading Manchuria in 1931 and the reaction of the League of Nations ▶

20 The rise of Nazi Germany

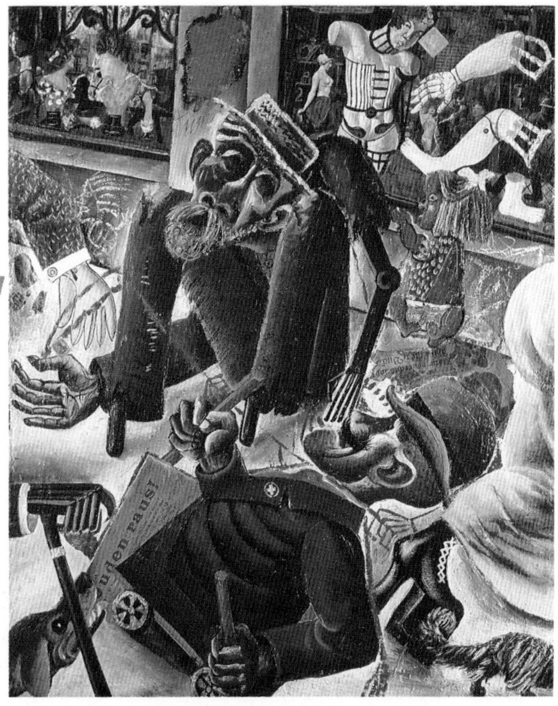
The German artist Otto ▶ Dix (see page 115) painted *Prager Strasse* (Prague Street) in Dresden in 1920

FOCUS

▶ *WHAT problems did Germany face after the war?* AT1B ■ AT1C ■
▶ *HOW and WHY did Hitler become dictator of Germany?* AT1B ■
▶ *HOW did Hitler change Germany?*
AT1A ■ AT1B ■ AT1C ■

20.1 Look at the painting *Prager Strasse*. What does the picture tell you about the attitude of Germany to its former soldiers in the years immediately after the First World War? AT3/L5
20.2 Who suffered most when the value of the German mark fell? Who gained? AT1B/L6
20.3 List the similarities between Hitler's Nazi Party and Mussolini's Fascists? AT1C/L5
20.4 How would a Nazi Party government have broken the terms of the Treaty of Versailles? AT3/L4
20.5 Source 20.C talks about the 'November Criminals'. Who were they? What does this tell you about the reasons for the Munich *Putsch*? AT3/L5

After the war

For months after the end of the First World War, Germany was a hotbed of revolution. Communists and right-wingers clashed in violent street battles. There was widespread unemployment. People condemned the Socialist Government for signing the Treaty of Versailles. They thought it was unjust to put all the blame on Germany for starting the war. They resented the loss of German territory. They objected to the huge amount of compensation which Germany had to pay to the Allied countries for war damage. When Germany fell behind with her payments at the end of 1922, the French and Belgian governments sent in troops to occupy the Ruhr coalfield. The German Army made no effort to stop them, much to the annoyance of right-wingers like Hitler. By November 1923, inflation was increasing at a colossal rate (Source 20.A). Postage stamps were valued in millions of marks. Workers used wheelbarrows to take away a week's pay.

Source 20.A Price of a loaf of bread: 1919–23

November:	1919	1920	1921	1922	1923
Marks	1	1.7	5.8	182	100 000 000 000

Inflation hit small businesses, farmers and the middle classes hard. Their savings had become worthless. It wasn't fair. Some of the people who lost their savings thought Hitler's Nazi Party might provide the remedy. Many factory workers, alarmed when their wages failed to keep pace with the cost of living, looked to Communism for a better deal.

The rise of the Nazi Party

In 1919, an ex-soldier called Adolf Hitler joined the German Workers' Party. His hot-blooded speeches against Jews and Communists soon helped him become its leader or *Führer*. It was known as the Nazi Party after the name was changed to *Nationalsozialistische Deutsche Arbeiter Partei* (National Socialist German Workers' Party) in 1920.

Hitler's Storm-Troopers stand behind barricades outside the War Ministry in Munich

Hitler in prison in 1924

Hitler's ideas and those of the Nazis were much the same as Italy's Fascists (see table on pages 128–9). The Nazis were very nationalistic. They always put Germany first. They wanted Germany and German-speaking Austria to unite. Germany needed more land for her growing population. Hitler planned a totalitarian system of government. Each person would work for the good of the State. Young people would serve as conscripts in the army. Newspapers would be censored. The Nazi Party would provide strong government.

The new party adopted the sign of the swastika as its symbol. It soon attracted many other ex-soldiers. Hitler copied Mussolini's Blackshirts and formed a private army of Nazi Storm-Troopers. This was the *Sturm Abteilung*, known usually as the SA. They were also called the Brownshirts because they wore jackboots and brown uniforms with swastika armbands. Several years later Hitler formed another private army, the *Schutz Staffeln* or SS. They wore black uniforms and owed their loyalty to Hitler personally as Führer.

The Munich *Putsch*

In November 1923, when inflation was at its peak, Hitler decided to act. He planned a rebellion (*putsch*) to seize power first in Munich and then in Berlin. It began on Thursday, 8 November 1923 (Source 20.B). On the following day, 9 November 1923, a strange assortment of Nazis marched through Munich led by the First World War commander, General Ludendorff (who had joined the Nazi Party), ex-Corporal Hitler and former air force pilot Hermann Göring.

Source 20.B From *The Daily Telegraph*

Munich: Thursday, 8 November 1923 *A nationalist demonstration was held in the great Burgerbrau beer cellars today. Herr Hitler, the Fascist leader entered the cellars with 600 men and announced the overthrow of the Bavarian government.*

Source 20.C Poster in Munich, 9 November 1923

Proclamation
to the German People!

The Government of the November
Criminals in Berlin has today
been deposed.
A provisional German
National Government has been formed.

Hitler and Ludendorff got no farther than the *Odeonplatz* in Munich when police barred their way. Shots rang out and sixteen Storm-Troopers and three policemen were killed. Several others were seriously wounded, including Göring. Hitler and Ludendorff were arrested and charged with treason. The *Putsch* was over. Hitler was tried and sentenced to five years imprisonment, but Ludendorff was acquitted. However, the Bavarian authorities felt much the same as Hitler and he spent only nine months in jail. During this time he wrote *Mein Kampf* ('My Struggle'), the book which later became compulsory reading for all Nazis.

dolf Hitler

Adolf Hitler was born in Austria in 1889 and died in 1945. After spending part of his youth in the slums of Vienna (where he blamed the Jews for his poverty), he went to live in Germany. When war broke out, he joined the German army, was gassed and won the Iron Cross for bravery. He was bitter and angry when Germany surrendered in 1918 and disgusted at the way ex-soldiers were treated. This is why the Nazi Party appealed to him. He soon made his mark there as a brilliant speaker with an extraordinary ability to charm and captivate an audience despite a rasping voice and mediocre appearance.

After the failure of the Munich Putsch in 1923 he reorganised the Party so successfully he was appointed Chancellor of Germany less than ten years later. In 1939 he led Germany into another world war and by 1942 ruled a vast empire. It stretched from Western France to the outskirts of Moscow and from Northern Norway to Southern Greece.

The Big City- *Otto Dix painted this Berlin night-club in about 1927*

20.6 What does the painting *The Big City* tell you about Berlin in 1927? AT3/L5

20.7 What was different about the way in which Germany agreed to the Treaty of Locarno compared with Versailles in 1919? AT1B/L5

Germany recovers

On his release from prison in December 1924, Hitler found that Germany had changed. American banks were helping Germany recover with large loans of money. Factories were booming. People were spending money and enjoying themselves. Most workers had a job at last. There was much less distress and poverty. The Nazi Party no longer had the same appeal.

When Germany signed the Treaty of Locarno in 1925, her position in Europe further improved (Source 20.D). Much to Hitler's disgust, Germany voluntarily gave up claims to the territories lost at Versailles and promised not to send troops into the Rhineland. Soon afterwards, Germany was admitted to the League of Nations. With the country now prospering and enjoying better relations with the other European powers, Germany was well on the road to recovery.

Women! Millions of men without work. Millions of children without food. Vote Adolf Hitler!

20.8 Why did Frau Speer vote for Hitler? What reasons for voting for Hitler are given by the election posters? Write a paragraph explaining what they tell us about Germany in the early 1930s. AT3/L6

Source 20.D From *The Times*, 17 October 1925

The light of a new dawn is at last breaking upon the world. The war is over at last. Under British guarantee, France and Germany promise not to make war against each other.

The Great Depression

In October 1929, however, the value of American shares fell sharply during the Wall Street Crash. Germany was badly hit by the Great Depression which followed (page 130). American banks now needed the money they had loaned to Germany. People in Germany spent less. German factories could no longer sell all the goods they produced. Many works shut down and unemployment rose sharply (see also Source 20.M on page 137). There were 1.7 million Germans out of work in 1928, 3.1 million in 1930, 4.5 million in 1931 and 5.6 million in 1932. Newsreel film shows poor people in Germany sifting through slag heaps in search of coal. Queues of people lined up for free soup. Banks failed. What was to be done?

Work, freedom and bread! Vote National Socialist!

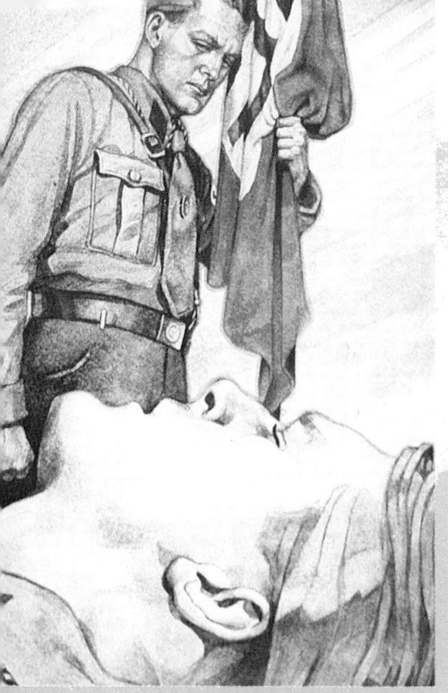

A Nazi painting of an SA man killed in street fighting with the Communists

Electing the Nazis

The Communists and National Socialists both had drastic solutions to offer. They fought in the streets and broke up each other's meetings as they tried to win the votes of the German people in the elections to the Reichstag, the German Parliament. You can see from the pictures and sources on these pages how the Nazis persuaded the German people to vote for them.

Source 20.E *Manchester Guardian*, 30 March 1932

Although the Nazis, like the Reichsbanner [the Socialist equivalent of the SA], *are forbidden to wear uniforms in Germany, they go about Brunswick as they do in any other city, in their brown uniforms – a brown shirt, brown riding breeches and leggings. If there is any trouble, the SA lorry dashes to the spot, the storm troops leap down. Blows from cudgels, knives, knuckle dusters are dealt out right and left. Heads are cut open. Arms raised in self defence are broken or bruised and crouching backs or shoulders are beaten black and blue. Sometimes shots are fired and knives are drawn. In a few moments all is over. The Nazis scramble back into their lorry and are off.*

Source 20.F The Nazi Election Campaign in July 1932

As I walked through the Berlin streets, the Party flag was everywhere in evidence. Huge posters and Nazi slogans screamed forth messages about honour and duty, social justice, bread, liberty, and the beauty of sacrifice – all showing the remarkable skill with which Hitler had been softening up the masses.

Source 20.G By Albert Speer, a Nazi Minister

It must have been during these months [1930–31] *that my mother saw an SA parade in the streets of Heidelberg. The sight of discipline in a time of chaos, the impression of energy in an atmosphere of universal hopelessness, seem to have won her over. At any rate, without ever having heard a speech or read a pamphlet, she joined the party.*

At first progress was slow (Source 20.H). Only 12 Nazis were elected to the Reichstag in 1928 when Germany was doing well. In 1930, however, they gained 6 million votes and won 107 seats to become the second largest party. Meanwhile, the German Government seemed powerless to do anything to relieve the country's misery. Two years later (July 1932), as unemployment continued to rise sharply, the Nazis became the largest party in the Reichstag with 230 out of the 608 seats. It was not an overall majority but it was enough to ensure that Hitler could block the work of a non-Nazi government. After yet another election in November 1932, President Hindenburg had little choice. He invited Hitler to become the new German Chancellor (Prime Minister) on 30 January 1933.

Source 20.H Elections to the Reichstag

Percentage of German people voting for each party

	20 May 1928	14 Sept 1930	13 July 1932	6 Nov 1932	5 March 1933
National Socialists	2.6%	18.3%	37.3%	33.1%	43.9%
Socialists	29.8%	24.5%	21.6%	20.4%	18.3%
Communists	10.6%	13.1%	14.5%	16.9%	12.3%
All other Parties	57.0%	44.1%	26.6%	29.6%	25.5%

20.9 Use Source 20.H and Source 20.M on page 137 to draw a graph showing how the Nazi share of the vote grew with the rise in unemployment. AT1A/L5 AT3/L6

20.10 What did the Nazi artist who drew the picture of the two SA men want people who saw it to feel? In what ways is it biased? AT1C ■ AT2/L5

20.11 What use is a propaganda picture like this when studying history? AT2 ■

20.12 Use the Sources to explain how and why the National Socialists became the largest party in the Reichstag. AT3/L6

Hitler as Chancellor

On 4 February 1933, Hitler held a secret meeting with top army officers and told them of his plans (Source 20.I).

Source 20.I Hitler's policy: 4 February 1933

- *Get rid of Communism for good.*
- *Win over the youth of the nation.*
- *Rebuild the armed forces.*
- *Bring back conscription.*
- *Abolish elections to the Reichstag.*
- *Fight against the Treaty of Versailles.*

'The Führer speaks' from a Nazi cigarette-card album published in 1933

Hitler called a new election for March, telling colleagues it would be the last. The new Reichstag would provide the two- thirds majority he needed under German law to pass an Enabling Act giving him the powers of a dictator. Despite his control of German radio and the press, over 56 per cent of the people voted against him (Source 20.H). When the Reichstag met after the election, Socialist representatives said they were met by the SA and SS (Source 20.J).
Not surprisingly, 153 Reichstag members voted with the Nazis. They soon had cause for regret. On 14 July 1933, Hitler banned all political parties other than the Nazi Party and sent many Socialists and Communists to concentration camps.

Source 20.J The Enabling Act

We were received with wild choruses: 'We want the Enabling Act!' Youths with swastikas on their chests eyed us insolently, blocked our way, in fact made us run the gauntlet, calling us names like 'Centre pig', 'Marxist sow'. The place was crawling with armed SA and SS men. They surrounded us in a semicircle along the walls of the hall, hissed loudly and murmured: 'Shut up!', 'Traitors!', 'You'll be strung up today.'

Hitler as dictator

Concentration camps had been set up to 're-educate' enemies of the State. The first prisoners were Communists and Socialists as well as Jews. Their heads were closely shaven and they lived in tightly-packed dormitory blocks under a system of rigid discipline (Source 20.K).

Prisoners at Dachau in 1938

Dachau Concentration Camp, near Munich, is a reminder of the evils of Nazi rule ▼

Source 20.K
Dachau in the 1930s

Physical punishment consisted of whipping, frequent kicking (abdomen or groin), slaps in the face, shooting, or wounding with the bayonet. Prisoners were forced to stare for hours into glaring lights, to kneel for hours, and so on. A Communist worker who by then had been at Dachau for four years spoke to me out of his rich experience: 'Listen you, make up your mind. Do you want to live or do you want to die? And whenever you have a minute, don't blabber, read by yourself, or flop down and sleep.'

20.13 How was a Nazi concentration camp different from an ordinary prison?
AT1C/L5

20.14 Write down the reasons which might lead you to question whether Sources 20.J and 20.K provide reliable evidence of Nazi intimidation and brutality?
AT1C/L7 AT2/L7 AT3/L7

Hitler starting the work on a new motorway (autobahn) *in 1933*

20.15 Draw a graph to show the unemployment figures in Source 20.M. Compare it with the graph you drew for Britain (page 130). Write down reasons for the differences you notice.
AT1A ■

Hitler was just as ruthless with his own party. On 29 June 1934, the 'Night of the Long Knives', he accused the SA of treachery and used the SS to round up and shoot many of its leaders including the SA chief, Ernst Röhm, one of his oldest friends and a hero of the Munich *Putsch.*

The Nazis also began a systematic persecution of the Jews. Shop windows were smashed, synagogues were destroyed, people were beaten up in the street and Jewish children were ridiculed at school. Cartoonists drew grotesque pictures of Jewish money-lenders, to whip up hatred. '*Achtung! Juden!* ('Warning! Jews!') was painted across shop windows. Books were burned and the works of Jewish writers and composers banned. You can read more about this in Chapter 24.

Controlling the workers

Hitler made sure that the factory workers were well looked after. They were not allowed to strike, trade unions were banned and many trade union leaders were sent to concentration camps. But in return, the German Labour Front which took their place provided many benefits, such as holidays with pay and better working conditions. Slogans – 'Fight against noise!' and 'Clean workers in a clean works!' – put pressure on factory owners to improve working conditions. The 'Strength Through Joy' organisation helped workers to go on sea cruises and holidays abroad. It built health resorts and spas, ran coach tours, provided cheap sporting facilities and even manufactured the Volkswagen (the 'People's car'). Young men served six months in the Labour Service Corps (Source 20.L), often working in the fields 'stripped to the waist in all weathers.'

Source 20.L The Labour Service Corps at Nuremberg

6 September 1934 *Hitler sprang his* Arbeitsdienst, *his Labour Service Corps, on the public for the first time today. It turned out to be a highly trained, semi-military group of fanatical Nazi youths. Standing there in the early morning sunlight which sparkled on their shiny spades, fifty thousand of them, with the first thousand bared above the waist, suddenly made the German spectators go mad with joy when, without warning, they broke into a perfect goose-step. Spontaneously they jumped up and shouted their applause. Then the Labour Service Corps formed an immense chorus and chanted:* 'We want one Leader! Nothing for us! Everything for Germany! Heil Hitler!'

Large-scale building projects, such as motorways and new government buildings, as well as the manufacture of tanks, aeroplanes and warships (pages 140–1), provided hundreds of thousands of new jobs. This was at a time of high unemployment in other parts of the world. You can see the effects of Hitler's policies in Source 20.M. For workers who had at last found a job it was easy to ignore the fact that Germany was now a police state.

Source 20.M Unemployment in Germany

1928	1929	1930	1931	1932	1933	1934	1935	1936	1937	1938
8.4%	13.1%	15.3%	23.3%	30.1%	26.3%	14.9%	11.6%	8.3%	4.6%	2.1%

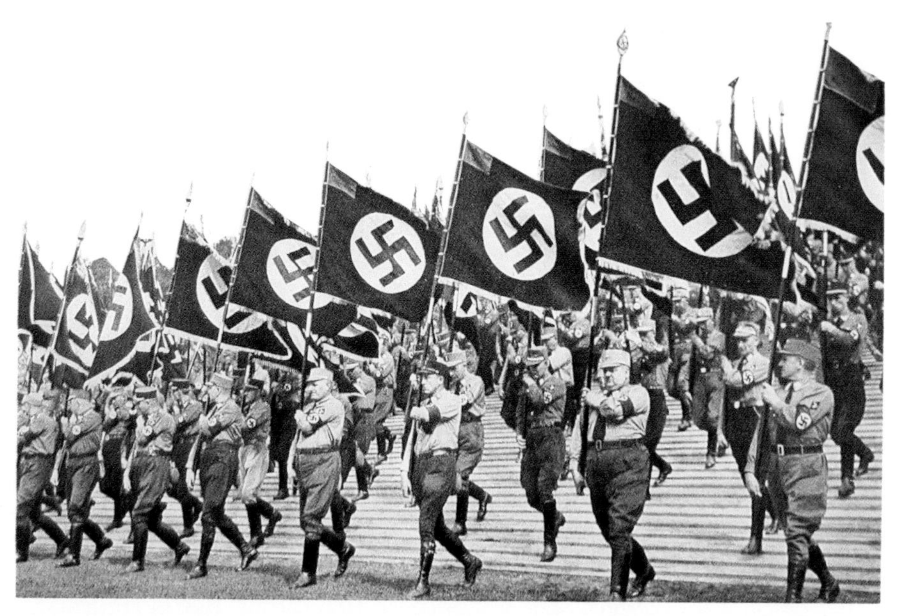

Flags and elaborate standards featuring the Swastika were always in evidence at Nazi Party rallies

'Hitler Girls' greet the Führer at Odenwald in Germany in 1932

Tightening Hitler's grip on Germany

The Nazis used education and youth training to ensure the next generation was Nazi through and through (Sources 20.N and 20.O). Hitler believed the German people could be divided into two classes. The pure-bred Germans, tall and blonde, were the Aryans. They were the 'Master Race'. People who were not Aryans, such as the Jews, were inferior and to be treated as slaves. This is why children were taught to hate and despise the Jews. Children were brought up to have complete faith in Hitler. They were trained to be obedient to the State. One-sided education like this is called indoctrination.

Source 20.N From a book published in 1937

At the age of ten, each little boy gets a brown shirt with the pfennigs he has saved. Henceforth he belongs to the Young Folk. The little girl will join the Union of German Maidens, and is supposed to be dressed in a uniform of white blouse and blue skirt. After four years of this, the boy of fourteen joins the Hitler Youth. When grown up, the boy goes to camp for six months' compulsory labour service, for the most part working stripped to the waist, in the fields. This is followed by two years' service in the army as a conscript.

Source 20.O Hitler Worship in Berlin

That day tens of thousands of young men and women, uniformly dressed in brown or white, lined the terraces of the huge Olympic Stadium in Berlin. Every now and then their movements, combined with the colour of their clothes, spelled out in living brown and white letters, slogans glorifying Hitler, such as 'Live and die for our Führer'. Patriotic hymns rose like anthems.

The leader of the Youth, its High Priest, Baldur von Schirach, then got up. In simple and direct words he told them of the sanctity of their mission. Every neck was stretched, every eye shone. One felt that these young people were burning with religious zeal. Von Schirach had compared the Führer to the Messiah. When Hitler appeared, late as usual, a sort of hysteria took hold of the crowd. The first shouts which they let out before they declared their faith were like sobs.

20.16 How do the photographs of the 'Hitler Girls' and the SA men back up what you can find out from the written sources? AT3/L6

20.17 Pick out all the words in Source 20.O which are connected in any way with religion. Why do you think the author used these words? What do they tell you about Hitler's Germany? AT1C ■

20.18 Most of the black and white photographs in this chapter were taken by Nazi photographers. How does this make a difference to their value as a record of Nazi Germany? AT2 ■

20.19 Why do you think Hitler was so successful in persuading the German people to accept the Nazi Party? Write a reasoned account, giving examples of Nazi propaganda methods. AT1B ■

20.20 Look at Source 20.P. Why do you think some British politicians opposed to Communism ignored the brutality of the Nazi regime in the 1930s? Did they have any excuse? AT1C ■

20.21 What does the painting tell you about a German town just before the outbreak of war in 1939? AT3/L5

20.22 Name some of the ways in which Hitler's Germany differed from Britain today. AT1A ■ AT1C ■

Propaganda

Propaganda played a big part in tightening Hitler's grip on Germany. The Reichminister responsible, Dr Josef Goebbels, was an expert. He made sure the German people only heard praise for the regime, never criticism. They were only told the news the Nazis wanted them to hear. Goebbels used posters, newspapers, pamphlets, books, films and radio to whip up support for the Nazis. 'If you tell a lie,' he once said, 'tell a big lie. If you tell a big lie often enough people will believe it.' Nazi propaganda urged everyone to tune in to the State-controlled radio. 'All Germany listens to the Führer' was the message on the posters.

SA men 'in conversation with the Führer'

At the Nuremberg rallies in September each year, there were impressive parades (Source 20.L). Thumping marches, patriotic songs, torchlight processions and goose-stepping soldiers carrying giant swastikas thrilled the German crowds. They shouted the slogans of the Nazi Party, such as 'Ein Volk, ein Reich, ein Führer!' ('One People, One Country, One Leader!').

Hitler Youth on the march

Despite the fact that many leading Jewish scientists and musicians had already fled from Germany, foreign leaders were impressed by the Nazis. They ignored the journalists, clergy, opposition leaders, Communists, and trade unionists who had been sent to concentration camps. A Conservative MP called Sir Henry Channon went to Berlin in 1936 and said of his first glimpse of Hitler, 'I was more excited than when I met Mussolini'. In December 1937 Channon met a leading Government minister called Lord Halifax (Source 20.P).

Source 20.P By Sir Henry Channon, MP

5 December 1937: *I had a long conversation with Lord Halifax about Germany and his recent visit. He told me he liked all the Nazi leaders, even Goebbels, and he was much impressed, interested and amused by the visit. He thinks the regime absolutely fantastic, perhaps even too fantastic to be taken seriously.*

This painting shows a small German town festooned with flags and banners to celebrate Hitler's 50th birthday on 20 April 1939

Time Line

1919 Treaty of Versailles

1920 Nazi Party founded

1923 Munich Putsch

1928 Low unemployment; Nazis win 12 seats in Reichstag

1930 3 million unemployed; Nazis win 107 seats in Reichstag

1932 6 million unemployed; Nazis win 230 seats in Reichstag

1933 Hitler becomes Chancellor; Germany becomes a one-party state; Hitler is its Führer

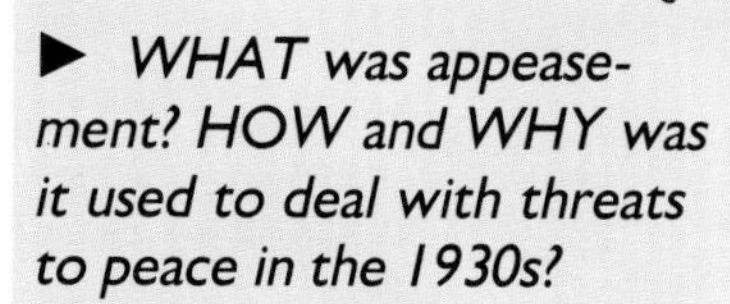

21 The march to War

This cartoon by Low shows the British Foreign Secretary, Anthony Eden, trying to stop soldiers led by Hitler and Mussolini

▶ *WHAT was appeasement? HOW and WHY was it used to deal with threats to peace in the 1930s?* AT1B ■ AT1C ■

▶ *WHAT were the short and long-term causes of the Second World War?* AT1B ■

21.1 Use the cartoon by Low to explain what was meant by appeasement. AT3/L5

21.2 How was Germany depicted in the Soviet poster? AT3/L3

21.3 What reasons help to explain why Hitler was allowed to break the Treaty of Versailles when he rearmed the German armed forces? AT1B ■

21.4 Write one or two sentences to say why each of these was an example of appeasement:
(a) the Anglo-German Naval Agreement.
(b) Sir Henry Channon's attitude to the Nazis (Source 21.A).
(c) Anthony Eden's attitude to the Abyssinian Crisis. AT1B/L5

Appeasement

In the 1930s, the policy of most Western politicians was one of appeasement. This means trying to stop a war by giving way on some points in the hope that this will be enough to satisfy the country threatening military action. British and French politicians did not want to repeat the mistakes of 1914, when war began because the statesmen did not talk to each other first. They could not forget friends killed in the trenches. Britain's Anthony Eden told the League of Nations there is 'no dispute between nations that cannot be settled by peaceful means'. He made the mistake of thinking that Hitler or Mussolini were reasonable men. As you have seen, Hitler was determined to tear up the Treaty of Versailles (Source 20.l). Britain and France let him get away with it.

One reason why they did so was their fear of Russian Communism. Hitler was a tyrant but so too was Stalin. During the Great Depression there were real fears in both Britain and France that demonstrations by unemployed or striking workers could lead to a repeat of the Russian Revolution. The Russians made no secret of wanting to start Communist revolutions in other countries (page 129).

Mussolini and Hitler were both anti-Communist. Many important people in Britain and France found it easy to excuse the evils of Fascism for this reason. For instance, Harold Nicolson described the views of his fellow MP, Sir Henry Channon in September 1936 (Source 21.A).

Source 21.A

At luncheon we discuss the Nazis. The Channons think we should let gallant little Germany glut her fill of the Reds in the East and keep France quiet while she does so. Otherwise we shall have not only Reds in the West but bombs in London, Kelvedon [where the Channons had a country house] and Southend.

German rearmament

Under the terms of the Treaty of Versailles (page 127), Germany had been restricted to a small army and navy and prevented from building submarines or an air force. One of Hitler's first actions, therefore, was to reverse this. Germany could not become strong without a strong

Source 21.B Hitler speaking about the Bolsheviks

We are only safe against the Bolsheviks if we have armaments which they respect. Hundreds of my party comrades have been murdered by Bolsheviks. German soldiers and civilians have fallen in the fight against Bolshevik risings.

Hitler and Mussolini took great pride in their armed forces. Both thought of themselves as inspired military leaders and usually wore military uniforms when seen in public

Source 21.C Anthony Eden at the League of Nations

I cannot believe that, in present world conditions, military action could be considered a possibility.

army. He made no secret of this. He withdrew from the League of Nations in 1933 and left the conference on disarmament. He told Göring to create a German Air Force (*Luftwaffe*) and in March 1935 said he was going to form an army of half a million men. Nine days later Sir John Simon and Anthony Eden went to Berlin to see him. Hitler told them his actions were aimed at the Soviet Union, not the West (Source 21.B).

Hitler said he wanted a navy thirty-five per cent the size of the Royal Navy. Three months later Britain and Germany signed the Anglo-German Naval Agreement which allowed this. France protested in vain that she should have been consulted, since Britain was allowing Germany to break the terms of the Treaty of Versailles.

Abyssinia

Later the same year (1935), Mussolini invaded Abyssinia (Ethiopia). He was determined to put right the wrong done to Italy in 1919 when the Allies refused to give her an African colony. However, times had changed since the 'Scramble for Africa' in the 1880s (page 60). Abyssinia had been a member of the League of Nations since 1923.

For months, the great powers knew what Mussolini was planning to do. He even sent his troop-ships carrying soldiers through the British-controlled Suez Canal. The League of Nations condemned Mussolini and half-heartedly agreed to ban trade with Italy. Mussolini later told Hitler that if oil had been banned as well he would have had to call off the invasion. Despite the bravery of the Abyssinian soldiers, the result was never in doubt. But when the Ethiopian Emperor Haile Selassie asked the League of Nations to honour its pledges (Source 19.F), Britain's Foreign Secretary, Anthony Eden, gave him his reply (Source 21.C).

The Abyssinian Crisis had two main effects. Firstly, the League played little part in subsequent talks held to avert war. Secondly, it pulled Mussolini closer to Hitler. On 21 October 1936, Italy signed a pact with Germany. Mussolini said the link between Berlin and Rome was an axis (line) around which all peaceful states in Europe could gather. Later the same year, Germany signed another treaty with Japan to stop the spread of Communism. Mussolini signed this treaty as well. The German Foreign Minister said Germany and Italy would defeat Communism in Europe. Japan would do the same in the Far East.

This Soviet poster was painted in 1935. The Russian slogan warned Hitler that if he put his 'pig's snout into Russia's back garden', he would meet overwhelming resistance ▶

The Rhineland

On 8 March 1936, Hitler broke the Treaty of Versailles again when he sent soldiers into the Rhineland. His top generals warned him this would mean war with France, but Hitler proved them wrong. The French did nothing apart from appealing to the League of Nations. Afterwards, Hitler told his interpreter, Dr Paul Schmidt, of his fears (Source 21.D)

German troops marching into Austria

Source 21.D

The forty-eight hours after the march into the Rhineland were the most nerve-racking in my life. If the French had then marched into the Rhineland, we would have had to withdraw with our tails between our legs, for the military resources at our disposal would have been wholly inadequate for even a moderate resistance.

Guernica *was painted by Pablo Picasso after the Spanish town of that name was destroyed by German bombers in April 1937*

Bit by bit, Hitler was eating away at the Treaty of Versailles. But many people still gave him the benefit of the doubt. When the Olympic Games were held in Berlin in August 1936, an American journalist said, 'I'm afraid the Nazis have succeeded with their propaganda'. Thousands of visitors went away impressed. The *JEWS NOT WELCOME* signs had disappeared, the streets were clean and the trains ran on time.

Spanish Civil War

But another crisis had already begun. In July 1936, the Fascist General Francisco Franco led an army revolt against the elected left-wing Republican government of Spain. Franco's supporters, many of them priests, landowners, shopkeepers and factory owners, were afraid that Spain would soon turn Communist. The civil war which followed lasted nearly three years and ended with the deaths of over half a million Spaniards and 20 000 foreign volunteers. Left- wingers from Europe and North America fought with Republicans. Right-wingers fought for the Fascists. A substantial number of these 'volunteers' were German and Italian soldiers. Mussolini and Hitler supplied Franco with weapons, ammunition and aircraft. Stalin supplied Russian arms, weapons and troops to the Republicans. This interference in Spain's civil war caused an outcry but there was little the other powers could do to stop it.

21.5 Use Source 21.D to help explain why Hitler marched his troops into the Rhineland in 1936. AT3/L5

21.6 Use Picasso's painting and the written sources to write a paragraph saying why the bombing of Guernica made such an impression on the world in 1937. AT3/L6

21.7 What part did the Spanish Civil War play in the lead-up to the Second World War? AT1B ■

21.8 What was the point of the *The Statue of Freiheit* cartoon? What was the cartoonist's attitude to the Nazis? AT1C/L6

21.9 What reliable evidence is there that the Austrians did, or did not, want to unite with Hitler's Germany? AT2 ■ AT3/L7

In some ways the war was a rehearsal for the Second World War to come. Hitler and Mussolini tried out new weapons. When German bombers destroyed the town of Guernica in northern Spain, people were horrified (Sources 21.E and 21.F).

Source 21.E Newspaper headlines, April 1937

FRANCO WIPES OUT TOWN:
800 VICTIMS OF BARBARIC AIR RAID

Fugitives Fall Under Bullets Of Swooping Rebel Planes

AIR RAID WIPES OUT BASQUE TOWN – RELAYS OF BOMBERS

THE TRAGEDY OF GUERNICA – Town destroyed in air attack

PRIEST BLESSES CITY AS BOMBS FALL

Source 21.F By Noel Monks in the *Daily Express*

I walked this evening through the still-burning town. Hundreds of bodies had been found in the debris. Most were charred beyond recognition. At least two hundred others were riddled with machine-gun bullets as they fled to the hills. I stood beside the smouldering Red Cross hospital of Josefinas. The bodies of forty-two wounded soldiers and ten nurses lay buried in the wreckage. They never had a chance. The wounded were killed in their beds, the nurses were killed on duty.

The war came to an end in March 1939 with the surrender of Madrid. Many Republicans were executed in the reprisals which followed. Franco was now the third Fascist dictator in Europe. He owed his victory partly to the support he got from Germany and Italy. Despite this, he did not repay Hitler and Mussolini by declaring war on Britain and France in 1939 or 1940. Spain remained neutral throughout the war.

Anschluss

In the Spring of 1938, Hitler united Germany with German-speaking Austria. *Anschluss* (see page 127) had been forbidden at Versailles, so Hitler made it look as if the desire for union came from Austria rather than from Germany. The Austrian Chancellor, Kurt von Schuschnigg, was forced to admit Nazis into his government. In March, when he tried to hold a referendum for Austrians to vote on whether they wanted to be independent or not, Hitler threatened an invasion. Schuschnigg called off the referendum and resigned. The Austrian Nazi leader, Arthur Seyss-Inquart, took his place and invited the German Army to enter Austria in order 'to help preserve the peace'. At dawn, on 12 March 1938, German troops crossed the border (Source 21.G).

Source 21.G From a British book published in 1938

Cheers greeted German troops as they arrived over the frontier and came into Austrian towns. Swastikas hung from windows. Crowds gave the Nazi salute. Buttonholes, not bullets, greeted the marching men as they penetrated further into the land where Hitler was born.

On 13 March 1938, Seyss-Inquart announced that Austria was now a province of Germany's Third Reich. Three days later Hitler drove through Vienna with crowds trying to break through the police cordons. According to journalists, they shouted, 'We want to see our Führer! Hitler! Hitler!' A British reporter said the older men and women had 'tears of joy in their eyes.' A month later, ninety-nine per cent of Austrians entitled to vote said 'Yes' to *Anschluss*. By then the persecution of Austria's Jews had already begun.

The Statue of Freiheit, *was published in* Punch *on 6 April 1938.* Freiheit *is the German word for freedom or liberty*

The Munich Crisis

When the old Austro-Hungarian Empire broke up in 1918, the Sudetenland, where three million Germans were living, became part of Czechoslovakia. Urged on by local Nazis, the people of the area claimed with some justice that they did not get a fair deal from the Czechs. They wanted to join Germany instead. When Hitler encouraged them, the Czechs stationed troops in the region in May 1938. Alarm bells rang again in Paris and London. France and Britain both warned Hitler that Czechoslovakia had their full support. When the Soviet Union proposed a military alliance to guarantee Czech freedom, however, neither the British nor the French would support the idea. At that time (1938) thousands of so-called 'enemies of the State' were being executed in Moscow. The Soviet Union was hardly the defender of liberty and freedom.

Hitler drives into the Sudetenland in October 1938

This cartoon 'Whose turn next?' *was published in* Punch *on 18 May 1938*

In August and early September, Hitler moved troops close to the Czech border and made a violent speech issuing threats. People began to think there could be a major war since Britain and France had both made their position clear. This is why Neville Chamberlain, the British Prime Minister, went to Germany. But Hitler wouldn't listen. The Czechs agreed to meet many of Hitler's demands, but it was still not enough for the Führer who seemed intent on war.

On Monday, 26 September 1938, Hitler made yet another vicious attack on the Czech leaders before a vast crowd of 30 000 people. He threatened an invasion by the following Monday if his demands were not met (Source 21.H).

Source 21.H
Adolf Hitler: Monday, 26 September 1938

Our patience is at an end. Benes [the Czech President] *will have to surrender this territory to us on October 1. It is the last territorial claim which I have to make in Europe, but it is the claim from which I do not recede and which I shall fulfil, God willing.*

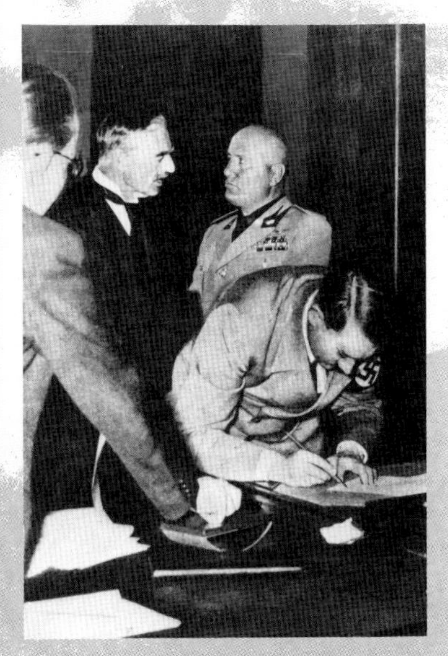

Hitler signs the Munich Peace Treaty

21.10 What does the cartoon 'Whose turn next?' tell you about British attitudes to Hitler in May 1938?
AT1C/L6 AT3/L5

21.11 Write a paragraph describing the different attitudes to the Munich agreement illustrated in Sources 21.L and 21.M. How do you account for the differences?
AT1C ■

21.12 How do Sources 21.J and 21.K differ in saying how the famous 'piece of paper' came to be written?
AT2/L5

21.13 Source 21.J was written two days after the talks by one of the two people taking part. Source 21.K was published thirteen years later by the interpreter, the only person to understand fully what was said by both men. Is it possible to say which account of the meeting is correct?
AT2 ■ AT3 ■

Source 21.L *The New York Times*

Let no man say too high a price has been paid for peace in Europe until he has searched his soul and found himself willing to risk in war the lives of those who are nearest and dearest to him.

By this time, Czech and German troops were both ready for war. The French, too, had stationed soldiers along the German border and the Royal Navy was on full alert. The atmosphere in Europe was electric. Most people feared the worse. Air-raid shelters were dug in London's parks. Gas masks were issued. Children were even evacuated from London.

At this late stage, just as most people had given up hope, Mussolini persuaded Hitler to call a last-minute conference in Munich to see if a peaceful solution could be found. Chamberlain and his supporters were delighted. Chamberlain flew to Munich and the four great powers – Britain, France, Italy and Germany – agreed that the Sudetenland should become German. When Chamberlain returned to London he was acclaimed as a hero. 'I believe it is peace for our time' he said, and waved a piece of paper at the crowd cheering him at the airport. You can find out more about that 'piece of paper' in Sources 21.I, 21.J and 21.K. As you can see from Sources 21.L and 21.M, reactions to the Munich agreement were mixed.

Source 21.I Neville Chamberlain, 30 September 1938

This morning I had another talk with the German Chancellor, Herr Hitler. And here is the paper which bears his name upon it as well as mine. We regard the agreement signed last night, and the Anglo-German Naval Agreement, as symbolic of the desire of our two peoples never to go to war with one another again.

Source 21.J Letter by Neville Chamberlain, 2 October 1938

I asked Hitler about 1 in the morning whether he would care to see me for another talk. He jumped at the idea. I had a very friendly and pleasant talk. At the end I pulled out the declaration, which I had prepared beforehand, and asked if he would sign it. As the interpreter translated the words into German, Hitler frequently said 'Yes, Yes' and at the end 'Yes, I will certainly sign it.'

Source 21.K Account of the meeting by Hitler's interpreter, Dr Paul Schmidt, in 1951

Hitler looked pale and moody. He listened absent- mindedly to Chamberlain's remarks, contributing little to the conversation. Towards the end Chamberlain drew the famous Declaration from his pocket. Slowly, emphasising each word, I translated this statement to Hitler. I did not share Chamberlain's impression, expressed in a private letter of his now published, that Hitler eagerly assented to this declaration. My own feeling was that he agreed to the wording with a certain reluctance, and I believe he signed only to please Chamberlain.

Source 21.M A Cockney bus conductor

It'll have the whole world against us now. Who'll trust us? We helped make it a country and then Chamberlain comes along and wants to buy that swine off. There'll be a war sooner or later, then there'll be nobody to help us.

The expansion of Hitler's Germany by October 1939

Poland

The Munich Crisis had two main effects. On the one hand it encouraged both Hitler and Stalin to think that neither Britain nor France was prepared to go to war to defend Europe's frontiers. On the other hand, it finally convinced the British and French governments that despite all the talk of 'peace in our time' they might soon have to go to war in earnest. This is why the British Government put extra money and effort into strengthening its armed forces. Free air-raid shelters were issued to many Londoners in February 1939. In March, Britain and France both made pledges to defend Poland against a German invasion. In April, the British Government announced plans to conscript young men into the armed forces.

The reason for these warlike moves was simply the realisation, at last, that Hitler intended to dominate Europe. In March 1939, the jackbooted soldiers of the German Army had marched into Prague, the Czech capital, after Goebbels prepared the way with anti-Czech propaganda, such as the newspaper headline 'Bloody Terror of the Czechs'. The takeover of Czechoslovakia was different from Hitler's other invasions. It was the first time that German troops had marched into non-German territory. There was no longer the excuse that the Treaty of Versailles had been unfair to Germany.

Hitler then claimed the right to acquire part of Poland in order to link Germany with East Prussia and the free port of Danzig which also had a Nazi government. Talks were held between Britain, France and the Soviet Union with a view to forming an alliance against Hitler. But all sides were reluctant to go ahead. When war loomed closer in August, it was too late. The Soviet Union had found another ally.

Stalin and Hitler drawn by a cartoonist after the signing of the Soviet- German Non-Aggression Pact

21.14 What evidence is there that Hitler did not expect Britain to go to war? AT3/L5
21.15 Do you think this is likely to be a reliable source of evidence? AT3/L7
21.16 Make a list of the long-term causes of the Second World War. AT1B/L5
21.17 What were the short-term causes of the war? AT1B/L5
21.18 Compare the map of Europe with the map on page 127? How had Hitler changed the boundaries of Europe by the end of September 1939? AT1A ■

A crowd in Munich listening to Hitler announcing the invasion of Poland in a radio broadcast, 1 September 1939

The Soviet-German Non-Aggression Pact

On 23 August the world was shocked to hear that the Soviet Union and Germany had signed a non-aggression pact. This meant that they both agreed not to attack each other in the event of war. In other words, the Communist, Joseph Stalin, was telling the world that the Nazi leader, Adolf Hitler, his sworn enemy, could invade Poland without fear of retaliation from the Red Army. What the world was not told, however, was that both powers had signed a secret agreement to divide Poland in two.

Feverish attempts were made in both Paris and London to avert a war but without success. On Friday, 1 September 1939, German troops invaded Poland. Using tanks and warplanes they swept through the Polish defences and advanced towards Warsaw.

Two days later, on Sunday, 3 September 1939, Hitler's interpreter, Dr Paul Schmidt, was told to take Ribbentrop's place at the German Foreign Office in Berlin. An important document was being delivered by the British ambassador. It was an ultimatum. It gave Hitler just two hours to agree to withdraw his troops from Poland. You can see what happened next in Sources 21.N and 21.O.

France declared war later the same day. The Second World War had begun.

Time Line

1917 Bolshevik Revolution

1918 End of First World War

1919 Treaty of Versailles

1920 League of Nations founded

1922 Mussolini in power in Italy

1925 Treaty of Locarno

1928 Kellogg-Briand Pact

1931 Japanese attack Manchuria

1933 Hitler becomes German dictator; German rearmament begins

1935 Anglo-German Naval Agreement; Italy invades Abyssinia

1936 Spanish Civil War; Hitler marches troops into Rhineland

1937 Guernica bombed by Nazi planes

1938 *Anschluss*; Munich Crisis

1939 Czechoslovakia taken over by Hitler; Soviet-German Pact; invasion of Poland; start of Second World War

Source 21.N By Dr Paul Schmidt, Hitler's interpreter

Berlin: 9.00 a.m., 3 September 1939 *I took the ultimatum to the Chancellery, where everyone was anxiously awaiting me. When I entered the next room Hitler was sitting at his desk and Ribbentrop* [the German Foreign Minister] *stood by the window. Both looked up expectantly as I came in. I stopped at some distance from Hitler's desk, and then slowly translated the British Government's ultimatum. When I finished there was complete silence.*

Hitler sat immobile, gazing before him. He was not at a loss, as was afterwards stated, nor did he rage as others allege. He sat completely silent and unmoving.

After an interval which seemed an age, he turned to Ribbentrop, who had remained standing by the window. 'What now?' asked Hitler with a savage look, as though implying that his Foreign Minister had misled him about England's probable reaction.

Source 21.O BBC broadcast by Neville Chamberlain

London: 11.15 a.m., 3 September 1939 *I am speaking to you from the Cabinet Room at 10 Downing Street. This morning the British Ambassador in Berlin handed the German Government a final note stating that, unless we heard from them by eleven o'clock that they were prepared at once to withdraw their troops from Poland, a state of war would exist between us. I have to tell you that no such undertaking has been received, and that consequently this country is at war with Germany.*

22 The impact of War

▶ *HOW was the Second World War fought?* ATIC ■
▶ *WHAT was the experience and impact of war in Europe and in other parts of the world?* ATIB ■ ATIC ■
▶ *WHAT part did the wartime leaders play in the conduct of the war?* ATIB ■ ATIC ■

The phoney war

Hitler's army moved so rapidly and with such devastating effect across Poland, a new word *Blitzkrieg* (meaning 'lightning war') was used to describe it. Tanks, dive-bombers and fighter aircraft shocked the Poles. It was all over in five weeks. By then, Stalin had invaded Poland from the east to claim the share agreed a month earlier in August. Hitler then expected Britain and France to agree to peace, since there was nothing they could do now to recover Poland. However, by this time people looked on Hitler as evil (Source 22.A). Further appeasement was unthinkable. Even so, nothing happened. The French made no attempt to invade Germany. This war of waiting was called the 'Phoney War'. It lasted seven months.

Source 22.A From the *Daily Mirror*, 4 September 1939

WANTED!
For Murder . . . For Kidnapping . . . For Theft and for Arson
Adolf Hitler *alias* Adolf Shicklegruber,
Adolf Hittler or Hidler.

Last heard of in Berlin, September 3, 1939. Has a habit of raising right hand to shoulder level!

DANGEROUS!

This reckless criminal is Wanted – Dead or Alive!

The Phoney War ended when German forces invaded Denmark and Norway in April 1940. An Allied force sent to halt the Germans failed. Neville Chamberlain resigned as Prime Minister and Winston Churchill became Britain's wartime leader. On the day he took office, the Germans launched another all-out attack, this time on Belgium and the Netherlands.

Dunkirk and the fall of France

French and British troops rushed to the Low Countries to halt the German invasion. But it was a trap. The main German attack came instead through the Ardennes in southern Belgium which the French had thought too hilly for tank warfare. In a matter of days, German tanks raced through the hills to the Channel coast beyond. They cut off the British Army and a substantial French force as well.

Luckily for Britain, Hitler insisted that the leading tank units keep to his plan – to defeat France as soon as possible by advancing on Paris. Troops cut off by the advancing forces could be dealt with by those coming up behind. This delay gave the British Army time enough to retreat, since there was nothing more they could do to halt the German advance. While some soldiers defended the outskirts of Dunkirk, the rest escaped. Over 800 ships, most of them fishing boats, ferries and even private yachts manned by civilians, took 335 000 British, French and Belgian troops back to Britain between 27 May and 4 June 1940.

A column of German armoured vehicles advancing through Belgium in 1940

Winston Churchill

Winston Churchill was born in 1874. In 1900 he entered Parliament and in 1914 became the Government Minister in charge of the Royal Navy. In the 1930s he was one of the few politicians to speak out against appeasement. When war broke out in 1939 he was put in charge of the Navy once more. He became Prime Minister on 10 May 1940 when Chamberlain resigned.

Churchill enjoyed being Britain's war leader. He took an active part in taking important military decisions. His greatest value to the country, however, was as a tough, stirring and fiery speaker who could always raise the spirits of the people and of the troops. They called him 'Winnie'. When he died in 1965, most people agreed he had been the greatest Englishman of the twentieth century.

Source 22.B On the beaches at Dunkirk

Three long thin black lines protruded into the water. These were lines of men, standing in pairs behind one another far out into the water, waiting in queues till boats arrived to transport them, a score or so at a time, to the steamers and warships that were filling up with the last survivors.

On either side, scattered over the sand in all sorts of positions, were the dark shapes of dead and dying men, sometimes alone, sometimes in twos and threes. It remained a gamble all the time whether that sea, close though it was, would be reached in safety. Splinters from bursting shells were continually whizzing through the air, and occasionally a man in one of the plodding groups would fall with a groan.

British soldiers wait to be evacuated from Dunkirk in 1940

This poster featuring Winston Churchill was first published in May 1940

22.1 Use the painting and Source 22.B to write an imaginary account of what it was like to to be a soldier waiting to be evacuated from Dunkirk. AT3/L4

22.2 Who do you think were the heroes of Dunkirk? AT1C/L5

22.3 The Churchill poster and Sources 22.A and 22.C are all examples in their own way of British propaganda. Why? AT2/L5

22.4 Compare the painting of Dunkirk by an official war artist with the eyewitness account published in 1940 (Source 22.B). What facts about Dunkirk are the same in each case? What extra information does (a) the painting, (b) Source 22.B, provide? AT3/L6

Dunkirk was a massive defeat for Britain, of course. The British Army left behind most of its vehicles and equipment. But the survivors lived to fight another day. Churchill made a stirring speech in Parliament which made Dunkirk seem more like a victory than a defeat (Source 22.C).

Source 22.C Speech by Winston Churchill, 4 June 1940

We shall not flag or fail. We shall go on to the end. We shall fight in France. We shall fight on the seas and oceans. We shall fight with growing confidence and growing strength in the air. We shall defend our island whatever the cost may be.

We shall fight on the beaches. We shall fight on the landing grounds. We shall fight in the fields and in the streets. We shall fight in the hills. We shall never surrender.

After Dunkirk, French resistance collapsed. On 10 June, Italy declared war. On 14 June, German troops goose-stepped into Paris. On 21 June, the French Government surrendered. Germany occupied most of northern and western France. The rest of the country became neutral.

The Battle of Britain

After the fall of France, Britain was on her own. When Churchill rejected another peace offer, Hitler drew up a plan, Operation Sealion, to invade Britain. To be successful he needed command of the air. This is why German bombers, protected by fighters, attacked British ships and harbours in the English Channel. They intended to destroy the RAF *Spitfire* and *Hurricane* fighters sent up to shoot them down.

In August the *Luftwaffe* stepped up its campaign. This time RAF stations in southern England were bombed. Landing strips were damaged and radar masts, hangars and workshops destroyed. By the end of the month, the RAF was desperately short of fighter pilots. Two-thirds of its airfields in Kent and Sussex had been badly damaged.

Then, by mistake, a few bombs were dropped on Central London. The RAF bombed Berlin in return, doing little damage but infuriating the Nazis. Propaganda could not hide the fact that Berlin had been attacked. They would teach the British a lesson. Instead of bombing RAF stations, they would bomb London instead. The London Blitz (Source 22.D) which followed did a vast amount of damage and killed thousands of people (as you can see in Chapter 23) but it also gave the RAF time to repair its airfields and radar stations.

◀ The Battle of Britain *by the official war artist Paul Nash (page 114). Often, only the vapour trails from the aircraft told people a deadly battle was in progress overhead*

On 15 September 1940, Göring launched his biggest raid yet (page 168). Once again he failed to destroy the RAF. Two days later Hitler postponed Operation Sealion. Churchill had earlier paid tribute to the RAF: 'Never in the field of human conflict was so much owed by so many to so few', he said.

Source 22.E Aircraft lost in the Battle of Britain

	RAF	Luftwaffe
10 July – 23 August	264	576
24 August – 6 September	286	380
7 – 30 September	242	433
Total	792	1389

Source 22.D First day of the Blitz by a young Londoner

7 September 1940

Directly above me were literally hundreds of 'planes, Germans! The sky was full of them. Bombers hemmed in with fighters, like bees around their queen, like destroyers round the battleship, so came Jerry. My ears were deafened by bombs, machine-gun fire, the colossal inferno of machine after machine zooming in the blue sky. Squadron after squadron of Spitfires and Hurricanes tore out of the blue. One by one they tore the Nazi formations into shreds.

22.5 Write one or two sentences explaining why Hitler's decision to bomb London was a mistake. AT1B ■

22.6 How effective are Source 22.D and the picture in depicting the Battle of Britain? AT2 ■

22.7 Why do you think so many feature films have been made about the RAF in 1940, such as *Angel One Five* and *The Battle of Britain*?

22.8 Why is Source 22.E not enough in itself to say who won the Battle of Britain? AT2 ■ AT3 ■

22.9 Use Source 22.G to explain why sea and air power also played a part in winning the Battle of El Alamein. AT1C/L5 AT3/L5

22.10 What reasons might make you wonder whether Source 22.G can be trusted as a reliable and accurate source of information? AT2/L7 AT3/L7

22.11 How did the desert war differ from fighting in Europe? AT1B ■

Source 22.F From *The Diary of a Desert Rat*

Right on time the barrage bursts, the whole line leaps into life. The guns nearby crash incessantly, one against another, searing the darkness with gashes of flame.

Source 22.G By Field Marshal Rommel

Only three issues of petrol remained. It had been impossible to send any more across in the last weeks, partly because the Italian Navy had not provided the shipping and partly because of the British sinkings. This was sheer disaster. Experience had shown that one issue of petrol was required for each day of battle. Without it, the army was crippled.

The war in the desert

For a year or so after the fall of France, most of the land fighting involving Britain was in Africa. In September 1940, Mussolini ordered the army in the Italian colony of Libya to seize Egypt. To his dismay, the much smaller but better equipped British army heavily defeated the Italians, took 130 000 prisoners and drove the Italians halfway across Libya. In February 1941 Hitler came to Mussolini's rescue. He sent the *Afrika Korps* to Libya led by Erwin Rommel, one of the outstanding generals of the war.

Rommel's guns had a much longer range than the British. They could knock out a tank long before it could fire back. Since the desert gave little cover, Rommel's tanks usually won. Desert fighting was also different in other ways. Overheating and blowing sand caused machines to break down. Swarms of desert insects, lack of water, scorching sun and razor-sharp desert sand-storms made life intolerable for the soldiers.

By July 1942, Rommel had driven the British Eighth Army back into Egypt to the small desert town of El Alamein. General Bernard Montgomery was now in charge of the British Eighth Army – the 'Desert Rats'. Unlike most generals in the First World War, 'Monty' shared the same discomforts as his men. He demanded, and got, extra troops, new tanks and ample supplies of fuel and ammunition. By October, he was ready to go. At 9.40 p.m. on 23 October 1942, the Battle of El Alamein began (Source 22.F).

An Australian regiment attacks at night during the Battle of El Alamein

Rommel was on sick leave in Germany but rushed back to take charge. To his fury, he discovered he had a major problem on his hands (Source 22.G).

The Battle of El Alamein lasted nearly a fortnight. It ended in a stunning Allied victory. Rommel lost 59 000 men (dead, wounded or taken prisoner), 500 tanks and 400 guns. The Allies lost 13 000 men and 430 tanks. Four days later, American and British forces led by General Eisenhower (page 158) landed in North Africa and joined up with the Eighth Army to drive the enemy out. Both armies invaded Sicily in July 1943 and mainland Italy in September. Mussolini was overthrown and Italy surrendered. Hitler immediately sent troops there to halt the Allied advance.

Operation *Barbarossa*

Hitler now turned his attention to his old enemy, the Soviet Union. He told his generals, 'The sooner we smash Russia, the better'. Hitler planned the German invasion, code-named 'Operation Barbarossa', for May 1941 but delayed the start by six weeks in order to attack Greece and Yugoslavia first. This was a fatal mistake.

You can see what happened in Sources 22.H and 22.I. Source 22.H comes from the private diary kept by Dr Josef Goebbels, the Nazi Minister for Propaganda. He wrote the entry you can see here as he was preparing to broadcast the announcement that Operation Barbarossa had started.

The German army advances into the heart of Russia

Source 22.H From *The Goebbels Diaries*

Sunday, 22 June 1941 *The attack will begin at 3.30 a.m. 160 Full Divisions along a 3000 kilometre-long battlefront. Everything is well prepared. The biggest concentration of forces in the history of the world. The Führer seems to lose his fear as the decision comes nearer. It is always the same with him. He relaxes visibly. All the exhaustion seems to drop away. We pace up and down in his salon for three hours.*

I go over to the Ministry of Propaganda. It is still pitch dark. I put my colleagues in the picture. Total amazement in all quarters. Most had guessed half, or even the whole truth. Everyone sets to work immediately. Radio, press and newsreel are set in motion. Everything runs like clockwork.

3.30 *Now the guns will be thundering. May God bless our weapons! Outside on the Wilhelmplatz, it is quiet and deserted. Berlin and the entire Reich are asleep. I have half an hour to spare, but I cannot sleep. I pace up and down restlessly in my room. One can hear the breath of history.*

Soviet propaganda poster

Source 22.I By German General Guenther Blumentritt

The infantry had a hard time keeping up. Marches of twenty-five miles [40km] *in the course of a day were by no means exceptional, and that over the most atrocious roads. Great clouds of yellow dust were kicked up by the Russian columns attempting to retreat. The heat was tremendous, though interspersed with sudden showers which quickly turned the roads to mud before the sun reappeared and as quickly baked them into crumbling clay once again.*

It was appallingly difficult country for tank movement – great virgin forests, widespread swamps, terrible roads, and bridges not strong enough to bear the weight of tanks. The resistance also became stiffer, and the Russians began to cover their front with minefields; it was easier for them to block the way because there were so few roads.

The German armies advanced as far as Leningrad (St Petersburg) and the outskirts of Moscow, but thanks to the delay in starting the campaign, failed to complete the conquest of Russia before the onset of winter. It caught the Germans unprepared. They were still wearing summer uniform and their tanks and vehicles were unable to cope with the intense cold. This allowed the Russians to fight back with some success.

Josef Stalin

Josef Stalin was born in 1879 and died in 1953. He played an important part in planning the Bolshevik Revolution in 1917 and by 1922 had become General Secretary of the Communist Party. This powerful post gave him the power he needed to take Lenin's place when the Russian leader died in 1924.

Stalin ruled the Soviet Union for 25 years. Thousands perished as he turned the backward Soviet Union into a modern society. Nonetheless, his leadership during the war helped the Soviet Union to win. Foreign observers thought him a very impressive figure indeed, even when compared with Churchill or Roosevelt, the other two great Allied war leaders.

22.12 What facts (not opinions) does Goebbels tell us about the German invasion in Source 22.H? AT2/L3

22.13 Look at the Russian propaganda poster. How did Stalin want the Russian people to see him? AT2/L5

22.14 Use Source 22.I and the pictures to write a paragraph saying what difficulties the Russian climate and landscape put in the way of the invading German forces. AT3/L6

22.15 Why was the painting on the right called *Summer Soldiers*? Use the picture to show how unprepared the German soldiers were for the Russian winter. AT3/L5

22.16 Why do you think the German authorities prevented *Summer Soldiers* from being shown during the war? AT1C ■

22.17 What does Source 22.H tell you about (a) Hitler, (b) Goebbels? AT3/L5

22.18 We know that Goebbels, as Minister for Propaganda, twisted the truth and often told vicious lies to glorify the Nazi regime and make people hate its enemies. How does this affect Source 22.H? Is it likely to be reliable and accurate? AT3/L7

The following spring the German offensive began again, but with a change of plan. Hitler ordered them to seize the Soviet oilfields beyond Stalingrad. Once again the Russian winter intervened. The outstanding Soviet general of the war, Marshal Zhukov, led the Germans into a trap. He cut off the German Sixth Army and forced them to surrender on 31 January 1943.

This picture of the Russian Front in winter, Summer Soldiers, *was painted by a German artist called Franz Eichorst*

That same month another Russian army relieved Leningrad after a devastating siege in which hundreds of thousands of Russians died. In July 1943, after a colossal tank battle – the world's biggest – at Kursk in central Russia, the Red Army began to drive the German armies back. By July 1944, the Russians had 6 million men in uniform compared with the 4 million German soldiers fighting on the Russian Front. This was where most of the fighting in the Second World War took place – at first in Russia and then in the countries of Eastern Europe and in Eastern Germany as the Red Army advanced steadily towards Berlin and Vienna.

Pearl Harbor

The United States stayed neutral for over two years and watched as Hitler overran Europe. But the American President, Franklin Delano Roosevelt, was not neutral when it came to supplying friendly countries with arms. He supported Britain's stand against Germany by 'lending' American destroyers and other weapons.

America had pressing problems of her own to solve. Her relations with Japan were getting worse. The Japanese Government was militarist at this time. This means it was controlled by the army. The Japanese had been preparing their country for war for ten years. Japan had few raw materials, such as coal, iron ore and oil. She was short of space. Her people needed more land for their farms and cities. After their disappointment at Versailles (page 128) they invaded Manchuria in 1931 and China in 1937.

When Japanese troops entered French Indochina (Vietnam) in July 1941, the Americans suspected that the Japanese intended to take over south-east Asia. This is why Roosevelt banned the export of oil to Japan and made it difficult for the Japanese to trade. Talks were held to try to solve the dispute. While these were going on, six Japanese aircraft carriers steamed in secret across the Pacific to launch a surprise attack on the US Naval Base at Pearl Harbor in Hawaii (Source 22.J).

Pearl Harbor after the Japanese raid

Source 22.J News report, 7 December 1941

War struck suddenly and without warning from the sky and sea today at the Hawaiian islands. Japanese bombs took a heavy toll in American lives. Wave after wave of planes streamed over Oahu which the army said started at 8.10 a.m. Honolulu time and which ended at around 9.25, an hour and 15 minutes later.

It was Sunday morning. The Japanese warplanes came in low and completely surprised the Americans, killing 2300 people, destroying 200 aircraft, sinking four battleships and badly damaging four others. Luckily the three American aircraft carriers based at Pearl Harbor were at sea. Roosevelt called it 'a date that shall live in infamy'. Britain joined him in declaring war on Japan. Four days later, Germany and Italy declared war on the United States. The world was now well and truly at war.

The Japanese launched attacks soon afterwards on the Philippines, Thailand, Hong Kong, Malaya and Burma. They captured Singapore in February 1942 and took thousands of British and Commonwealth soldiers prisoner. By June, they were in control of a vast empire in the Far East (see map on page 174).

Franklin Delano Roosevelt

Franklin Delano Roosevelt was born in 1883. In 1921 he was struck down by poliomyelitis. Despite the handicap of ruling America from a wheelchair, he was elected President of the United States for a record twelve years from 1933 to his death in 1945. During the war he was the inspiration behind the American war effort and threw himself wholeheartedly into the planning of the Allied campaigns. Despite declining health, he insisted on going to the wartime conferences with Churchill and Stalin (pages 178–9). The last of these, at Yalta, was held only two months before his death in 1945.

◀ *Changi jail held many of the soldiers captured at Singapore. The prisoners suffered terribly from inadequate food, harsh treatment and the hardship of being made to do hard labour in a tropical climate. Many of them died.*

22.19 Use the painting of Changi jail to describe the horrors of a Japanese prisoner-of-war camp. AT3/L5

22.20 How do you know that Source 22.K is an eyewitness account? What difference does this make to the way we look at the information it contains? AT2 ■

22.21 Compare Source 22.K with the painting. How do they each have something different to tell us about the Battle of Midway? AT3/L6

22.22 Are they likely to be accurate sources of information about Midway? AT3 ■

Midway

Only six months after Pearl Harbor, the Americans struck back. Their experts read Japanese coded messages indicating that an attack was being launched to capture the American base at Midway in the middle of the Pacific. In secret, the three American aircraft carriers based at Pearl Harbor sailed to Midway to wait for them.

On 4 June 1942, American *Dauntless* dive-bombers from the US carriers changed the course of the war in the Pacific (Source 22.K). They surprised and sank the four Japanese aircraft carriers with the Japanese invasion fleet and forced the troopships, battleships and other warships to turn back for home. The Japanese Navy never recovered from this massive defeat – as you will see in Chapter 25.

Source 22.K By Mitsuo Fuchida, a Japanese pilot

Midway: 10.30 a.m., 4 June 1942 *The terrifying scream of the dive-bombers reached me first, followed by the crashing explosion of a direct hit. At that instant a look-out screamed 'Hell-Divers!' I looked up to see three black enemy planes plummeting towards our ship. Bombs! Down they came straight towards me! There was a blinding flash and then a second explosion, much louder than the first. I was shaken by a weird blast of warm air. I got up and looked at the sky. The enemy planes were already gone from sight.*

Midway: 10.30 a.m., 4 June 1942. ▶ *This wartime painting shows the Japanese aircraft carriers on fire*

The war at sea

The Battle of Midway proved that command of the air was all-important in the war at sea. Command of the water below sea-level was also of great importance, as Britain discovered to its cost soon after the outbreak of war. German U-boats torpedoed and destroyed hundreds of merchant ships despite the use of the convoy system (page 97).

On the surface, the Royal Navy was greatly superior to the German Navy. As in the First World War, they tried to keep the German warships bottled up inside the North Sea so that they could stop merchant ships bringing food and raw materials to Germany. Those German warships which did escape, such as the *Graf Spee* (December 1939) and the *Bismarck* (May 1941) caused immense disruption to Atlantic shipping until they were caught and sunk.

The war in the air

The casualty rate among bomber crews was high. In 1942, they had only a one in three chance of surviving a tour of duty (about 25 missions)

When civilians died in air-raids, the enemy (Allied or German) was accused of terror bombing. In fact, it made much more sense to hit factories or docks rather than homes. But it was hard to find a specific target at night or even during the day. Cloud, mist and smoke from factory chimneys often obscured the target area. Taking action to avoid fighter aircraft, barrage balloons (page 166), searchlights and anti-aircraft guns made it even more difficult as well as making it dangerous.

By the end of 1941, British experts worked out that in some cases only one bomber in ten was getting close enough even to drop its bombs within 5 miles of the selected target! This is why RAF Bomber Command was told by the Government to aim instead at 'destroying the morale of the civil population'. In other words, they were to bomb towns and cities in general as well as the factories where people worked.

The newly appointed chief of Bomber Command, Air Chief Marshal Sir Arthur 'Bomber' Harris, set out to improve the accuracy of the raids. He sent special Pathfinder aircraft ahead of the main force to find and mark the target with flares. This policy was highly successful. Many great German cities, such as Cologne and Hamburg, were badly damaged in this way. The fires caused by incendiary bombs used up the oxygen in the air. Fresh air sucked in to replace it caused horrific firestorms.

22.23 What was the attitude of the writer of Source 22.L to the war in the air? AT1C/L6

22.24 How do Sources 22.M, 22.O and 22.P differ in describing the reasons for the raid on Dresden? AT3/L6

22.25 Was Churchill being fair in his comment on the Dresden air-raid (Source 22.P)? What arguments could 'Bomber' Harris have used to defend his decision? AT2 ■

22.26 Look at Source 22.L and at the pictures. If it was 'evil' of Hitler to bomb Britain's historic cities, was it also evil to bomb German historic cities, such as Dresden and Nuremberg? AT1C/L7

22.27 Use the sources to explain why the exact number of casualties of the Dresden air-raid will never be known. AT3/L6

Source 22.L Diary of a woman living near Coventry

Saturday 18 April 1942

The great news today is that American planes have raided Japan and Tokyo and Kobe have been bombed. Horrible as it sounds, this is really a good thing.

Wednesday 29 April 1942

Last night it was York. According to Hitler, all our beautiful ancient towns are to be bombed. What an evil mind he has.

The bomber crews flying thousands of metres high, found it difficult to imagine the terror their raids were causing. An Australian said the burning city below was unreal. 'We could not hear it or feel its breath', he said. To most people at that time, the bomber crews were heroes (Source 22.L). They were the only Allied servicemen taking the war to Nazi Germany itself and showing the German people the penalty for supporting Hitler.

Bomber Command also carried out special precision-bombing raids. These included the 'Dambusters' raid when special bouncing bombs were used to burst the walls of two dams in the Ruhr industrial region of Germany. They also attacked the secret rocket factory at Peenemünde in 1943.

By 1944, the Allied air forces were winning the war in the air. Formations of over a thousand bombers were raining bombs down on Germany's large industrial cities. The worst air-raid took place on 13 February 1945 only weeks before the end of the war. The historic and beautiful city of Dresden lay in the path of the advancing Russian army. 'Bomber' Harris launched a huge air-raid on the city. You can read what happened and why it caused controversy in Sources 22.M to 22.P.

Estimates vary as to how many people died in the Dresden air-raid. Some say 200 000, others 25 000

The ruins of Nuremberg after the war. When 795 bombers raided the city in March 1944, 95 were shot down and another 71 badly damaged. About 55 000 members of the RAF bomber crews and 550 000 Germans died in the air-raids on Germany. Some 65 000 people died in the German raids on Britain.

Source 22.M *The Independent on Sunday*, 31 May 1992

Jeffrey Chapman remembers vividly the briefing [instructions] *given to 582 Squadron in February 1945. 'Dresden,' the briefer said, 'is a very old German city with a great many buildings of wooden construction. It will burn well and you are loaded with maximum incendiaries* [fire bombs]. *It is believed to be crowded with refugees from the Russian Front.'*

Source 22.N By a victim of the raid

Because of the flying sparks and the firestorm I can't see anything at first. In front of me is something that might be a street, filled with a hellish rain of sparks which look like enormous rings of fire when they hit the ground. It's hot. Hot! My hands are burning like fire. I just drop my suitcase. I am past caring, and too weak.

I spent all the daylight hours searching for my fiancé. Dead, dead, dead everywhere. Some completely black like charcoal. Women in aprons. Women with children sitting in the trams as if they had just nodded off.

Source 22.O *Evening Standard*, 14 February 1945

The raids were in support of Marshal Koniev's troops who are less than 70 miles [112 km] *away. The Germans may be using Dresden as their base. Telephone services and other means of communication are almost as essential to the German Army as the railways and roads which meet in Dresden. Its buildings are needed for troops and offices evacuated from other towns. Dresden has large munition workshops in the old arsenal.*

Source 22.P Winston Churchill in March 1945

It seems to me that the moment has come when the question of bombing German cities simply for the sake of increasing the terror should be reviewed.

D-Day

Stalin had urged Churchill to invade Europe, so the Germans would have to fight on two fronts. After the Americans entered the war, they too put the case for an Allied invasion, by the end of 1942. But Churchill insisted that plans must be drawn up in advance.

The Allied invasion of Europe, code-named 'Operation Overlord', was planned by General Dwight Eisenhower, Supreme Allied Commander.

For months American and British soldiers trained for their part in the invasion. Engineers assembled PLUTO, an underwater pipeline, to supply oil for the tanks. They also built a floating harbour called MULBERRY which could be towed across to Normandy to make it easier to unload supplies and reinforcements. Ingenious efforts were also made to deceive the Germans about the time and place of the Allied landings. False guns, warplanes and landing craft were assembled near Dover to make the Germans think the landing would be near Calais. The French Resistance (local people who risked their lives to sabotage the German war effort) blew up telephone lines and railways to hamper the Germans when they sent reinforcements to Normandy.

Bad weather postponed the invasion by 24 hours but a favourable forecast, even though it was raining at the time, persuaded Eisenhower at last. 'OK. Let's go,' he said. On Tuesday 6 June the vast armada sailed – the greatest naval invasion in history. You can see what happened in the painting and in the sources. It caught the Germans completely by surprise. By the time they recovered, the Allied soldiers were ashore.

US army vehicles drive through the ruins of a town in Normandy

Source 22.Q BBC Broadcast by Thomas Treanor

7 June 1944 *We came sliding and slowing in on some light breakers and grounded. I stepped ashore on France. Walking up a beach where men were moving casually about, carrying equipment inshore. All up and down the broad beach as far as I could see, men, jeeps, bulldozers, and other equipment were moving about like ants. A few columns of black, greasy smoke marked equipment which had been hit by shellfire and set afire.*

Source 22.R By an American soldier

We were late in getting to the beaches. Our rope ladders got wet on the way over. We were dumped out and had to wade several hundred feet in to the beach, and all the time the Germans were firing at us from the top of the big bluff we had to storm. Some of us were shot crossing the sand to the foot of the cliff. When we climbed, the Germans shot down at us.

22.28 Use the sources and the painting to write a description of what it was like to take part in the D-Day landings. AT1C/L4 AT3/L4

22.29 Look at the photograph and the painting showing Allied army vehicles driving through Normandy. How different would your impression be of the Allied advance if you chose to use one of these pictures rather than the other? AT2/L6 AT3/L6

22.30 Does this mean either or both of these pictures is unreliable as a source of information? AT2/L7 AT3/L7

American painting of the D-Day landings in Normandy ▼

Time Line

1939 Hitler invades Poland; Phoney War
1940 Dunkirk; fall of France; Battle of Britain
1941 Hitler invades the Soviet Union; Pearl Harbor; world at war
1942 Fall of Singapore; Allied victories at Midway and El Alamein
1943 German defeat at Stalingrad; Allied invasion of Italy; Soviet victory at Kursk
1944 D-Day landings; Paris liberated
1945 End of war in Europe; death of Hitler

22.31 Look at the maps. Draw a map or make a tracing to show which areas of Europe were captured by German forces in 1940–2 and later recaptured by the Allies in 1943–5. Which areas were still in German hands at the end of the war? AT1A/L5

Canadian painting of troop carriers advancing through Normandy at dusk

Victory in Europe

In August the Allies broke through the opposing German forces and launched a rapid advance across northern France and the Low Countries. There were temporary setbacks when the Germans fought back but by March 1945 Eisenhower's armies had crossed the Rhine from the west. At the same time the Red Army was advancing on Berlin from the east. On 25 April 1945, American and Russian soldiers met at Torgau on the river Elbe.

Five days later Mussolini was executed by Partisans (the Italian Resistance). The next day Hitler committed suicide. Berlin fell to the Russians on 2 May and on 8 May it was all over. Germany had surrendered. Schools closed all over Britain as people celebrated VE (Victory in Europe) Day.

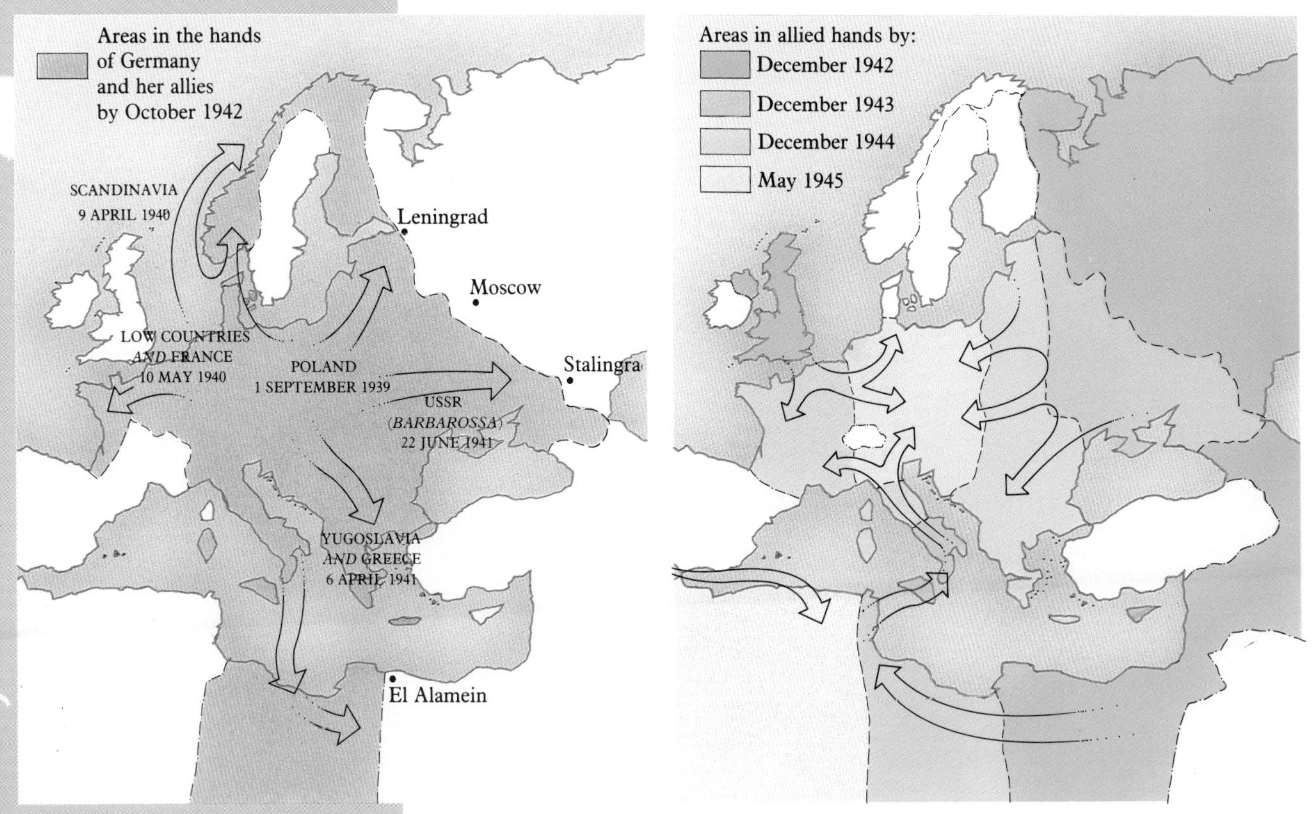

The Second World War in Europe 1939–45

23 The Home Front in Britain

▶ *WHAT was the impact of the war on people in Britain?* ATIB ■

▶ *HOW did the war change the way people lived?* ATIA ■

Conscription

By the time the war started in September 1939, part-time and former soldiers had been called up to rejoin their regiments. Together with the regular soldiers already serving in the army, they formed the expeditionary force which fought in France in the Spring of 1940. Many of these were the soldiers who returned in the small ships from Dunkirk. Conscription had been introduced five months before the outbreak of war. By the end of 1940 some two million men had been recruited into the armed forces. Men in jobs which were vital to the war effort were excused. These were called *reserved* occupations, such as farm work and working in a coal-mine.

After December 1941 women who were single and between 20 and 30 could also be conscripted into the armed services, police, fire service or made to work in factories. In fact, so many women volunteered for the Wrens (WRNS – Women's Royal Naval Service) and to a lesser extent, the WAAF (Women's Auxiliary Air Force) and the ATS (Auxiliary Territorial Service), that very few women had to serve in the armed forces against their will.

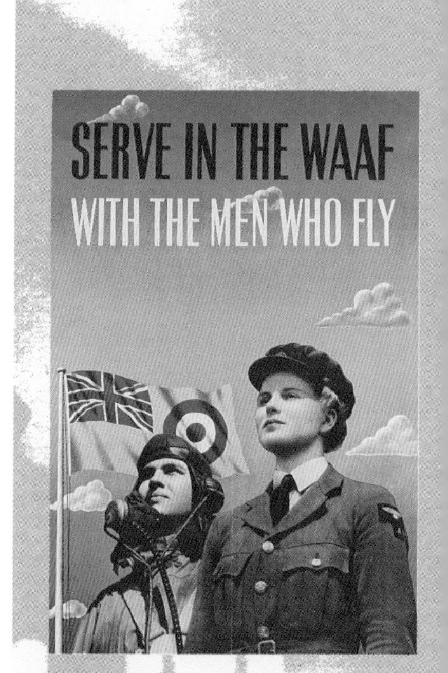

Preparations for war

Many precautions for war had been taken long before Hitler marched into Poland. Air-raid shelters made from corrugated iron had been built in many back gardens. Arrangements had also been made to make sure that everyone knew they had to black out their windows at night. Thick curtains were made. On hot nights in summer the air inside was unbearable. ARP (Air-Raid Precautions) wardens patrolled the streets looking for chinks of light from a window. Government restrictions also meant that motorists could not use their car head-lights during an air-

Source 23.A

The classrooms were filled with children, parcels, gas masks. The children were excited and happy because their parents had told them they were going away to the country. Many had never seen green fields.

Evacuees from London

23.1 Your grandparents or great-grandparents may be able to remember the Second World War. Ask them about, (a) gas masks, (b) air-raids, (c) holidays in wartime, (d) the blackout, (e) rationing, (g) listening to the radio, (h) going to the cinema. Write a report summing up your findings and saying whether you think recollections like this are accurate or not. AT2 ■ AT3/L5

23.2 Look at the 'Serve in the WAAF' poster. How did the RAF encourage women to volunteer? AT1C/L6

23.3 What do Sources 23.B, 23.C and 23.D tell you about Britain and the British people at the start of the war? AT3/L6

23.4 Look at the poster urging people to fight for 'Your Britain'. What attitude do you think the Government hoped this poster would produce in the people who read it? AT1C/L6

raid. They were told to park their cars and keep their side lights on. Gas-masks were also issued since it was thought the Germans would be certain to drop bombs containing poison gas. They were wrong. The masks were never needed.

Evacuation

The Government also expected that hundreds of thousands of people would be killed when the *Luftwaffe* raided Britain's industrial cities. This is why children, disabled people and pregnant women were evacuated (moved) to the countryside as soon as war seemed likely. Between 1–3 September 1939 over 1 million people left the cities. Whole schools went together (Source 23.A).

On arrival, the children were billeted (housed) in local homes. Many of the evacuees came from neglected city slums which had suffered high unemployment during the long years of the Depression (page 130). Some country-dwellers claimed to be shocked at their appearance (Source 23.B). In fact, many of the evacuees were shocked as well (Source 23.C).

Source 23.B Report from a Women's Institute in 1940

Except for a small number the children were filthy, and in this district we have never seen so many verminous children lacking any knowledge of clean and hygienic habits. Furthermore, it appeared they were unbathed for months. One child was suffering from scabies and the majority had it in their hair and the others had dirty septic sores all over their bodies.

Source 23.C Two evacuees remember East Anglia

(1) 'No indoor toilets, no bathrooms, no electric. It was like going back to the olden days for us. We never imagined people could live like that.'

(2) 'No modern conveniences. Outside lavatory – an earth closet. Water from a well! Baths in a tin bath in front of the fire!'

Most of the children got on well with their hosts, but others could not get used to country life. A few never settled and were 'always sad'. Some ran away and returned to their homes. Others complained that the countryside was too dark at night and asked where the cinemas were! As the 'Phoney War' dragged on (page 148), the children drifted back home. Of the 6700 evacuees sent to Cambridge in September, only half were still there two months later. By June 1940, there were less than 2000 left.

Government offices and many private firms also moved into the country. Great works of art and historic documents were taken to safe places, such as the cave in North Wales where the National Gallery's paintings were stored during the war. Those who could afford it went to North America or sent their children there for the duration of the war (Source 23.D).

Source 23.D A child is sent to Canada

24 June 1940 *At 8.15 we set out for Euston. Honor and I had the child* [aged 4] *between us. At the station there was a queue of Rolls-Royces and liveried servants and mountains of trunks. It seemed that everyone we knew was there on the very crowded platform.*

This cartoon by Donald Zec infuriated the Government when it was printed in the Daily Mirror *in 1942. Churchill objected to the caption* 'The price of petrol has been increased by one penny – Official'.

Rationing

Soon after the war began, an official propaganda campaign was launched (Source 23.E) to encourage people to save money and raw materials. They were told old corsets could be used to make parachutes and frying pans turned into steel helmets. They could save hot water by sharing baths and using no more than five inches (12cm) of water. A cartoon on a poster showed a woman having a bath brimful of hot water with Mussolini at her side singing, 'I like-a da bath that is full to the brim/Hot water for England keeps me in the swim'. In 1940, the iron railings round gardens and public parks were taken by the Government and melted down as scrap. This didn't stop the park-keepers in Manchester from locking the park gates at night to show they were shut!

Source 23.E Wartime slogans

'LET YOUR SHOPPING HELP OUR SHIPPING'

'WASTE NOT, WANT NOT'

'IS YOUR JOURNEY REALLY NECESSARY?'

'MAKE DO AND MEND'

'PLOUGH NOW! BY DAY AND NIGHT'

'WINGS FOR VICTORY'

'KILL THE SQUANDERBUG'

'TURN YOUR POTS AND PANS INTO SPITFIRES AND HURRICANES'

'LEND DON'T SPEND'

'LET "DIG FOR VICTORY" BE THE MOTTO OF EVERYONE WITH A GARDEN'

'SAVE WASTE PAPER: EVERY SCRAP SHORTENS THE SCRAP!'

23.5 Look at the photograph of the concrete pillbox. What evidence of the Second World War can still be seen in your home area? AT3/L4

23.6 What were the arguments in favour of rationing? AT1B/L5

23.7 Conscription, the blackout and rationing meant that the Government took much greater control of people's everyday lives than it did in peacetime. Write a paragraph explaining why these controls were necessary. AT1C/L5

An Emergency Food Office during the War. People who had been bombed out were issued with temporary ration books. Without coupons, you were unable to buy food. ▶

Source 23.F
A Midlands woman in 1941

Friday 18 July *In Leamington this morning we had a good deal to do and shopping takes a long time. People take their ration books to the shops and they have to have the coupons cancelled as well as being served with bits of this and that.*

23.8 What do the slogans in Source 23.E tell you about wartime Britain? AT3/L5
23.9 Why do you think the television comedy series *Dad's Army* about the Home Guard was so popular? AT2/L5
23.10 The Government said Donald Zec's cartoon accused the oil companies of making profits from petrol which seamen had risked their lives to bring to Britain. The *Daily Mirror*, in reply, said this was nonsense. The cartoon urged people to save petrol. Which do you think it was? Give your reasons. AT2/L7

A World War II concrete pillbox

Other economies were also made. Men's suits had fewer pockets and no turn-ups to the trousers. Women's skirts and dresses were shorter. Non-essential foods disappeared from the shelves. Many wartime children saw their first bananas years after the war had ended. As food became scarce, the price went up and some goods were hidden from view and reserved for regular customers only or for friends of the shop-keeper. This was widely seen as being unfair. An opinion poll two months after the start of the war showed that over sixty per cent of people were in favour of rationing. Buying foods with a ration-book would mean that everyone, rich or poor, would have the same right to a minimum amount of food, clothing, petrol and sweets.

On 2 November 1939 the Ministry of Food announced plans to ration butter and bacon. Seven weeks later sugar and meat were rationed as well. In future, people would have to register with a grocer and a butcher in order to get their weekly ration. Even buying a ham sandwich at a snack bar meant giving up half a coupon. People who lived through the war years (and for several years of rationing afterwards) can still recall vividly phrases such as 'it's on the ration', 'it's on points' or 'have you got your coupons?'

Rationing was also inconvenient (Source 23.F). The Minister of Food said it was 'fair shares all round' but this did not stop some people from buying and selling goods on the black market. Farmers reared pigs in secret and sold 'off-the- ration' pork and bacon at high prices.

The Home Guard

The Local Defence Volunteers (LDV) – later called the Home Guard – were recruited in 1940 to help defend Britain against invaders. Many of the volunteers (who could be any age between 17 and 65) were former soldiers who had fought in the First World War. At first they lacked weapons and had to train with wooden rifles or even broom handles. Nor did they have uniforms – as yet. This is why many ex-soldiers turned out in their old uniforms. This caused problems in one village when six former generals turned up in uniform!

Concrete pillboxes – as they were called – were built as local strongpoints for use by the Army and the Home Guard against an enemy. Road signs were removed to confuse enemy parachutists. Beaches were covered in barbed wire and concrete gun emplacements were built on the cliffs. Even church bells were banned from ringing. They were only to be rung as a sign that the country was being invaded.

The war effort

Everyone had to do their bit for the war effort. The war came first. After the German invasion in May 1940, for instance, the Whitsuntide holiday was cancelled. All factories and shops worked normally. The huge numbers of workers needed in factories making aircraft, tanks, guns, ammunition, uniforms and other products for the war effort meant that unemployment all but disappeared. There were nearly 2 million people out of work at the start of 1939. By 1945 this number was down to less than 100 000. As in the First World War, women were asked to do much of the extra work. Posters urged: 'Women of Britain. Come into the Factories'. Many volunteered to join the Women's Land Army (Source 23.G). The land under cultivation grew as every available field and common was ploughed up to grow crops. The rise in food production was remarkable (Source 23.H).

Source 23.G The Land Army Song

Back to the land, we must all lend a hand.
To the farms and the fields we must go.
There's a job to be done,
Though we can't fire a gun
We can still do our bit with a hoe.

Some men were conscripted to work in the coal mines instead of serving in the armed forces. Their names were drawn out of a hat. They were called Bevin Boys after Ernest Bevin, the Minister of Labour who introduced the scheme. Along with the other mineworkers, they were sometimes asked to work on Sundays as well as during the rest of the week. People vied with each other in telling stories about devotion to duty. A Minister told Parliament about a factory worker who was afraid he couldn't get to work before 8.00 a.m. because his wife started work at another factory at 7.00 a.m., while the grandmother who looked after their child during the day only came off her night shift then!

Source 23.H Agricultural production: 1939–45

Farm crops	Output in 1939	Output in 1945
Wheat, barley, oats Potatoes	3 300 000 tonnes 4 400 000 tonnes	7 250 000 tonnes 8 850 000 tonnes

23.11 How was the wartime poster below designed to encourage people to work for the war effort? Is this advertising or propaganda?
AT3/L5

23.12 What similarities are there between the painting *Ruby Loftus screwing a breech-ring* and the photograph on page 122 showing a woman worker operating a machine during the First World War?
AT2/L5

23.13 What is the value of a realistic painting like this compared with a photograph of a similar scene?
AT3/L6

23.14 Use the painting of *War Weapons Week in a Small Town* (opposite) to describe in detail some of the ways in which everyday life had been changed by the war.
AT1C/L5 AT3/L5

◀ *This painting by Dame Laura Knight,* Ruby Loftus screwing a breech-ring, *was painted in 1943. Ruby Loftus had become highly skilled at performing an extremely tricky engineering task in a weapons factory. Posters of this painting were later published to show the type of skilled work being done successfully by women factory workers*

Source 23.I Clement Attlee (Churchill's deputy) in 1942

The work that women are performing in munition factories has to be seen to be believed. Precision engineering jobs which a few years ago would have made a skilled turner's hair stand on end are performed with dead accuracy by girls who have had no industrial experience.

Source 23.J Proportion of jobs done by women

Aircraft factories	Engineering works	Chemical plants
40% women	35% women	52% women

Source 23.K Aircraft production in Britain

1938	1939	1940	1941	1942	1943	1944
2800	8000	15 000	20 000	24 000	26 000	26 500

War Weapons Week in a Small Town. *Scenes like this were a familiar sight during the war. People were asked to give or lend money to help the war effort. Notice the concrete road blocks in the middle of the street*

23.15 Use the facts and figures in these sources to draw graphs and make a list of facts showing the effect of the war effort on Britain. AT3/L6

Civilians under attack

Despite the blackout, the evacuation, the issue of gas masks and the building of air-raid shelters, the first civilian casualties in an air-raid did not occur for seven months. When they did come, the air-raids on Britain's cities killed thousands of people and did a great amount of damage. Eleven days after the start of the London Blitz on 7 September 1940, the Germans boasted that they had destroyed the will of Londoners to continue with the war (Source 23.L).

Source 23.L German radio: 18 September 1940

The legend of British self control and coolness under fire is being destroyed. All reports from London agree in stating that the people are seized by fear – hair-raising fear. The 7 000 000 Londoners have completely lost their self-control. They run aimlessly about in the streets and are the victims of bombs and bursting shells.

In fact, reactions were mixed. Most Londoners were very frightened but took it calmly. People kept up their spirits by joking about the raids. A bombed-out shopkeeper put up a sign which read 'More open than usual'. You can see what it was like to live through the Blitz in the pictures and sources on pages 166–7.

An all-woman crew raises a barrage balloon above Coventry in 1943. If an enemy bomber came in too low, it got entangled in the cables and crashed

The Elephant and Castle Tube Station, like many others on the Underground, was used as an air-raid shelter. A woman worker complained 'Dirt is everywhere. The floors are never swept and are filthy. People are sleeping on piles of rubbish '

Britain during the Blitz

Other towns and cities were bombed as well as London. One of the worst of these raids was on Coventry on 15 November 1940 when 449 German bombers destroyed much of the city. Bristol, Liverpool and Southampton were bombed later the same month and Birmingham, Manchester and Sheffield in December 1940. By the end of the year, 22 000 people had been killed in the German air-raids on Britain.

Source 23.M From a diary of the war years

Saturday, 7 September 1940 *Mark this day in your memory. It has seen the opening of the first serious air attack on London. There stood St Paul's with a semicircular background of red. The flames looked perilously near the dome. To the left the pall of smoke was black.*

Source 23.N Official Government Report in 1942

London: Sunday evening, 29 December 1940 *During these hours the flames seemed to be roaring and raging from one end of the City to the other. The glare was like daylight, and the streets were filled with showers of sparks.*

London firemen tried to put out the raging fires which swept through the City of London on 29 December 1940 (Sources 23.N and 23.O). It was probably the worst night of the Blitz

Source 23.O The London Blitz from the Thames

London: Sunday evening, 29 December 1940 *An unforgettable sight. The whole of London seemed involved, one great circle of overwhelming disaster. One could not pick out known buildings through the great clouds of smoke, except when there was a sudden spurt of yellow flames which lit a church tower.*

Source 23.P Official Government Report in 1942

There was never a trace of public panic. But the Blitz was not a picnic, and no fine slogan about 'taking it' should hide the realities of human fear and heartache. So far was all this from panic that it took three months for the population of Central London to drop by about 25 per cent from a little over 3 000 000 in August to 2 280 000 at the end of November.

Many thousands of people were made homeless during the Blitz

The London Blitz

Swansea after three heavy raids

Doodlebugs and rockets

There was a second Blitz in 1944 when the first V1 flying bombs (popularly knows as *doodlebugs* or *buzz bombs*) were launched in June. These were short, pilotless aircraft travelling at about 600kph which made an unmistakable droning sound as they came in low over England. When the jet engine stopped, people ducked to the ground or ran for shelter. They knew they had just 15 seconds before a tonne of high explosives hit the ground.

The flying bombs were launched night and day, so air-raid warnings were of little use. When one of these bombs hit the Guards' Chapel in London on 18 June 1944, 119 people were killed. Another 198 people were killed in London twelve days later. Over a million people left London again to escape the onslaught. But by the end of July fighter aircraft, anti-aircraft guns and barrage balloons successfully stopped most of the *buzz bombs* reaching London. On 28 August, for instance, only 4 out of 94 flying bombs got through.

Hitler, however, had another secret weapon ready to be unleashed on Britain. On 8 September 1944 a German V2 rocket carrying a tonne of high explosive was launched from Holland and landed in London three minutes later, killing three people. One V2 killed 160 people in a London shopping centre and another fell on a cinema in Antwerp killing 567 people, including many Allied soldiers. Churchill hid the news of the rockets from the British people for two months. But after a hundred V2 attacks, he told Parliament in November (Source 23.Q). The news was commented on in the press (Source 23.R)

Source 23.Q Winston Churchill in Parliament

No official statement about the attack has hitherto been issued. The reason for this silence was that any announcement might have given information useful to the enemy.

Source 23.R *Evening Standard*, 10 November 1944

The rocket travels at an enormous speed and no warning of its approach can be given. For the time being the answer is: (1) An all-out bomber offensive against V2 launching sites, factories and experimental stations (2) As we thrust deeper into Holland and Western Germany more and more launching sites will fall into our hands.

23.16 How was the barrage-balloon picture painted 'as propaganda to recruit the right sort of women for Balloon Command'? AT2/L5

23.17 How and why do Sources 23.L and 23.P disagree? AT2/L5

23.18 Use the pictures and sources to write a report saying what effect the bombing raids had on Britain. AT3/L4

23.19 Use Sources 23.Q and 23.R to say why you think news of the V2 rocket was concealed from the public. AT3/L6

23.20 Why were Hitler's V-weapons a serious threat to Britain in 1944? AT1B ■

This American cartoon was called 'A Madman's Dream'

Wartime propaganda

Both sides used propaganda to boost people's spirits and give them a reason for fighting the war and doing their utmost for the war effort. Victories were made to seem greater than they really were. When the *Luftwaffe* raided Britain on 15 September 1940 (page 150), newspapers and broadcasts gave wildy exaggerated estimates of the number of German aircraft shot down. These varied from 189 to 183 although in reality the Germans only lost 56.

As in the Great War (page 113), the Government also used censorship to keep people from hearing the really bad news – as the American journalist H. R. Knickerbocker discovered to his cost during the London Blitz on 12 September 1940 (Source 23.S). Censorship was also used to suppress anything which might harm the war effort, such as the 'petrol costs lives' cartoon on page 162. The Government nearly closed the *Daily Mirror* down after this incident.

Source 23.S By Harold Nicolson, a British MP

12 September, 1940 *Knickerbocker dashes up to me aflame with rage. He says he has the best story in the world and the censors are holding it up. It is the story about the time-bomb outside St Paul's Cathedral which may go off at any moment and destroy the great work of Sir Christopher Wren. 'Cannot the American people be brought in to share my anxiety?' Also why is he not allowed to mention the destruction of Bond Street and the Burlington Arcade, so dear to many Americans?*

Wartime entertainment

The cinema was one of the most popular forms of wartime entertainment. The Government closed cinemas and theatres at the start of the war but soon allowed them to reopen. Even when the air-raids began, many still remained open. The Windmill Theatre in London's West End boasted afterwards 'We never closed!' When the siren for an air-raid sounded during one film, the manager told the audience they could get their money back. 'Few moved, I can tell you,' said one woman. 'Who cared if a bomb did drop? One would go out happy!'

23.21 Describe some of the main features of wartime Britain. AT1C/L4

23.22 How did BBC Radio play an important part in wartime Britain? AT1C/L5

23.23 Source 23.U describes the holiday of a ten-year old boy but it was written nearly 50 years later. Is there any reason to question whether what it says is accurate or not? AT3/L7

23.24 Compare the Nazi cartoon *Entente Cordiale* with the American cartoon *A Madman's Dream*. How did each cartoonist show the enemy leaders on the other side? Write a short description of each cartoon saying why it is propaganda. AT2/L5

23.25 What examples of British propaganda are there in this chapter? AT2/L5

23.26 What use is propaganda in history if it does not always tell the truth? AT3/L7

The ATS Dance Band in 1944

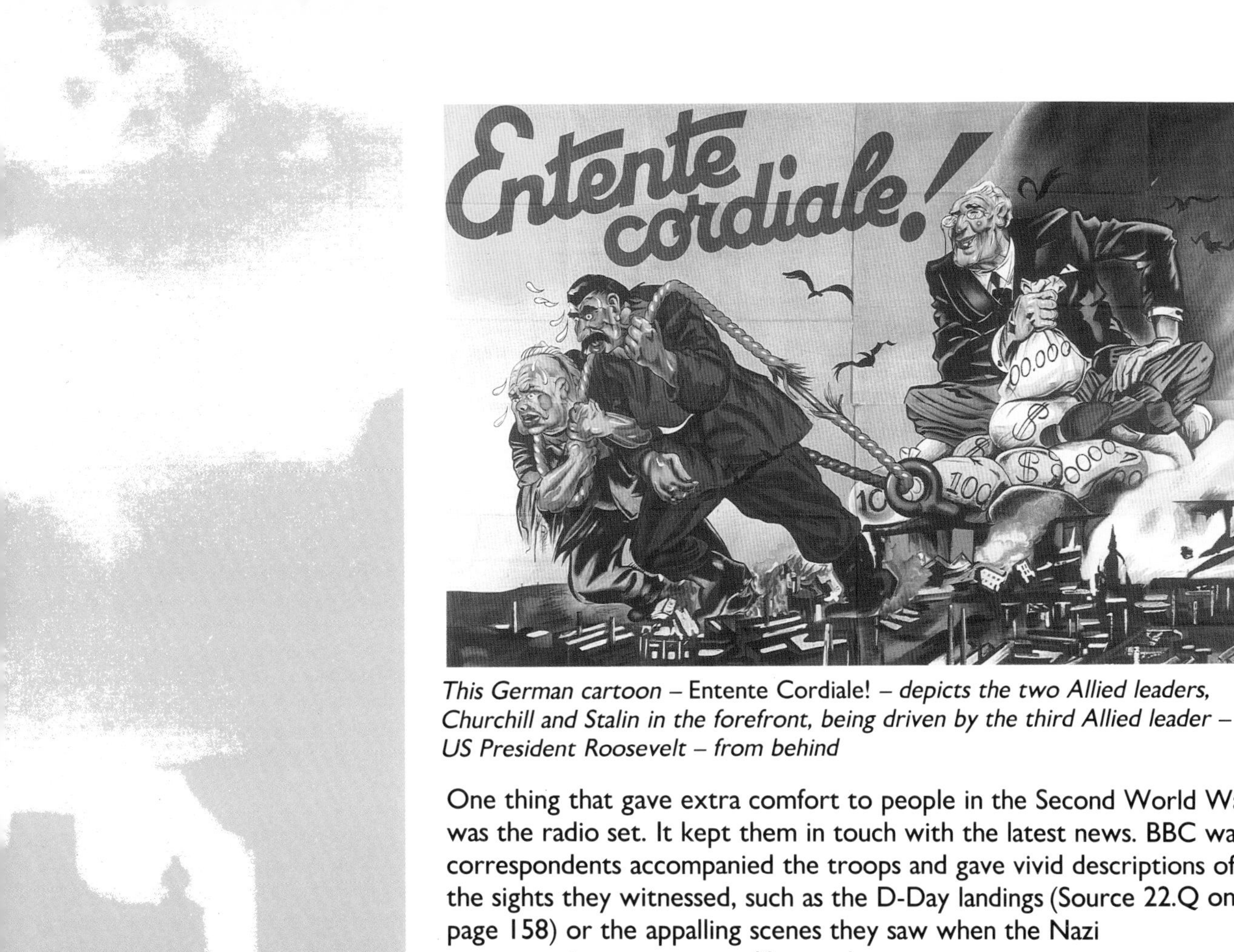

This German cartoon – Entente Cordiale! *– depicts the two Allied leaders, Churchill and Stalin in the forefront, being driven by the third Allied leader – US President Roosevelt – from behind*

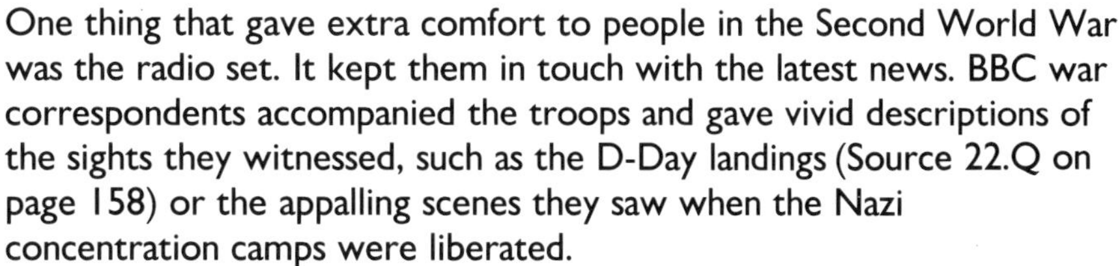

One thing that gave extra comfort to people in the Second World War was the radio set. It kept them in touch with the latest news. BBC war correspondents accompanied the troops and gave vivid descriptions of the sights they witnessed, such as the D-Day landings (Source 22.Q on page 158) or the appalling scenes they saw when the Nazi concentration camps were liberated.

People who lived through these war years still remember the popular songs. Twice a day, *Music While You Work* broadcast the latest dance band hits to offices and factories. Other popular radio shows included *Workers' Playtime* (a variety programme for factory workers), *Happidrome*, *Garrison Theatre* and *Band Waggon*. Some of the first situation comedies were heard on radio during these war years. They included *Much Binding-in-the-Marsh* about an incompetent RAF Station and the very popular *ITMA (It's That Man Again)* which starred Tommy Handley. *ITMA* was one of the first programmes to get most of its laughs from the use of catchphrases, such as Colonel Chinstrap who was always looking for a drink – 'I don't mind if I do'.

Going to dances was another popular leisure-time activity. In a television interview in 1992, an East Anglian woman recalled the dances she went to at a nearby US air base (Source 23.T).

Source 23.T

We used to go to the dances at Kimbolton. Reason why we used to go was because the Americans had bowls of cigarettes and candy bars all around and the girls used to stuff their pockets and take them for the girls in the hostels who did smoke.

Wartime holidays (Source 23.U) meant putting up with a lot of restrictions. Ration books had to be given in to the hotel or boarding house. Nonetheless, the chance to take a short holiday was important, especially for people under strain with their war work.

Source 23.U A wartime holiday in July 1943

As soon as we got off the train at Hunstanton Station [Norfolk], *we heard a woman telling her son, 'Breathe in Brian!' The signs of war were everywhere. The pier was closed and so were many of the hotels. There was barbed wire on the beach and on the cliffs. The town seemed full of men and women in uniform and there were lots of Americans about. I remember lying on the cliffs gazing at the sky. Hundreds of bombers droned overhead heading out across the coast. It was only much later I realised they were going to bomb Hamburg.*

24 Persecution of the Jews

▶ *HOW and WHY did the Nazis persecute the Jews?* ATIB ■ ATIC ■
▶ *WHAT was the Final Solution? HOW and WHY did the Nazis try to achieve it?* ATIB ■ ATIC ■

Enemies of the Jews

Hitler claimed he had hated the Jews ever since his youth in Vienna before the First World War. He made this hatred perfectly clear in 1924 when he wrote *Mein Kampf* (Source 24.A). Most of the other Nazi leaders were just as prejudiced – as you can see in Source 24.B

Source 24.A Adolf Hitler in *Mein Kampf* written in 1924

The Jew is and remains a sponger, who, like a germ, spreads over wider and wider areas as some new area attracts him. Wherever he sets himself up, the people who welcome him are bound to be bled to death sooner or later.

Source 24.B Dr Josef Goebbels in 1930

The Jew is the real cause for our loss of the Great War. He is responsible for our misery and he lives on it. He has spoiled our race, undermined our customs, and broken our power. We are enemies of the Jews because we belong to the German people.

When the Nazis seized power in Germany in 1933, the Jews were among the first of their targets. They immediately ordered a boycott of Jewish-owned shops (Source 24.C).

Source 24.C

From Saturday, April 1 1933, A BOYCOTT. Don't buy in Jewish shops or warehouses! Don't engage Jewish lawyers. Avoid Jewish doctors! Show the Jews that they cannot disgrace Germany's honour without being punished. Those who ignore this appeal prove that they sympathise with Germany's enemies.

The works of Jewish writers and composers were banned (such as the music of Mendelssohn). Great Germans, such as Albert Einstein, the scientist, and Bruno Walter, the conductor, fled or were forced to leave Germany because they were Jews. Nearly 40 000 Jews left Germany in 1933, over 20 000 in each year between 1934 and 1937, 40 000 again in 1938 and double that number in 1939.

The Nazis believed that the people of Aryan descent – those from Northern Europe (Germany and Scandinavia) – were the Master Race. They were shown on Nazi posters as tall, lean, athletic, blonde and blue-eyed. This was, of course, a complete nonsense – as any picture of the Nazi leaders will make plain, such as Hitler himself or Goebbels. Nonetheless, the Nazis wanted to pass a law to make sure that only people with 'pure' German blood could become German citizens. This is why Hitler announced a new race law at Nuremberg in September 1935. Marriages between a Jew (anyone with at least one Jewish grandparent) and a German were forbidden. This even applied to existing marriages. As you can imagine, it caused a lot of distress. It was nothing, however, when compared to the horrors to come.

On 9 November 1938, the Nazis launched a new campaign of terror against the Jews after a German diplomat in Paris had been murdered by a young Jew (Source 24.D). The first day of this campaign was later

Nazi poster advertising the Eternal Jew *exhibition in Munich in 1937*

24.1 Use the sources to say why the Nazis were prejudiced against the Jews. AT3/L6
24.2 What things in the poster 'The Eternal Jew' tell you that this is Nazi propaganda? What did the artist want people to think? AT2/L5
24.3 Draw a bar chart to show the number of Jews who fled from Germany between 1933 and 1939. Use the Sources to explain the variations in the length of the columns in your chart. AT1B/L5
24.4 What type of Nazi is shown in the American poster above?
24.5 Compare the two posters. In what ways are they similar? In what ways are they different? AT2/L6
24.6 Look at the photograph of Dachau. What do you think the sculptor of this memorial wanted people to think when they looked at this work? AT1C ■

An American poster

called Crystal Night because thousands of Jewish glass windows had been smashed. Jews were beaten up in the streets. New regulations were brought in (Source 24.E) stopping Jews from using many public buildings.

Source 24.D From a Berlin newspaper

Berlin: November 10, 1938 *The announcement of the death of the diplomat and party member vom Rath by the cowardly hand of the Jewish murderer has aroused spontaneous anti-Jewish demonstrations throughout the Reich. The German People's deep indignation has given rise to powerful anti-Jewish activities. In many places Jewish shop windows have been smashed and the show-cases of Jewish shopkeepers wrecked. The synagogues from which teachings hostile to the State and People are spread, have been set on fire and the furnishings destroyed.*

Source 24.E Jews banned from public places

Police decree of November 28th, 1938 *No Jew may set foot in or drive through the streets, squares, parks, or buildings which have been barred to Jews. In Berlin Jews are barred from all theatres, cinemas, cabarets, public concert halls, museums, amusement parks, all sports grounds including the skating rink, all public and private swimming pools.*

Exterminating the Jews

Many Jews were sent to concentration camps like Dachau (see photograph below) before 1939. But the Holocaust – the mass murder of millions of Jews in special camps – did not begin until midway through the Second World War. Before that time, however, the Nazis had already begun to eliminate the Jewish peoples they overran as they advanced through Poland and Russia. Both of these countries had large Jewish populations. A German builder called Hermann Graebe told the Nuremberg War Tribunal in 1946 of the mass executions he had seen near Dubno in the Ukraine in October 1942. The 5000 Jews living in the town had been taken by SS men to a building site and shot in groups, twenty people at a time. Barbaric executions like these horrified the world. They were used in Allied propaganda, such as the poster above, to convince everyone of the evil they were fighting.

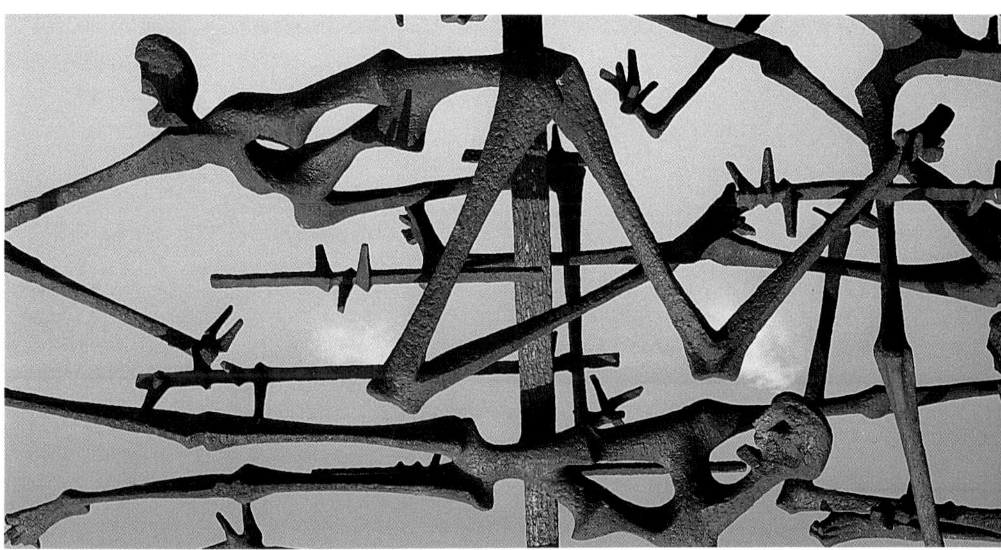

Memorial to the thousands of Jewish and non-Jewish victims who died at Dachau Concentration Camp near Munich in Germany

The Final Solution

As the Allied armies advanced through Europe in 1944–5, they were horrified to discover gas chambers in the Nazi concentration camps. They found thousands of corpses in a pit at Bergen-Belsen and a vast pile of shoes at Auschwitz. The troops were so incensed, they rounded up local Germans and made them walk round the camps to see for themselves what had been done in their name (Source 24.F).

Source 24.F By an American serviceman

When the people saw what the camp was like and were led through the torture chambers and past the ovens, men and women screamed out and fainted. Others were led away crying hysterically. All swore that during the past years they had no idea of what had been going on in the camp just outside their town.

And yet, one heard other stories. One heard that it would be impossible not to know what was happening, that the greasy smoke and the unmistakeable odour of burning bodies could be detected for miles around such concentration camps, that villagers got up petitions to have the camps moved elsewhere. I never knew what to believe.

The Allies found it hard to come to terms with the scale of the horrors they had uncovered. Eventually they worked out that as many as six million Jews may have died in the Nazi concentration camps. Two million died in the gas chambers at Auschwitz in Poland alone. As you can see from the photograph, Aushwitz had a special railway line for the Jewish people who made their last journey on earth to the camp. The Nazis called this blood-chilling extermination programme The Final Solution.

The story of Auschwitz began in 1941 when Rudolf Hoess, the commandant of what was then a concentration camp in Poland for prisoners of war, was ordered by the SS Chief, Heinrich Himmler, to convert it into an extermination camp (Source 24.G). In cold blood, Hoess and Himmler's assistant, Adolf Eichmann, drew up plans (Source 24.H).

Source 24.G Himmler's orders in 1941

The Führer has ordered the final solution of the Jewish question and we – the SS – have to carry out this order. I have selected Auschwitz for this task both because of its good communications and because the area can be easily sealed off and hidden. You will maintain the strictest silence concerning this order. After your meeting with Eichmann send me the plans for the proposed installations at once.

Source 24.H By Rudolf Hoess, Commandant of Auschwitz

We [Hoess and Eichmann] *discussed how the extermination was to be carried out. Gas was the only feasible method, since it would be impossible to wipe out by shooting the large numbers involved. In any case, shooting would place too heavy a burden on the SS men who had to carry it out, particularly in view of the women and children involved.*

Eichmann and Hoess decided that the gas Cyclon B, which was used for pest control at Auschwitz, would prove suitable. When the trains crowded with Jews arrived at the camp, they were surrounded by SS guards. The barbed wire which sealed the sliding doors to the waggons

24.7 How do we know that the Nazis did not want anyone to know about The Final Solution? AT3/L4

24.8 How and why did the mass extermination programme begin? Draw up a Time Line like the one on page 159 to show the steps which led to The Final Solution. AT1A ■

24.9 What was the reaction of the Commandant of Auschwitz when he received Himmler's instructions? Was he only obeying orders? AT3/L5

24.10 Look at the painting of Belsen. What does it tell you about the Nazi concentration camps? AT3/L5

24.11 At Dachau a huge slogan warns visitors, '*THOSE WHO CANNOT REMEMBER THE PAST ARE CONDEMNED TO REPEAT IT*'. Despite this, some people object to the fact that Nazi concentration camps have been preserved instead of being destroyed. Why? Do you think the Dachau slogan justifies the use of these camps as museums of the holocaust? AT2/L7

The one-way only railway line to Auschwitz

was released and the prisoners were separated into two groups – those who were fit for work and those who were 'unfit'. The unfit prisoners were taken to a block labelled 'Shower'. They could see the shower jets in the ceiling above. An eyewitness after the war said that the prisoners were told they were going to have a bath after their long journey. Sometimes they were promised a drink of hot coffee. Packed inside the gas chambers they realised the truth only too late. Within minutes they were dead. The bodies were cremated at night in order to preserve secrecy but the fumes could not be concealed.

On 4 October 1943 Himmler said, 'This is a glorious page of our history which never has and never will be written'. He was wrong. It was. But when the trials for war crimes began after the war, onlookers were horrified to discover that the camp commandants, prison guards, doctors and assistants brought to trial looked little different from other people in court. It terrified observers to think that ordinary Germans should have been persuaded so easily to take part in such horrible crimes. Almost without exception, the former guards claimed they were only obeying orders. If they had disobeyed them, they said, they would have been executed themselves.

The women's compound at Belsen

25 Dropping the atom bomb

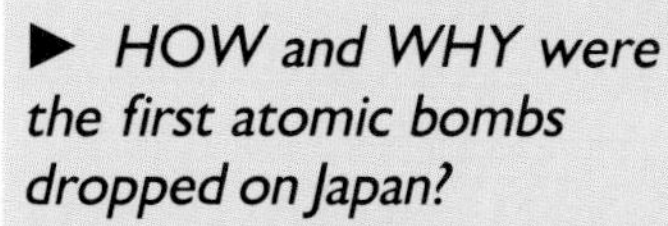

▶ *HOW and WHY were the first atomic bombs dropped on Japan?*

ATIB ■ ATIC ■

▶ *WHAT effect did this have on Japan and the rest of the world?*

ATIA ■ ATIB ■ ATIC ■

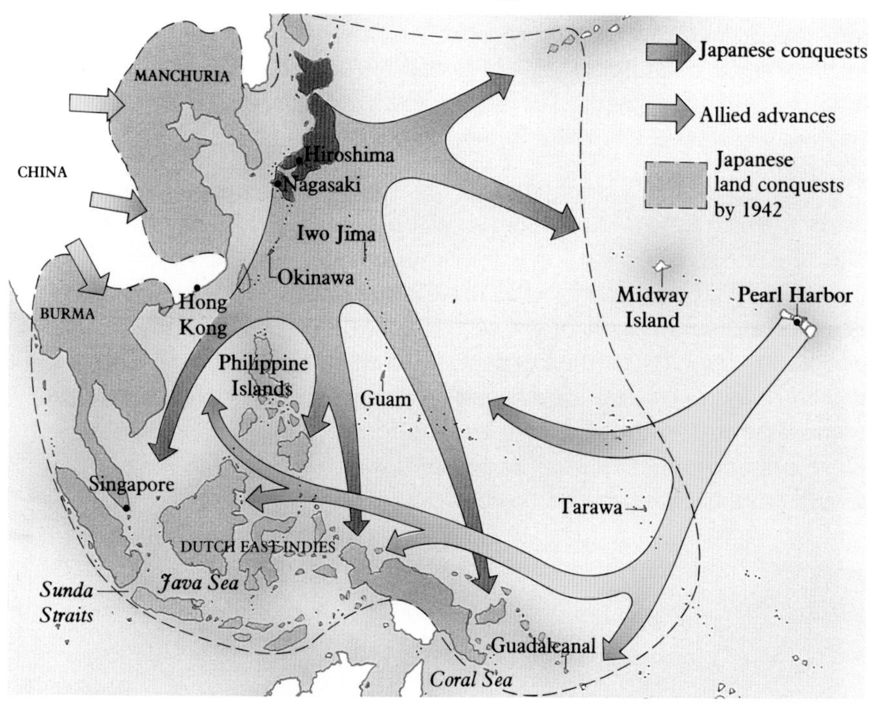

Map of the war in the Pacific

The war against Japan

By the middle of 1942 the Japanese had carved out a large empire for themselves in the Far East. But after the Battle of Midway (page 155), the Allies began to push them back. Using landing craft and aircraft carriers, American marines recaptured the Pacific islands. They landed on Guadalcanal in 1942 and by early 1945 had recaptured the Philippines. Each new island they took brought them closer to Japan. They called it 'island-hopping'.

The Allied armed forces in the Far East were greatly helped when the victory in Europe meant that every effort could now be used to defeat Japan. Allied commanders made plans to invade southern Japan with 650 000 men in November 1945 (Operation Olympic) and to land a million men on central Japan in March 1946 (Operation Coronet). They forecast at least 250 000 American dead and another 500 000 wounded. This was because the Japanese defenders of the islands of Iwo Jima and Okinawa, captured in March and June 1945, had fought to the last man. Many had committed suicide sooner than be taken prisoner. Over 100 000 Japanese and 12 000 Americans died on Okinawa alone.

By the start of August 1945, however, the chances of winning the war had greatly improved. The Japanese were already seeking peace. The Emperor Hirohito had appointed Admiral Suzuki as Prime Minister on 7 April 1945. Suzuki had argued for peace, not war, in the 1930s. In June the Emperor told him to try 'to end the war as soon as possible' although Japan's military leaders opposed this. Suzuki's Government secretly asked the Soviet Union (which had not yet entered the Pacific war) to help her negotiate peace with the West. When US President Truman insisted on unconditional surrender in July (see page 178), the Japanese rejected his terms.

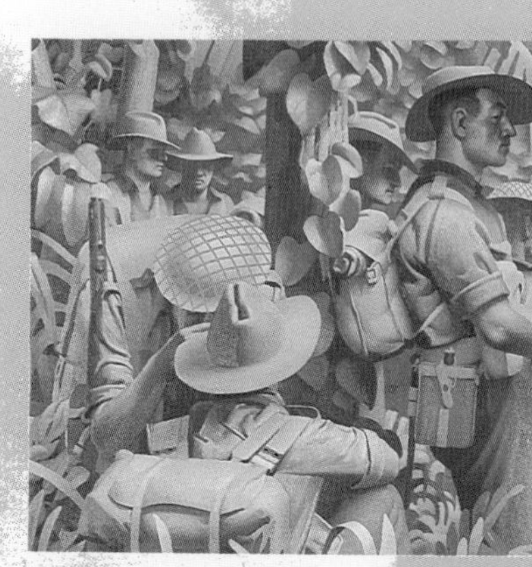

An Australian patrol in the jungle. Many of the soldiers fighting in the tropical forests of the Far East found the stifling, wet heat unbearable. The dense undergrowth meant a different type of warfare from that used in Europe or North Africa

25.1 How was fighting in a tropical forest different from fighting in a desert (page 151)?

AT1B/L5

25.2 Look at the painting *The Two-Thousand-Yard Stare*. Why do you think it is called this? What does it tell you about the war in the Pacific?

AT3/L5 AT1C/L6

American landing craft approach the Philippines in 1944

25.3 Compare *The Two-Thousand-Yard Stare* with *Summer Soldiers* on page 153. What do the two pictures have in common? AT3/L6 AT1C/L7

American soldier in the Pacific with 'The Two-Thousand-Yard Stare'

Even at this late stage, further help was on its way. Russian troops from Germany were travelling by rail across Siberia to the Far East. This was because Stalin had promised the Allies earlier (page 179) that he would declare war on Japan three months after the defeat of Hitler. When at last he did so, on 8 August 1945, the Americans had already dropped the atomic bomb which would end the war.

Source 25.A By Captain Parsons on the *Enola Gay*

When the bomb fell away, we began putting as much distance between us and the ball of fire which we knew was coming as quickly as possible. There was a terrific flash of light, brilliant as the sun. That was the first indication I had that the bomb worked. Each man gasped. What had been Hiroshima was going up in a mountain of smoke.

First I could see a mushroom of boiling dust apparently with some debris in it up to 20 000 feet [6000 metres]. *The boiling continued for three or four minutes as I watched. Then a white cloud plumed upwards from the centre to some 40 000 feet* [12 000 metres]. *An angry dust cloud swirled and spread all round the city. There were fires on the fringes of the city, apparently burning as buildings crumbled and gas mains broke.*

Hiroshima and Nagasaki

At 9.15 a.m. on Monday, 6 August 1945, an American superfortress bomber, the *Enola Gay*, dropped an atomic bomb on Hiroshima, a large industrial city in southern Japan (Sources 25.A and 25.B). The bomb killed 80 000 people and destroyed 80 per cent of the city's buildings. Many people at the time, and since, thought the Allies should have given the Japanese a warning beforehand. But an American minister explained that the scientists were always afraid the first bombs they dropped might be 'duds' and fail to go off. US Navy Captain, William Parsons, was on the *Enola Gay*. His description of the dropping of the atom bomb on Hiroshima was given to the *Daily Telegraph* the following day (Source 25.A). The view from the ground was different (Source 25.B).

While the Japanese Government considered how to react to the Hiroshima bomb, a second bomb was dropped on Nagasaki on 9 August 1945, killing another 40 000 people. The Japanese had no way of countering these weapons. On 14 August the Japanese Emperor announced the surrender of Japan.

Source 25.B Report by a Japanese journalist

Suddenly a glaring whitish pinkish light appeared in the sky followed almost immediately by a wave of suffocating heat and a wind which swept away everything in its path. Within a few seconds the thousands of people in the streets and the gardens in the centre of the town were scorched by a wave of searing heat. Many were killed instantly. Others lay writhing on the ground screaming in agony from the intolerable pain of their burns. Everything standing upright in the way of the blast – walls, houses, factories and other buildings – was annihilated and the debris spun round in a whirlwind and was carried up into the air. Trams were picked up and tossed aside. Trains were flung off the rails as though they were toys. Trees went up in flames. The rice plants lost their greenness. The grass burned on the ground like dry straw.

Explosion of the atomic bomb over Nagasaki, 9 August 1945

25.4 Use Sources 25.A and 25.B on page 175 and Sources 25.C and 25.D to describe the dropping of the atomic bomb on Hiroshima and its effects on the city. AT3/L4 AT1C/L5

25.5 Use these sources to compare atomic warfare with an earlier war, such as the First World War (Chapters 13 and 15) or the Napoleonic Wars. What 'progress' had been made by 1945? AT1A ■

25.6 How did Churchill and Truman contradict themselves in Sources 25.E, 25.F, 25.G and 25.K? AT2/L5

25.7 One writer said 'The bomb that fell on Hiroshima fell on America, too.' What did he mean? AT1C ■

25.8 How did distrust of the Soviet Union play a part in persuading the Allies to use the bomb? AT1C/L5

Effects of the bomb

Source 25.C From *Hiroshima Diary*, by Dr Hachiya

Scorching winds howled around us, whipping dust and ashes into our eyes and up our noses. Our mouths became dry, our throats raw and sore from the biting smoke pulled into our lungs. Coughing was uncontrollable. The streets were deserted except for the dead. Some looked as if they had been frozen by death while in full flight; others lay sprawled as though some giant had flung them from a great height.

Source 25.D By Dr Tabuchi, a colleague of Dr Hachiya

It was a horrible sight. Hundreds of injured people who were trying to escape to the hills passed our house. The sight of them was almost unbearable. Their faces and hands were burnt and swollen; and great sheets of skin had peeled away from their tissues to hang like rags on a scarecrow.

Hiroshima six months after the dropping of the atom bomb

25.9 How does this help to explain the attitude of the Soviet writer in Source 25.L? AT2/L7

25.10 What evidence is there that dropping the atomic bomb was needed to persuade the Japanese to agree to peace? AT3/L6

Should the bomb have been used?

Ever since 6 August 1945, people have argued about whether the atomic bombs should have been used or not. You can see what US President Truman (the man responsible) thought in Sources 25.E and 25.F. Winston Churchill was in no doubt that it was the right decision (Source 25.G). Other Allied leaders, such as Admiral Leahy, President Truman's chief adviser, were not so sure (Source 25.H). You can see other verdicts and another extract by Churchill in Sources 25.I to 25.M.

Source 25.E By Admiral Leahy, who was with President Truman

Truman was excited over the news. He shook Captain Graham's hand and said, 'This is the greatest thing in history'.

Source 25.F By US President Truman in the 1950s

The atom bomb was no great decision. It was merely another powerful weapon in the arsenal of righteousness. The dropping of the bombs stopped the war, saved millions of lives.

25.11 What evidence is there that the war was almost over by then anyway? AT3/L6

25.12 Was the dropping of the atomic bomb on Hiroshima 'a senseless, cruel and barbarous crime' or was it 'a miracle of deliverance'? What do you think? AT1C/L7

Source 25.G By Winston Churchill writing in 1953

Up to this moment we had planned an assault upon Japan by terrific air bombing and by the invasion of very large armies. To quell the Japanese resistance man by man and conquer the country yard by yard might well require the loss of a million American lives and half that number of British. Now all this nightmarish picture had vanished. Moreover we should not need the Russians. We had no need to ask favours of them.

At any rate, there never was a moment's discussion as to whether the atomic bomb should be used or not. To bring the war to an end at the cost of a few explosions, seemed a miracle of deliverance.

Source 25.H By Admiral Leahy

My own feeling was that, in being the first to use it, we had copied the barbarians of the Dark Age. I was not taught to make war in that fashion and wars cannot be won by destroying women and children.

Source 25.I By President Truman's daughter

The final testimony for the rightness of Dad's decision on the atomic bomb comes from the Japanese themselves. Cabinet Secretary Sakomizu said the atomic bomb 'provided an excuse for surrender'. Hirohito's adviser, Marquis Kido said, 'The atomic bomb made it easier for us, the politicians, to negotiate peace'.

Source 25.J By one of the leading scientists involved

The bomb simply had to be a success – so much money had been spent on it. The relief to everyone concerned when the bomb was finished and dropped was enormous.

Source 25.K By Winston Churchill writing in 1953

By the end of July 1945 the Japanese Navy had virtually ceased to exist. The land was in chaos and on the verge of collapse. It would be a mistake to suppose that the fate of Japan was settled by the atomic bomb. Her defeat was certain before the first bomb fell.

Source 25.L A Soviet verdict on Hiroshima in 1977

On the 6 August, without any military necessity, an American plane dropped an atomic bomb on the Japanese city of Hiroshima, causing the deaths of many thousands of civilians, including women, children and old men. It was a senseless, cruel and barbarous crime against not only the Japanese people, but also mankind as a whole.

Source 25.M In a Hiroshima hospital, 15 August 1945

This unexpected message left me stunned. It had been the Emperor's voice and he had read the Imperial Proclamation of Surrender. Silence reigned for a long time. By degrees people began to whisper. Someone shouted, 'How can we lose the war!' Following this outburst, expressions of anger were unleashed. 'Only a coward would back out now.' 'I would rather die than be defeated!' 'What have we been suffering for?' I began to feel the same way – fight to the bloody end and die. The one word – surrender – had produced a greater shock than the bombing of our city.

26 The impact of peace

▶ *WHAT effect did the Second World War have on Europe?*

ATIA ■ ATIB ■ ATIC ■

▶ *WHAT part did the wartime conferences play in deciding the shape of Europe after the war?*

ATIB ■

Planning for peace

As you have seen (page 147), the Second World War began for Britain when the then Prime Minister, Neville Chamberlain, declared war on Germany on 3 September 1939 after Hitler had invaded Poland. He did so because he had promised to protect 'Poland's existing frontiers'. When the war ended in 1945, however, a large part of Poland was taken by the Soviet Union with the agreement of Chamberlain's successor, Winston Churchill. What had happened, as in most wars, was that the aims of the nations taking part had changed. Many of the promises made were never kept.

The Allies began preparing for peace long before the war ended. They had to agree on what to do with the lands they recaptured or conquered. It was unthinkable, for instance, to let Italy keep Ethiopia (formerly Abyssinia) which she seized in 1935 (page 141). This is why the Allied leaders met to hold wartime conferences to plan their next moves and to sort out what they would do after the war.

"Here you are! Don't lose it again!"

Donald Zec drew this cartoon for the Daily Mirror *in 1945*

Casablanca

The first of these conferences was held in Casablanca in North Africa after the Allied landings in Morocco in November 1942 (page 151). Churchill and Roosevelt met to decide what to do next (Source 26.A).

Source 26.A Decisions of the Casablanca Conference, 14–24 January 1943

- *British and US armies in North Africa to invade Italy after defeating the enemy forces in Libya and Tunisia.*
- *Britain to join wholeheartedly in the war against Japan after the defeat of Hitler.*
- *The Allies to demand the unconditional surrender of the enemy. This meant they would not discuss peace terms at all.*

The Teheran Conference in 1943

Teheran

The first conference with Stalin was held later the same year (1943) in Teheran, capital of Iran. You can see the main decisions the Allied leaders took in Source 26.B.

Source 26.B Decisions of the Teheran Conference, 29 Nov – 1 Dec 1943

- *Allied invasion of France to take place in May or June 1944.*
- *The Soviet Union to declare war on Japan after the defeat of Hitler.*
- *A new World Organisation to replace the League of Nations.*
- *The Polish frontier with the USSR to be moved further to the West. Poland to be given part of Germany in compensation.*

Source 26.C Stalin at Yalta

He is very quiet and restrained and spoke very much to the point. He's obviously got a very good sense of humour – and a rather quick temper! I have never known the Russians so easy and accommodating. In particular Joe has been extremely good. He is a great man, and shows up very impressively against the background of the other two ageing statesmen.

Source 26.E

The truth is that on any and every point, Russia tries to seize all that she can and she uses these meetings to grab as much as she can get.

26.1 How did the decisions of the wartime conferences change what had been agreed at Versailles in 1919 (page 127)? AT1A ■
26.2 What was Donald Zec's cartoon (opposite) saying?
26.3 Why do you think one of Churchill's chief advisers said it was 'foolishness' to demand unconditional surrender? What was he afraid of? AT1C/L5
26.4 Was it 'foolishness' in view of the Nazi treatment of the Jews? AT1C/L6
26.5 Compare Source 26.C with Source 26.E. How and why did Stalin's attitude change? AT1A ■

The Potsdam Conference

Yalta

The second meeting between Stalin (aged 64), Churchill (aged 69) and Roosevelt (aged 62, but seriously ill) was held in the Russian Black Sea holiday resort of Yalta when the war was nearly over in Europe. The Allies had to make important decisions about the shape of Europe after the war (Source 26.D). Stalin wanted to clear up the question of what to do with Poland. The British diplomat Sir Alexander Cadogan thought him 'much the most impressive of the three men' (Source 26.C).

Source 26.D Decisions of the Yalta Conference, 4–11 February 1945

- *Eastern boundary of Poland with the USSR to follow the line agreed with Hitler in 1939. Poland to be given part of eastern Germany up to a line following the rivers Oder and Neisse.*
- *Free elections to be held in nations liberated by the Allies.*
- *The USSR to declare war on Japan within three months of defeating Hitler. In return, the USSR to regain territories lost in 1904–05.*
- *United Nations Organisation to go ahead (see page 184).*
- *US, British, French and Soviet Occupation Zones to be formed in Germany after the war.*
- *Germany to pay war damages of about $20 000 million to the Soviet Union and other victims of Nazi aggression.*

Potsdam

The last of the Allied conferences was held two months after the end of the war in Europe in a palace near Berlin. Eastern Europe was then in Russian hands. The Western leaders wanted to see democratic elections held there but had no power to insist that this be done. In any case, the atmosphere had changed. By now, the Allies were very suspicious of Soviet aims in Europe. In fact, it seems highly likely that Truman dropped the atomic bomb only four days after the end of the Conference to stop Stalin acquiring an empire in the Far East as well as in Europe. Sir Alexander Cadogan shared these suspicions. He thought Stalin was being 'very tiresome' now (Source 26.E).

Source 26.F Decisions of the Potsdam Conference, 16 July – 2 August 1945

- *The boundary line following the rivers Oder and Neisse to be the German frontier with Poland until a peace treaty is signed.*
- *A Council of Foreign Ministers to draw up peace treaties with Germany, Austria and Italy.*
- *Nazi war criminals to be prosecuted.*
- *Payment of reparations by Germany to include equipment and machinery from German factories.*

When the Potsdam Conference was held in July/August 1945, one of the 'ageing statesmen' at Yalta – Roosevelt – had died. Another 'ageing statesman' – Churchill – was defeated in the British General Election while the Conference was being held. This is why the photograph shows the new Labour Prime Minister, Clement Attlee (on the left) and the new American President, Harry S. Truman (in the middle)

Refugees from Silesia in 1945

The refugee problem

After the war, the Allies had to deal with the immense problem of what to do to help starving people living in a Europe ripped apart by the conflict. Millions of refugees and returning soldiers, extensive bomb damage, looting of damaged buildings, crime, diseases (such as dysentery and typhoid fever) and the collapse of existing systems of law and order added to the chaos.

Most of the refugees had fled with what belongings they could carry to escape the advancing Red Army. Many were forced to leave their homes. As many as ten million Germans were on the move. Two million may have died. The survivors accused the Russian soldiers of raping women, looting homes, shooting people at random and forcing others to work as slave labour. Some of the accusations were true, others were invented. The Allies found it difficult to sort out which were fact and which were fiction. It seems clear, however, that many Russian soldiers did take revenge for the appalling atrocities inflicted on the Soviet Union when the Germans invaded the USSR in 1941 (page 152). Nor were the Allies free from blame. As you have seen (Source 22.M on page 157), thousands of refugees were knowingly killed in Dresden when that city was razed to the ground in February 1945. You can get some idea of what it was like to be a refugee from the diary of a woman who escaped from Vienna in April 1945 (Source 26.G).

Source 26.G

Vienna: 3 April 1945 *The train was packed. About noon, shortly after Krems* [30km from Vienna], *the first enemy fighters appeared. We crept into a tunnel and remained there for six hours while enemy bombers battered Krems to pieces.*

4 April *About 2.0 a.m. we boarded a freight train which consisted of open cars packed with people wrapped in blankets. They turned out to be refugees from Hungary.*

Linz: 5 April *The station area was one mass of ruins with crowds of people milling about. It was in an uproar. Nobody seemed to know where to go or what to do.*

Gmunden: 5 April *Much confusion as lorries keep arriving, loaded with fugitives from Vienna. Having nowhere to go, they are simply dumped and sit around on their bundles.*

Bad Aussee: 6 April *A recent arrival from Vienna told us that already yesterday the Russians were hanging Nazi party members from trees in Florisdorf, a suburb of Vienna.*

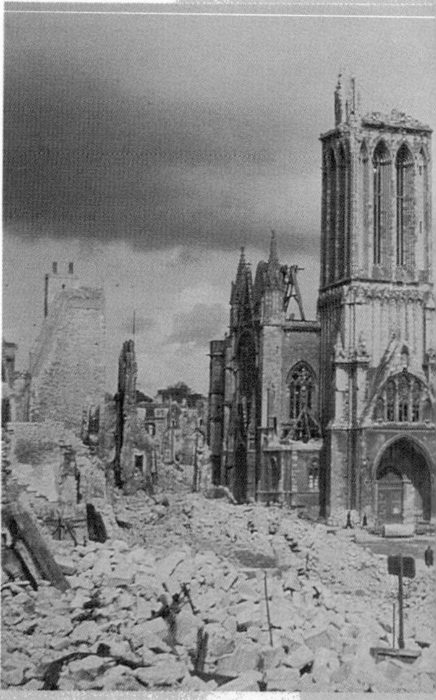

The ruins of Caen in Normandy in 1945. Scenes like this could be seen in hundreds of European towns and cities when the war ended. Reconstruction took many years. Some towns took the opportunity to design and build completely new city centres. Others, such as Warsaw (Poland), Tours (France) and Koblenz (Germany), painstakingly rebuilt many of their ancient buildings which had been badly damaged or destroyed during the war

26.6 Why was there a refugee problem after the Second World War? AT1B ■

26.7 Were the evacuees in Britain in 1939 (page 160) refugees as well?

By the end of 1945, as many as one in five of the Germans living in the British, French and American Occupation Zones was a refugee. In Europe as a whole there were about 20 million refugees or displaced persons. Many were labourers who had been taken from their homes in Occupied Europe and forced to work in German factories. Others were released prisoners of war trying to find their way home on foot. Some were Jews who had escaped from the concentration camps. The Allied troops and UNRRA, an organisation set up by the United Nations, tried to feed and clothe them. Camps were set up for them. Others lived by stealing or begging. It was years before the problem was resolved.

Over 3 500 000 German soldiers died during the war. This was about nine times as great as British losses. War memorials to those who died are not as prominent in Germany as they are in Britain. This war memorial at Garmisch-Partenkirchen in the Bavarian Alps is on a hillside overlooking the town

Rebuilding Europe

After the war in Europe, the British people elected a Labour Government to power. They wanted a fresh start to their lives, not a return to the unemployment and poverty of the 1930s. The war changed people's attitudes in other ways as well. Women wanted equal pay for equal work. The class system began to break down. It became rare for people to employ servants. Labour gave everyone, however rich or poor, the benefits of a Welfare State. They introduced free health care, free education and, for those in need, the right to an extensive range of social services, such as unemployment or disability benefit.

Like most other governments in Europe, Labour had difficult problems to solve, such as coping with shortages of fuel, housing and food and finding work for millions of returning servicemen and women. A vast rebuilding programme was needed to restore towns and cities and provide the homes that people needed. Factories and farms, docks and harbours, roads and railways, schools and hospitals, had all to be built or repaired. Huge sums of money were loaned by the Americans to help the countries of Europe recover. For years petrol, food and clothing were strictly rationed. It only ended in Britain on 2 July 1954 – nine years after the defeat of Germany!

One solution to the acute housing shortage after the war was an American idea. Prefabs (prefabricated houses) could be erected quickly to take the place of houses destroyed in enemy air-raids

The people of Europe set about the long and difficult task of rebuilding their shattered lives. Many had lost husbands, brothers and sons in the fighting. Millions of women had also died. As many as 8 million Russians, 6 million Poles, 2 million Germans and 1 million men and women from Yugoslavia were among the vast number of civilians who lost their lives in the war.

The Iron Curtain

The Second World War did not end with an impressive peace conference like Versailles (page 127). The Western Allies and the Soviet Union distrusted each other by the end of the war. Relations between the two sides got worse in the years which followed. This was called the Cold War because East and West treated the other as an enemy but without actually going to war. The Western Allies complained that they did not know what was happening in Eastern Europe (Source 26.H). The separation of Germany and Berlin into four Occupation Zones was one of the issues which divided them. As a result, Germany was not reunited until October 1990 – over 45 years after the end of the war.

A Russian soldier hoisting the hammer and sickle over Berlin

Denazification

One of the first Allied tasks was to search out the Nazis who had helped Hitler to plan and run the war. Many were wanted for war crimes. This rooting-out of Nazis was called *denazification*. Since the former members of the *Gestapo* and *SS* had discarded their uniforms and forged false papers, they were often able to merge with the refugees. Many escaped to South America. Those with special skills, such as the rocket experts, were recruited to work for either the Allies or the Russians.

You can see how the Allies tried to find the former Nazis in Source 26.I. Many innocent Germans suffered in the process and many of the guilty got away. The Austrian composer Anton Webern, for instance, was shot dead by an American soldier who mistook him for a criminal.

Punishing the guilty

When the war criminals were found, they were put on trial. Most got off more lightly than the men and women of Occupied Europe and the Ukraine who had collaborated with (worked with or helped) the Nazis. Some had betrayed their friends and some, like 40 000 of Russia's Cossacks, had fought for Germany in the war. The Cossacks were sent back to Stalin to almost certain execution. Thousands of French collaborators were also executed without trial. Women who had had German boyfriends had their heads shaven in public. The politicians who had collaborated were put on trial and some were executed, such as Pierre Laval, the French Prime Minister, and Vidkun Quisling, the Norwegian Fascist leader.

Stalin wanted to shoot the top 50 000 Nazi leaders on sight but the Allies insisted they be tried as war criminals in a court of law. The most famous of these trials was held at Nuremberg in 1945–6 when Göring, Hess, Ribbentrop and other top Nazi leaders were put on trial. The Allies would have tried Hitler, Goebbels and Himmler, too, but they had all committed suicide sooner than face capture and execution.

The Allies soon discovered a problem. What was a war crime? What was a normal act of war? There was no doubt that the wholesale extermination of millions of Jews and Russian prisoners of war was a war crime. So, too, was the mass execution of innocent civilians in reprisals, such as at Lidice in Czechoslovakia (where all the men in the village were shot after a top Nazi had been killed). But was it a war crime to be a clerk handling the documents of people who had been shot? And was it a defence for the accused Nazis and *SS* Guards to say 'I was only obeying orders' (see also page 173)?

Source 26.H By Winston Churchill in 1946

From Stettin in the Baltic to Trieste in the Adriatic, an Iron Curtain has descended across the Continent.

Source 26.I By a refugee from Vienna

We had to pass through the hands of a veritable chain of interrogators installed in three railroad cars. They asked us hundreds of questions and kept comparing our names with long lists to make sure that we had not been prominent Nazis. Finally we were allowed out of the last railway car, given a daub of white paint on each leg – to show that we had been 'whitewashed' – and, after a further long wait, told that we were free to go where we wished.

This painting by Dame Laura Knight, The Dock – Nuremberg, *shows the trial where the top Nazi leaders were tried for war crimes*

When a British officer refused to take part in the shelling of Le Havre in 1944, he was imprisoned for disobeying orders precisely because he thought it was a war crime to harm the helpless French civilians in the port.

26.8 How did Dame Laura Knight paint the Nuremberg Trial? AT3/L5

26.9 Compare the map below with the maps on pages 90, 127, 146 and 159. How did Europe change between 1914 and 1945? AT1A ■

26.10 Do you think it is possible to say what is a war crime and what is a normal act of war? Was the British officer right or wrong to disobey orders if he thought that by carrying them out he would commit a war crime? AT1C ■

26.11 Who was responsible for the war crimes? Was it, (a) the people who carried them out, (b) the people who gave the orders, or (c) both sets of people? AT1B ■

European boundary changes after the war

27 The United Nations

How the United Nations began

In August 1941, at a time when the United States was still neutral, Winston Churchill met US President Roosevelt on board a warship anchored off the Canadian coast. There they drew up a document describing the sort of world they wanted to see when the war was over. A British newspaper called it *The Atlantic Charter*. In it they said they wanted to defend the existing frontiers between nations. They thought all people should have the right to choose the type of government under which they wanted to live. They wanted the nations of the world to get together to ensure lasting peace by setting up 'a wider and permanent system of general security'.

Setting up the United Nations

What Churchill and Roosevelt had in mind was a more effective League of Nations (page 130). Two years later when they met Stalin at the Teheran Conference (page 178), the Allied leaders agreed to set up the United Nations. Representatives from the three countries held a conference in 1944 at Dumbarton Oaks (near Washington DC) to draw up plans. They decided it would have a General Assembly and a Security Council (just as the old League had had an Assembly and a Council).

There was one big sticking point on which they could not agree. This was over the right of one of the Great Powers in the Security Council to veto (turn down) any proposal which affected them personally. The Soviet Union insisted that all decisions must be agreed by everyone. The British delegate, Sir Alexander Cadogan, said that no other country in the world would agree to this if they couldn't have a veto as well (Source 27.A).

Source 27.A From the diary of Sir Alexander Cadogan

Thursday, 7 September 1944 *Ed Stettinius* [USA], *Gromyko* [Russia] *and I lunched together. Ed and I tried to hammer him on the main point – the Great Power Veto. But he was quite wooden on that. Best he could say was that we should 'leave the point open'. I explained to him again and again that this was an illusion and that, if one 'left it open' one simply wouldn't get a World Organisation.*

Wednesday, 13 September *Gromyko informed us his Government's final answer on voting question was definitely 'No'.*

The reason for the Soviet refusal was Stalin's fear that the Soviet Union would be outvoted by the West. The same problem cropped up at the San Francisco Conference (Source 27.B) in the summer of 1945. This time forty other nations took part besides Britain, the United States and the Soviet Union.

Source 27.B By an American delegate

May 23, 1945 *By hammering it out, we have found an answer which satisfies practically everybody. In my view, that is the great hope for the new League itself. If we do nothing more than create a constant forum* [meeting place for discussion] *where nations must face each other and debate their differences and strive for common ground, we shall have done infinitely much.*

► *HOW and WHY was the United Nations founded in 1945?* ATIB ■ ATIC ■

Signing the UN Charter in San Francisco in 1945

The United Nations Headquarters in New York

27.1 Look at Source 27.A. Why did the Great Powers disagree about the veto? Why was this of great importance for the future of the United Nations? AT1B ■

27.2 Compare Sources 27.B and 27.D. How did these writers differ in what they hoped the United Nations would achieve? Why were these differences important? AT1C/L6

27.3 Compare the League of Nations (page 130) with the United Nations (Source 27.C). What were the similarities? What were the main differences? AT1C/L5

27.4 Look at Source 27.E. What was the point of listing human rights when member states, such as the United Kingdom, could not even ensure that 'race, colour, sex,' would not be a barrier to progress in their own countries, let alone in the rest of the world? AT1C ■

The UN Charter

The Charter setting up the United Nations was eventually signed by representatives of fifty Allied nations on 26 June 1945 in San Francisco. It came into being officially on 24 October 1945 – later known as 'United Nations Day'. You can see the way the UN works in Source 27.C and how the leader of South Africa summed up its aims in Source 27.D.

Source 27.C The way the United Nations works

United Nations Secretary General
Runs the UN aided by officials from all the member states

Security Council
Takes day-to-day action on behalf of the General Assembly. Fifteen members – the five Great Powers (UK, USA, Russia, France, China) and ten other nations elected for 2 years at a time. All decisions have to be carried by nine members voting YES and none of the Great Powers voting NO (the *veto*).

General Assembly

- The Parliament of the United Nations.
- Each member state has one vote.
- Meets once a year in September.
- Special meetings can be held in an emergency.
- Important matters decided by a 2/3rds majority.
- Other decisions by a simple majority.

UN Organisations and agencies
Other organisations and agencies do much of the most valuable work of the UN, such as WHO (health) and UNESCO (education).

Source 27.D By General Smuts from South Africa

It provides for a peace with teeth; for the unity of peace-loving peoples against future aggressors; for a united front amongst the greatest powers, backed by the forces of the smaller powers as well.

Time Line

1941 Atlantic Charter
1943 Teheran Conference decides to form United Nations
1944 Dumbarton Oaks Conference
1945 End of Second World War; the United Nations is founded
1948 Universal Declaration of Human Rights

The Universal Declaration of Human Rights

The United Nations has often been criticised. Nonetheless it has had many successes. It has sent UN soldiers drawn from the armies of member-states to try to keep the peace in world troublespots, such as the Middle East in 1956 and in Croatia in 1992. Its importance in world affairs can be judged from the fact that unlike the old League of Nations, almost every country in the world is a member. One of its greatest achievements was in establishing the basic rights of every person on Earth. In 1948 the General Assembly of the United Nations gave its approval to the 'Universal Declaration of Human Rights'. You can see how it begins in Source 27.E.

Source 27.E Universal Declaration of Human Rights

All human beings are born free and equal in dignity and rights. They are endowed with reason and conscience and should act towards one another in a spirit of brotherhood.

Everyone is entitled to all the rights and freedoms set forth in this Declaration without distinction of any kind, such as race, colour, sex, language, religion, political or other opinion, national or social origin, property, birth or other status.

Teacher's notes

Flexibility
The three books in this series have been designed to be as flexible in use as possible. Each book can be used by individual pupils working on their own, by pupils working in small groups, or by pupils working together in class.

Taken together these books offer a wide variety of choice in selecting which combinations of options to teach. Yet they still provide coverage similar in depth and extent to that available otherwise from twelve separate topic books covering all five *core* study units and seven *optional* topics. They also provide the opportunity, not available otherwise, to cross-refer, to compare Britain during both World Wars, for instance, and to set the study of the Industrial Revolution firmly within the local context.

Choice of Optional Study Units
The choice of options offered by the series is as follows:

From Group A, a choice of:

either Castles and Cathedrals 1066 to 1500 **[Book 1]**
or The impact of the Industrial Revolution on a local area **[Book 3]**
or Britain and the Great War 1914 to 1918 **[Book 3]**

From Group B, a choice of:
either Reformation and Counter-Reformation in the sixteenth century **[Book 2]**
or The French Revolution and the Napoleonic era **[Book 2]**

From Group C, a choice of:

either Islamic civilisations: seventh to sixteenth centuries **[Book 1]**
or India from the Mughal Empire to the coming of the British **[Book 2]**

In accordance with the requirements of the National Curriculum, each optional study unit makes demands comparable to those of a core study unit, in historical knowledge, understanding and skills. Nonetheless, it has been assumed that, in general, rather more time in class will be needed to cover the five core study units.

Choice of Option Routes
As this table shows, the series makes possible a total combination of twelve different option routes.

	Option routes	1	2	3	4	5	6	7	8	9	10	11	12
Book One:	**Old World**												
CORE:	THE ROMAN EMPIRE	1	1	1	1	1	1	1	1	1	1	1	1
Option C:	Islamic civilisations	2	2	2	2	2	2						
CORE:	MEDIEVAL REALMS	3	3	3	3	3	3	2	2	2	2	2	2
Option A:	Castles and Cathedrals	4			4			3			3		
Book Two:	**Changing World**												
Option B:	The Reformation	5	4	4				4	3	3			
CORE:	MAKING OF THE UNITED KINGDOM	6	5	5	5	4	4	5	4	4	4	3	3
Option C:	Mughal India							6	5	5	5	4	4
Option B:	French Revolution				6	5	5				6	5	5
Book Three:	**Expanding World**												
CORE:	EXPANSION, TRADE AND INDUSTRY	7	6	6	7	6	6	7	6	6	7	6	6
Option A:	The impact of the Industrial Revolution		7			7			7			7	
Option A:	Britain and the Great War			7			7			7			7
CORE:	ERA OF THE SECOND WORLD WAR	8	8	8	8	8	8	8	8	8	8	8	8

These different option routes make it possible to use the same sets of books with classes following very different courses. Not only can the different teachers in a school use them to teach the options they prefer, but option changes can also be made easily from year to year (such as when new staff are appointed) without incurring the extra cost of purchasing new books and materials.

As envisaged in the National Curriculum, the work done on each topic can be expanded or modified to take account of pupils' interests; to make use of original documents, artefacts, pictures and music; and to take advantage of local study opportunities in the vicinity of the school.

The impact of the Industrial Revolution
Work for the Group A option, **The impact of the Industrial Revolution on a local area**, will depend very much on local circumstances, the potential offered by the home environment, the availability of appropriate local source materials – documents, printed sources, maps, pictures, photographs – and the feasibility of studying such a topic with each class. In this book a wide-ranging selection of photographs and sources has been chosen to show some of the possibilites available in most localities, however remote from the main centres of urban and industrial growth. The aim has been to stimulate and suggest rather than to prescribe or define specific local activities or assignments.

As you will see, the sections of text allocated to this topic have been added as an appendix to the main chapters from **Expansion, trade and industry** to which they relate. The illustrations and sources they contain are referred to in the main body of text. This material can obviously be used by all pupils irrespective of whether this is, or is not, their Group A topic.

Attainment Targets and Statements of Attainment

Questions, assignments and tasks have been set in the text. They test comprehension, expand historical ideas and concepts and can be used progressively to develop historical skills. Most have been tagged with a simple, unobtrusive code to indicate the relevant National Curriculum attainment target and level of attainment.

The different statements of attainment lettered (a), (b) and (c) in Attainment Target 1: *Knowledge and understanding of history* are shown by the codes **AT1A** (change), **AT1B** (causation and consequence), and **AT1C** (analysis of historical situations). **AT2** indicates Attainment Target 2: *Interpretations of history* and **AT3** indicates Attainment Target 3: *The use of historical sources.*

Similarly, the relevant Key Stage 3 statements of attainment are coded **L3**, **L4**, **L5**, **L6**, and **L7**. Thus **AT1A/L3** is the abbreviation for Attainment Target 1: *Knowledge and understanding of history*; Level Three: *'Describe changes over a period of time.'*

Each tagged question has a unique reference indicated by its chapter number and question number, such as 1.1 (chapter 1, question 1) and 18.12 (chapter 18, question 12). Tagged questions like these can be located in the relevant attainment level boxes on the Assessment Charts which follow (pages 188–91).

Differentiation by Outcome

Some tasks differentiate between different levels of attainment by outcome. In other words they differentiate according to the varying responses of pupils to the question which has been set. Levels of attainment can sometimes extend in theory, if not always in practice, across the entire range of attainment envisaged for pupils at Key Stage 3. Thus one pupil asked to explain the causes of the Second World War might give only a single simple reason (**AT1B/L3**); another might 'identify different types of cause and consequence' (**AT1B/L5**); while a third might 'show how the different causes are connected' (**AT1B/L7**).

Questions like these have been tagged in the text by the code for the Attainment Target only (**AT1A ■**). They are shown underlined in the Assessment Charts on pages 188–91 (18.12) and always appear in at least two or more adjacent attainment level boxes.

Please bear in mind, however, that the levels of attainment indicated in the text can only suggest. They cannot prescribe. The actual level of attainment will depend on the learning situation and the supplementary resources available in class. Accurate assessment of individual performance will always depend on the judgement of the teacher setting the task and on the level of interest and assiduity shown by the pupil or pupils.

Some questions carry two attainment target references. This is token recognition of the fact that many assignments can be classified under two or more attainment target headings. Many questions do not carry tags, even when it is obvious to which attainment target they are directed. This is partly to avoid further overcrowding the Assessment Charts and partly because some appropriate questions and assignments do not fit obviously into any of the existing statements of attainment.

Assessment Charts

The Assessment Charts which follow (pages 188–91) can be photocopied. When clipped together they will provide a continuous record of the pupil's achievements in history at Key Stage 3 and make it possible to identify at a glance the level of attainment reached in each attainment target.

Space has been provided to insert the pupil's name at the top of each sheet. The relevant question reference number can then be circled, struck-out, ticked or highlighted whenever a pupil satisfactorily completes an assignment or question. The blank panel in the bottom right-hand corner of each box can later be used to insert the date when the overall performance of the pupil is judged satisfactory at that level of attainment.

These boxes can also be used, of course, to record satisfactory achievement in exercises and assignments set independently of the books in the series. As you will see, the Assessment Chart for **The impact of the Industrial Revolution on a local area** has been left blank anyway, since the activites and assignments appropriate to this topic will depend very much on the opportunities provided by the local environment.

On completion of a study unit, a record of the highest level of attainment reached by a pupil in each attainment target can be transferred to the assessment chart for the next study unit by recording the date of achievement or highlighting or ticking the relevant box.

The acceptable completion of a single question or assignment, in itself, will not necesarily signify that a specific level of attainment has been achieved. Some questions are much more demanding than others. It will depend very much on circumstances – the nature and width of the assignment and the depth of understanding shown by the pupil.

Continuous Assessment

Opportunites for making valid assessments as part of an integral continuous process abound. They encompass every conceivable classroom learning situation – from the formal written exercise for every student in class to the informal, off-the-cuff question put to an individual pupil working on her own or in a group. Suitable opportunities may also occur during work on group or individual projects; during a visit to a museum; in a group or class discussion or during a simulation. Although a large number of questions have been tagged, this has only been done to ensure that as wide a range of assessment opportunities is provided as possible. This should be of particular value when making individual and informal assessments. It is not anticipated, however, that every tagged question will be needed for assessment.

References to Attainment Targets and Statements of Attainment are taken from *History in the National Curriculum* (England, DES, March 1991).

Name:

Assessment chart: Expansion, trade and industry

Level	Attainment target 1A	Attainment target 1B	Attainment target 1C	Attainment target 2	Attainment target 3
	Knowledge and understanding of history: Change	Knowledge and understanding of history: Causation and consequence	Knowledge and understanding of history: Analysis of historical situations	Interpretations of history	The use of historical sources
3	Describe changes over a period of time. 4.1 4.16	Give a reason for an historical event or development. 4.11 6.12	Identify differences between times in the past. 4.19	Distinguish between a fact and a point of view. 3.3	Make deductions from historical sources. 1.9 2.13
4	Recognise that over time some things changed and others stayed the same. 2.7 2.16 4.1 4.16 4.17 7.1	Show an awareness that historical events usually have more than one cause and consequence. 2.5 4.11 4.20 5.4 5.15 6.12	Describe different features of an historical period. 3.4 3.9 4.4	Show an understanding that deficiencies in evidence may lead to different interpretations of the past. 3.3 3.5 3.13 4.3 6.14 7.4	Put together information drawn from different historical sources. 5.16 6.8 7.19 8.2 9.13 10.14
5	Distinguish between different kinds of historical change. 1.3 2.2 2.4 2.7 2.8 2.14 2.16 3.14 4.17 4.18 5.1 5.14 6.13 8.5 9.3 9.19 10.3 10.9 10.15 10.18	Identify different types of cause and consequence. 1.15 2.11 2.20 3.12 4.10 4.11 4.18 4.21 5.11 5.15 5.17 6.12 7.5 7.16 8.6 8.7 8.9 9.18	Show how different features in an historical situation relate to each other. 1.11 2.3 2.9 2.10 3.4 3.9 4.8 4.18 5.2 6.6 6.16 6.22 7.8 8.1 8.3 8.8 9.1 9.11 10.1 10.6 11.1 11.5 11.12	Recognise that interpretations of the past, including popular accounts, may differ from what is known to have happened. 1.2 1.6 1.10 1.13 3.3 3.5 3.10 3.13 4.3 6.5 6.14 10.2	Comment on the usefulness of an historical source by reference to its content as evidence for a particular enquiry. 3.7 4.2 5.8 6.3 6.4 6.10 6.11 6.18 6.24 7.3 7.14 7.17 7.21 9.4 9.12 9.14 9.15 9.16 10.16 11.6 11.9
6	Show an understanding that change and progress are not the same. 1.3 1.5 1.12 2.2 2.4 2.6 2.8 3.14 5.14 6.13 6.23 8.4 8.5 9.3 10.3 10.15	Recognise that causes and consequences can vary in importance. 1.4 1.7 1.15 2.20 3.12 4.11 4.21 5.15 6.1 6.12 6.19 7.9 7.22 8.9 8.10 9.18	Describe the different ideas and attitudes of people in an historical situation. 1.16 1.17 3.9 5.12 5.19 6.17 6.22 6.26 7.10 7.13 7.18 7.20 9.17 9.23 10.1 10.6 10.11 10.12 10.13 10.17 10.18 11.1 11.7	Demonstrate how historical interpretations depend on the selection of sources. 3.3 3.5 3.11 3.13 4.3 4.5 5.21 6.7 6.14 6.27 9.8 10.2	Compare the usefulness of different historical sources as evidence for a particular enquiry. 1.14 4.12 5.20 5.21 6.15 6.20 6.28 7.20 9.5 9.6 9.7 9.8 9.9 9.12 9.22 9.24 10.8 10.18 11.2 11.4
7	Show an awareness that patterns of change can be complex. 2.2 2.4 2.6 2.8 2.19 3.14 5.3 5.6 5.7 5.14 6.2 6.13 6.23 8.5 9.3 10.3 10.15	Show how the different causes of an historical event are connected. 1.15 2.20 3.12 4.11 4.21 5.15 6.12 8.9 8.10 9.18	Show an awareness that different people's ideas and attitudes are often related to their circumstances. 3.8 5.18 6.22 7.6 7.13 10.1 10.6 10.12 10.13 10.17 11.1	Describe the strengths and weaknesses of different interpretations of an historical event or development. 1.18 3.6 4.6 6.14 6.23 7.11 10.2 10.4 11.10	Make judgments about the reliability and value of historical sources by reference to the circumstances in which they were produced. 1.18 6.15 6.21 6.25 6.28 7.11 9.2 9.10 9.12 10.2 10.4 10.5 11.3 11.10

Assessment chart: The impact of the Industrial Revolution on a local area

Name:

Level	Attainment target 1A	Attainment target 1B	Attainment target 1C	Attainment target 2	Attainment target 3
	Knowledge and understanding of history: Change	Knowledge and understanding of history: Causation and consequence	Knowledge and understanding of history: Analysis of historical situations	Interpretations of history	The use of historical sources
3	Describe changes over a period of time.	Give a reason for an historical event or development.	Identify differences between times in the past.	Distinguish between a fact and a point of view.	Make deductions from historical sources.
4	Recognise that over time some things changed and others stayed the same.	Show an awareness that historical events usually have more than one cause and consequence.	Describe different features of an historical period.	Show an understanding that deficiencies in evidence may lead to different interpretations of the past.	Put together information drawn from different historical sources.
5	Distinguish between different kinds of historical change.	Identify different types of cause and consequence.	Show how different features in an historical situation relate to each other.	Recognise that interpretations of the past, including popular accounts, may differ from what is known to have happened.	Comment on the usefulness of an historical source by reference to its content as evidence for a particular enquiry.
6	Show an understanding that change and progress are not the same.	Recognise that causes and consequences can vary in importance.	Describe the different ideas and attitudes of people in an historical situation.	Demonstrate how historical interpretations depend on the selection of sources.	Compare the usefulness of different historical sources as evidence for a particular enquiry.
7	Show an awareness that patterns of change can be complex.	Show how the different causes of an historical event are connected.	Show an awareness that different people's ideas and attitudes are often related to their circumstances.	Describe the strengths and weaknesses of different interpretations of an historical event or development.	Make judgments about the reliability and value of historical sources by reference to the circumstances in which they were produced.

Assessment chart: Britain and The Great War

Name:

Level	Attainment target 1A	Attainment target 1B	Attainment target 1C	Attainment target 2	Attainment target 3
	Knowledge and understanding of history: Change	Knowledge and understanding of history: Causation and consequence	Knowledge and understanding of history: Analysis of historical situations	Interpretations of history	The use of historical sources
3	Describe changes over a period of time. 12.11 15.25 17.20	Give a reason for an historical event or development. 13.3 15.24 18.1	Identify differences between times in the past.	Distinguish between a fact and a point of view. 16.4	Make deductions from historical sources. 12.1 12.6
4	Recognise that over time some things changed and others stayed the same. 12.11 15.25 17.1 17.20	Show an awareness that historical events usually have more than one cause and consequence. 13.3 14.1 15.8 15.24 17.5 18.1	Describe different features of an historical period. 15.3 17.7	Show an understanding that deficiencies in evidence may lead to different interpretations of the past. 15.10 16.4	Put together information drawn from different historical sources. 13.5 15.3 17.8
5	Distinguish between different kinds of historical change. 12.8 13.10 15.18 16.6 17.1 17.11 17.14 17.17 17.18 17.20	Identify different types of cause and consequence. 12.3 12.14 13.7 15.11 15.19 15.20 15.23 15.24 16.1 17.3 17.5 17.6 17.14 17.18 18.1	Show how different features in an historical situation relate to each other. 12.2 12.10 13.9 14.5 14.6 15.3 15.20 17.13 17.16 18.2	Recognise that interpretations of the past, including popular accounts, may differ from what is known to have happened. 12.4 13.1 13.6 13.8 15.2 15.10 16.4 16.5 16.7 17.2 18.3	Comment on the usefulness of an historical source by reference to its content as evidence for a particular enquiry. 13.2 13.4 15.3 15.9 15.12 15.13 16.3 17.4 17.9 17.19
6	Show an understanding that change and progress are not the same. 12.8 12.9 15.18 16.6 17.14 17.17 17.20	Recognise that causes and consequences can vary in importance. 12.15 13.7 15.11 15.19 15.20 15.24 17.5 17.12 17.14 18.1	Describe the different ideas and attitudes of people in an historical situation. 12.2 12.12 14.2 14.3 14.4 14.5 14.6 15.3 15.4 15.20 16.2 16.3 16.6 17.10 17.13 18.2	Demonstrate how historical interpretations depend on the selection of sources. 12.5 13.8 14.7 15.1 15.2 15.5 15.10 15.14 15.16 16.3 16.4 16.8 16.9 18.2 18.3	Compare the usefulness of different historical sources as evidence for a particular enquiry. 12.3 12.5 13.8 14.2 14.3 14.7 14.8 15.1 15.2 15.3 15.5 15.15 15.17 17.10
7	Show an awareness that patterns of change can be complex. 12.8 15.18 16.6 17.14 17.17 17.20	Show how the different causes of an historical event are connected. 12.16 13.7 15.11 15.19 15.20 15.24 17.14 18.1	Show an awareness that different people's ideas and attitudes are often related to their circumstances. 12.13 15.3 15.20 15.22 16.6 16.11 17.13 17.15 18.2	Describe the strengths and weaknesses of different interpretations of an historical event or development. 13.8 15.1 15.2 15.6 15.7 15.10 15.21 15.22 16.10 16.11 16.12 17.15 17.21 18.2 18.3	Make judgments about the reliability and value of historical sources by reference to the circumstances in which they were produced. 13.8 15.1 15.2 16.11 17.15 17.21

Name:

Assessment chart: The era of the Second World War

Level	Attainment target 1A	Attainment target 1B	Attainment target 1C	Attainment target 2	Attainment target 3
	Knowledge and understanding of history: Change	Knowledge and understanding of history: Causation and consequence	Knowledge and understanding of history: Analysis of historical situations	Interpretations of history	The use of historical sources
3	Describe changes over a period of time. 19.8 21.18 24.8	Give a reason for an historical event or development. 20.19 21.7	Identify differences between times in the past. 20.22	Distinguish between a fact and a point of view. 21.13 22.12	Make deductions from historical sources. 21.2
4	Recognise that over time some things changed and others stayed the same. 19.2 20.15 21.18 24.8 26.9	Show an awareness that historical events usually have more than one cause and consequence. 20.19 21.7 22.5 22.11 23.20	Describe different features of an historical period. 20.17 20.22 22.28 23.21	Show an understanding that deficiencies in evidence may lead to different interpretations of the past. 20.11 20.18 21.13 22.6 22.8 22.20 23.1	Put together information drawn from different historical sources. 20.4 22.1 22.28 23.5 23.18 24.7 25.4
5	Distinguish between different kinds of historical change. 19.2 20.9 20.15 20.22 22.31 24.8 26.1 26.5 26.9	Identify different types of cause and consequence. 19.7 19.12 20.7 20.19 21.3 21.4 21.7 21.16 21.17 22.5 22.11 23.6 23.20 24.3 25.1 26.6 26.11 27.1	Show how different features in an historical situation relate to each other. 19.4 20.3 20.10 20.13 20.17 20.20 20.22 21.11 22.2 22.9 23.7 23.14 23.22 25.4 25.8 26.3 27.3	Recognise that interpretations of the past, including popular accounts, may differ from what is known to have happened. 19.5 20.10 20.11 20.18 21.12 21.13 22.3 22.6 22.8 22.13 22.20 22.25 23.1 23.9 23.12 23.16 23.17 23.24 23.25 24.2 25.6	Comment on the usefulness of an historical source by reference to its content as evidence for a particular enquiry. 19.9 19.10 20.1 20.5 20.6 20.21 21.1 21.5 21.10 21.14 22.8 22.9 22.15 22.17 22.19 23.1 23.8 23.11 23.14 24.9 24.10 25.2 26.8
6	Show an understanding that change and progress are not the same. 19.2 20.15 20.22 25.5 26.1 26.5	Recognise that causes and consequences can vary in importance. 19.1 19.3 19.7 19.12 20.2 20.19 21.3 21.7 22.5 22.11 23.20 26.6 26.11 27.1	Describe the different ideas and attitudes of people in an historical situation. 19.4 19.5 19.11 20.10 20.17 20.20 20.22 21.8 21.10 21.11 22.16 22.23 23.2 23.4 24.6 25.2 25.7 26.4 26.10 27.2 27.4	Demonstrate how historical interpretations depend on the selection of sources. 20.11 20.18 21.9 21.13 22.6 22.8 22.20 22.25 22.29 23.1 24.5	Compare the usefulness of different historical sources as evidence for a particular enquiry. 19.6 20.8 20.9 20.12 20.16 21.6 21.13 22.4 22.8 22.14 22.21 22.22 22.24 22.27 22.29 23.3 23.13 23.15 23.19 24.1 25.3 25.10 25.11
7	Show an awareness that patterns of change can be complex. 19.2 20.15 20.22 25.5 26.1 26.5	Show how the different causes of an historical event are connected. 19.7 19.12 20.19 21.3 21.7 22.5 23.20 26.6 26.11 27.1	Show an awareness that different people's ideas and attitudes are often related to their circumstances. 19.4 20.10 20.14 20.17 20.20 20.22 21.11 22.16 22.26 24.6 25.3 25.7 25.12 26.10 27.4	Describe the strengths and weaknesses of different interpretations of an historical event or development. 20.11 20.14 20.18 21.9 21.13 22.6 22.10 22.20 22.25 22.30 23.1 23.10 24.11 25.9	Make judgments about the reliability and value of historical sources by reference to the circumstances in which they were produced. 20.14 21.9 21.13 21.15 22.10 22.18 22.22 22.30 23.23 23.26

Index